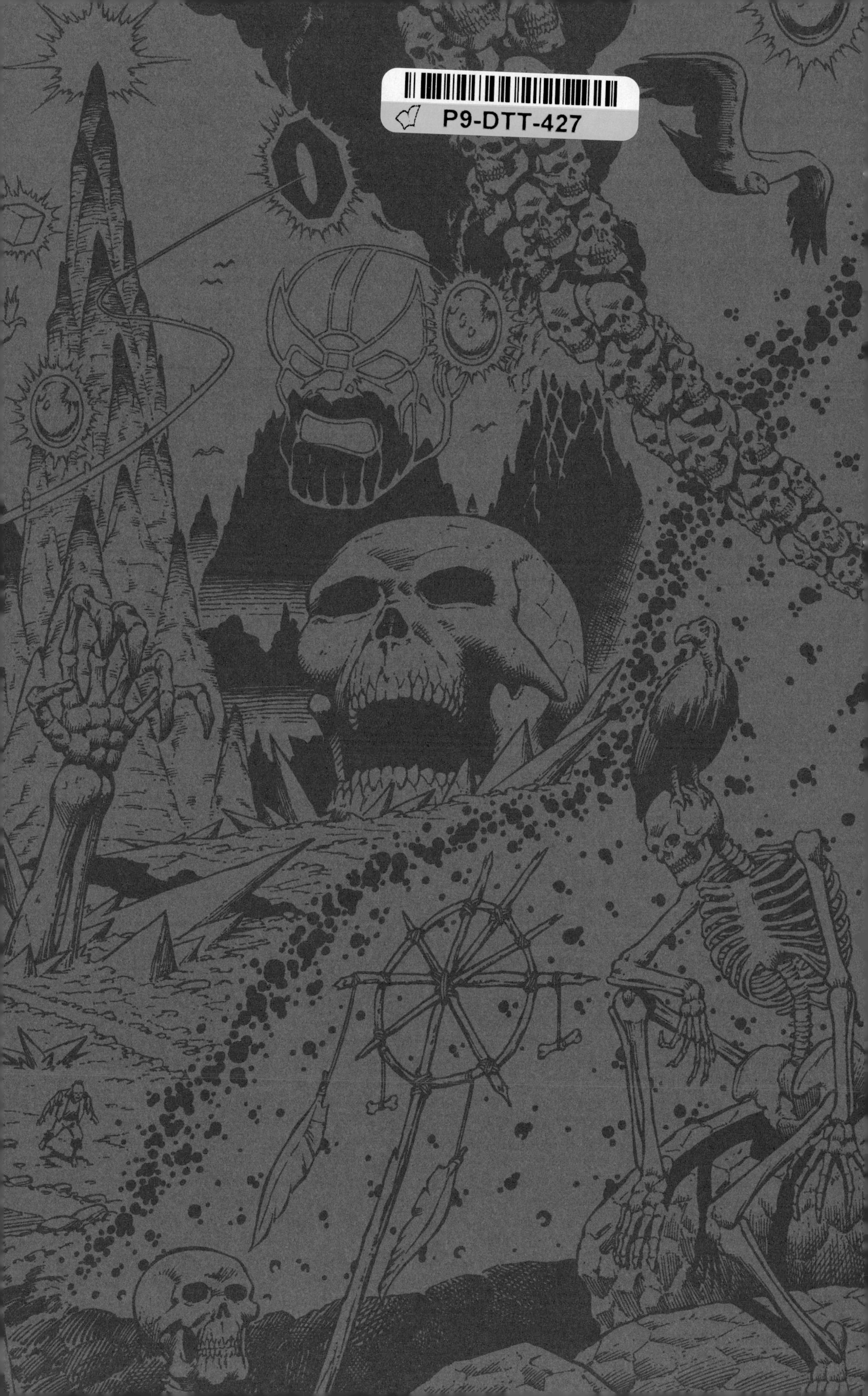

THANOS

THE INFINITY REVELATION

MARVEL OGN

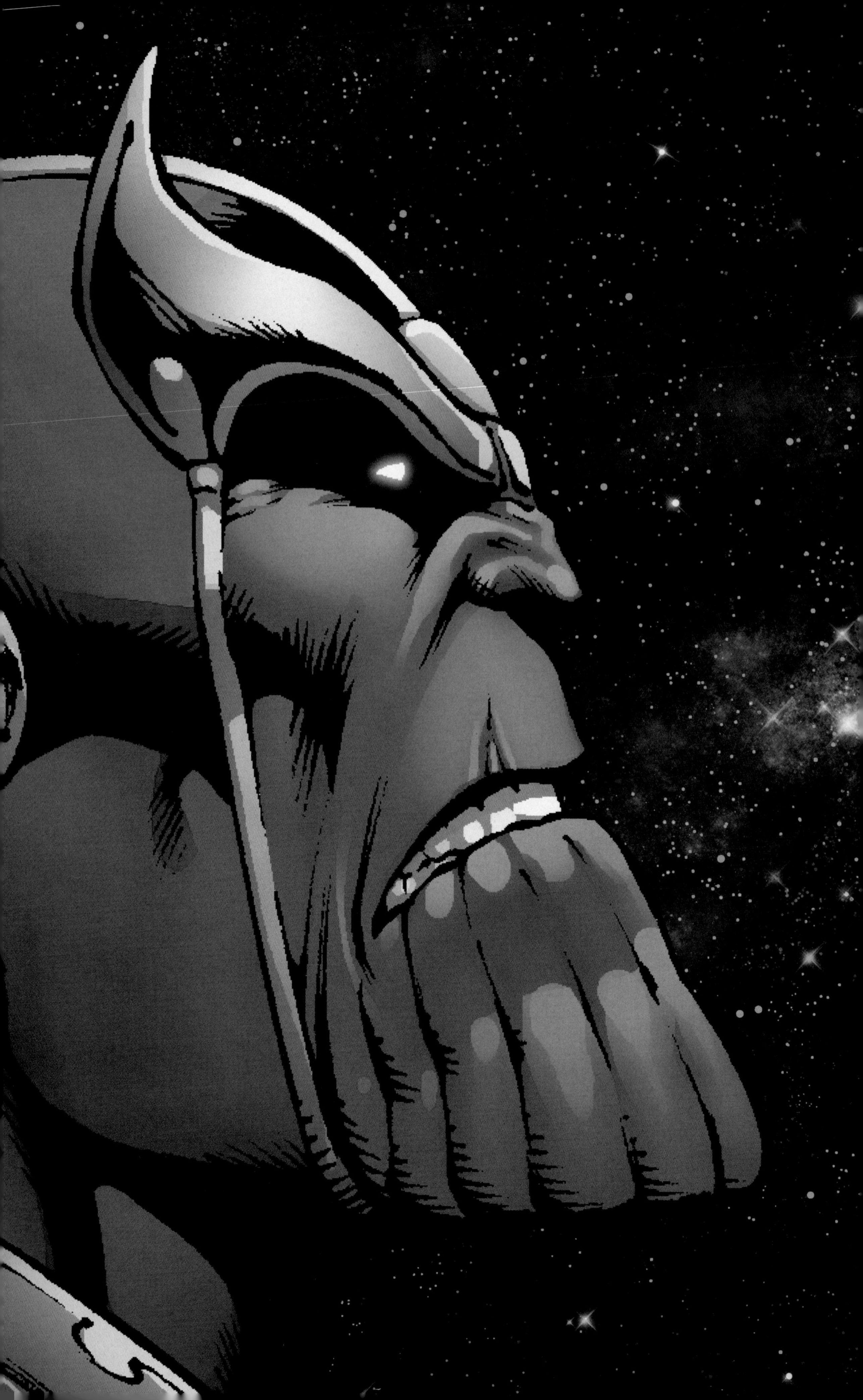

THANOS
THE INFINITY REVELATION

JIM STARLIN
writer and penciler

inker ANDY SMITH

color artists FRANK D'ARMATA with RACHELLE ROSENBERG

lettering VC's JOE CARAMAGNA

---

cover art STARLIN & ROSENBERG   book design JARED K. FLETCHER

assistant editor JAKE THOMAS   editors TOM BREVOORT with WIL MOSS

editor in chief AXEL ALONSO   chief creative officer JOE QUESADA

publisher DAN BUCKLEY   executive producer ALAN FINE

THANOS: THE INFINITY REVELATION. First printing 2014. ISBN# 978-0-7851-8470-6. Published by MARVEL WORLDWIDE, INC., a subsidiary of MARVEL ENTERTAINMENT, LLC. OFFICE OF PUBLICATION: 135 West 50th Street, New York, NY 10020. Copyright © 2014 Marvel Characters, Inc. All rights reserved. All characters featured in this issue and the distinctive names and likenesses thereof, and all related indicia are trademarks of Marvel Characters, Inc. No similarity between any of the names, characters, persons, and/or institutions in this magazine with those of any living or dead person or institution is intended, and any such similarity which may exist is purely coincidental. **Printed in the U.S.A.** ALAN FINE, EVP - Office of the President, Marvel Worldwide, Inc. and EVP & CMO Marvel Characters B.V.; DAN BUCKLEY, Publisher & President - Print, Animation & Digital Divisions; JOE QUESADA, Chief Creative Officer; TOM BREVOORT, SVP of Publishing; DAVID BOGART, SVP of Operations & Procurement, Publishing; C.B. CEBULSKI, SVP of Creator & Content Development; DAVID GABRIEL, SVP Print, Sales & Marketing; JIM O'KEEFE, VP of Operations & Logistics; DAN CARR, Executive Director of Publishing Technology; SUSAN CRESPI, Editorial Operations Manager; ALEX MORALES, Publishing Operations Manager; STAN LEE, Chairman Emeritus. For information regarding advertising in Marvel Comics or on Marvel.com, please contact Niza Disla, Director of Marvel Partnerships, at ndisla@marvel.com. For Marvel subscription inquiries, please call 800-217-9158. Manufactured between 5/9/2014 and 6/23/2014 by WORZALLA PUBLISHING CO., STEVENS POINT, WI, USA.

10 9 8 7 6 5 4 3 2 1

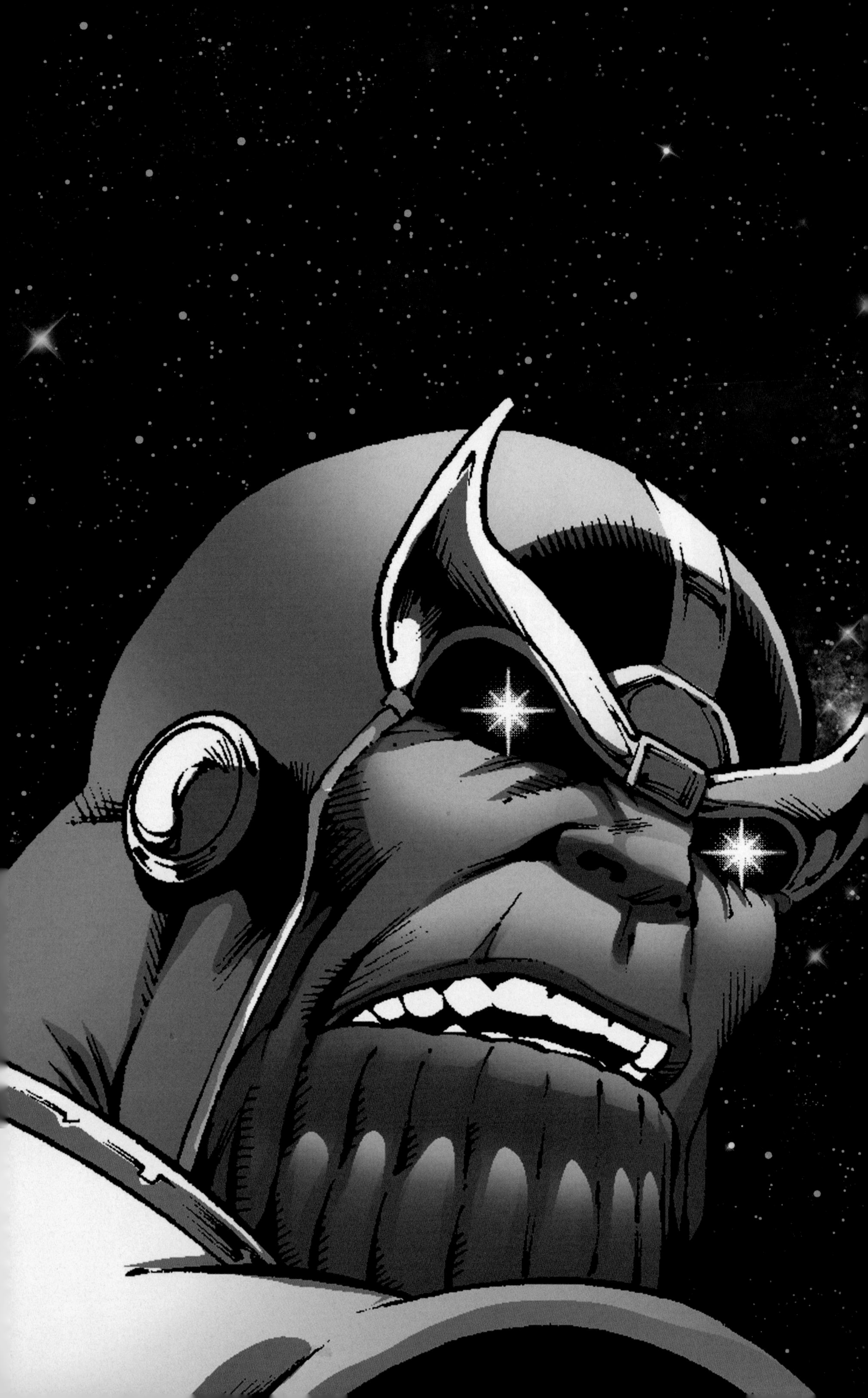

INTRODUCTION

◆

Thanos emerged from Jim Starlin's mind more than forty years ago, making his initial appearance in 1973 in one of Starlin's first comics, **Iron Man #55.** Since then, Starlin has returned to the Mad Titan again and again: in mid-'70s **Captain Marvel** and **Warlock** storylines, in an early-'90s sequence of stories involving the Infinity Gauntlet, in a handful of projects from the early 2000s, and now in **The Infinity Revelation.** Pay attention to that title, too. Starlin's always had an ear for religious language, and this graphic novel is a "revelation" both in the sense of a mystical vision and, perhaps, in the sense of the culmination of a long sequence of stories.

The Infinity Revelation is a resolution, but it's not **the** ending: Thanos has spent the past four decades courting Death — literally — in every imaginable way, and always being refused the finality of the grave. Starlin killed Captain Marvel in the very first Marvel graphic novel, but for the rest of his cosmic characters, death is inexorably coupled with rebirth, as derangement is with reason, eschatology with ontology, philosophy with fisticuffs.

Thanos' partner in this complicated dance of dualities, here as (almost) always, is Adam Warlock, who's perpetually emerging from his cocoon, even as Thanos pursues Death's embrace. Whenever Starlin comes back to Thanos and Warlock's dual orbit, he builds on the vision he constructed the previous time, deepening their story and the existential mysteries around it. On one page of **The Infinity Revelation** after another, there are echoes of his earlier comics about these characters. Their archetypal images recur like leitmotifs: light exploding from the center of darkness, a gigantic not-quite-human face hanging in the sky, geometrical forms suspended in space, the six Infinity Gems radiating their colors.

The Thanos/Warlock stories are halls of mirrors, full of Jungian doubles and shadow-selves and shadow-shadow-selves. That's never been more true than in this volume, in which Starlin blurs even the distinctions between originals and their doubles. If you read it carefully, you'll notice that certain characters don't appear quite the way we're used to seeing them, and some even change the way they look from panel to panel. As you'll see, this is all part of Starlin's grand plan. (A hint: You might want to take a glance at the cover of 1972's **Marvel Premiere #1,** the first issue in which Adam Warlock appeared under that name.)

Starlin has always paid homage to the work of Marvel's other architects — his contemporaries as well as his forebears. Jack Kirby and Steve Ditko have been part of Starlin's DNA as an artist all along, and parts of **The Infinity Revelation** explicitly recall Ditko's brambled mindscapes and Kirby's thunderous shows of force. But there's also imagery in this story that's descended from the look of the Marvel cosmos over the past decade — the era of **Annihilation** and **Infinity,** which were themselves inspired by Starlin's own work.

Speaking of the infinite: Starlin is known for his cosmic themes, and **The Infinity Revelation** is staged on so grand a scale that the personifications of Infinity and Eternity show up in its very first scene. Another one of his gifts, though, is the deftness with which he grounds his epic meditations in an unmistakable sense of place. He renders every location, from Thanos' ship Sanctuary VI to distant planets and realms of the unreal, with masterful certainty, even though none of them can escape the waves of transfiguration around which this story revolves.

As he's often done before, Starlin shows us almost all of this through Thanos' eyes. From our brutal, cruel narrator's perspective, there's scarcely such a thing as heroes or villains, just seekers after knowledge whose clashes transform their battlegrounds. **The Infinity Revelation** is as unsettling as it is thrilling. It's a vision of how mutable reality can be, and as densely concentrated a burst of Starlin's heady strangeness as anyone could hope to experience.

Douglas Wolk
May 2014

Douglas Wolk is the author of the Eisner Award-winning **Reading Comics: How Graphic Novels Work and What They Mean.** He writes about comics for the **New York Times,** the **Los Angeles Times, TIME** and elsewhere.

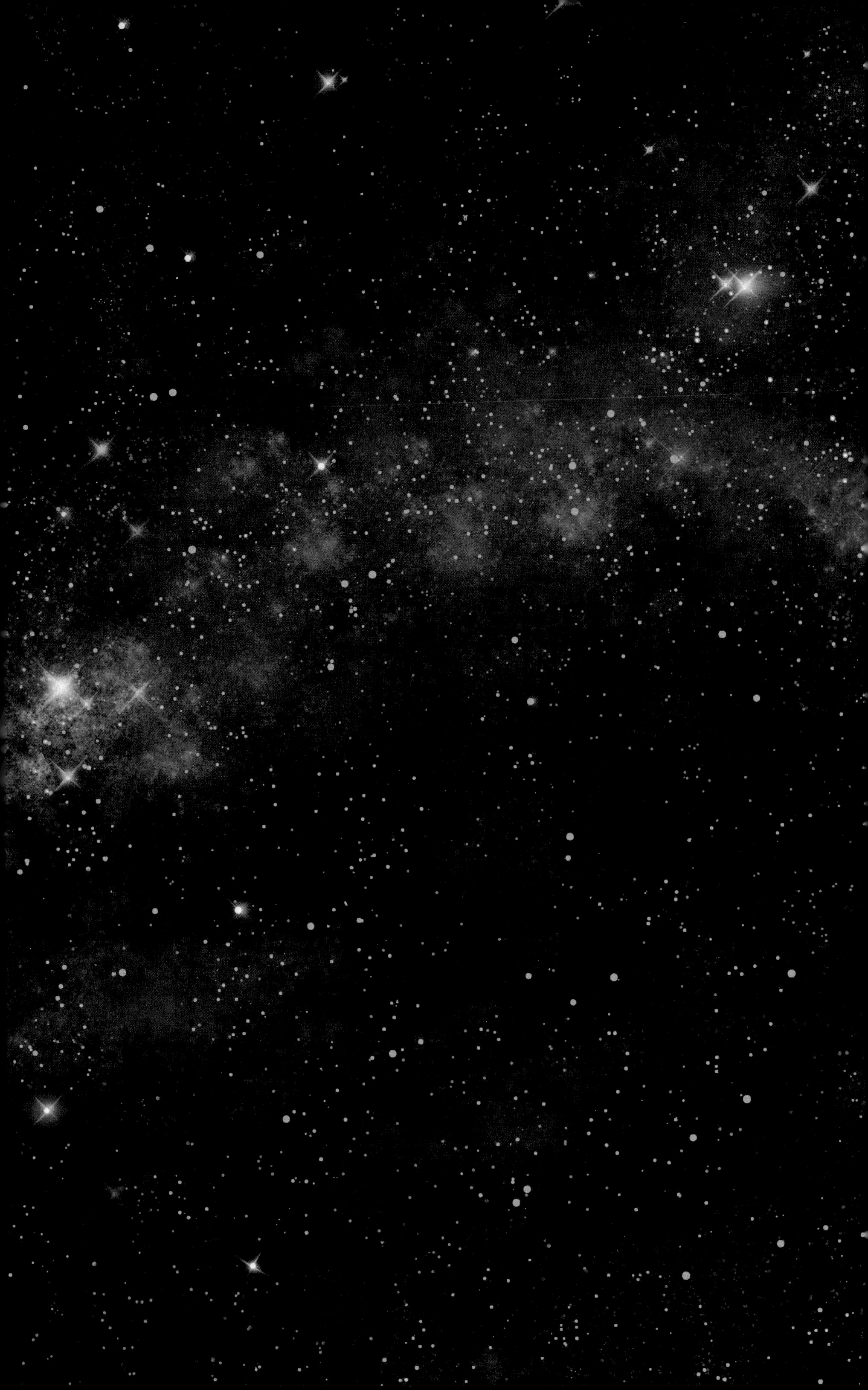

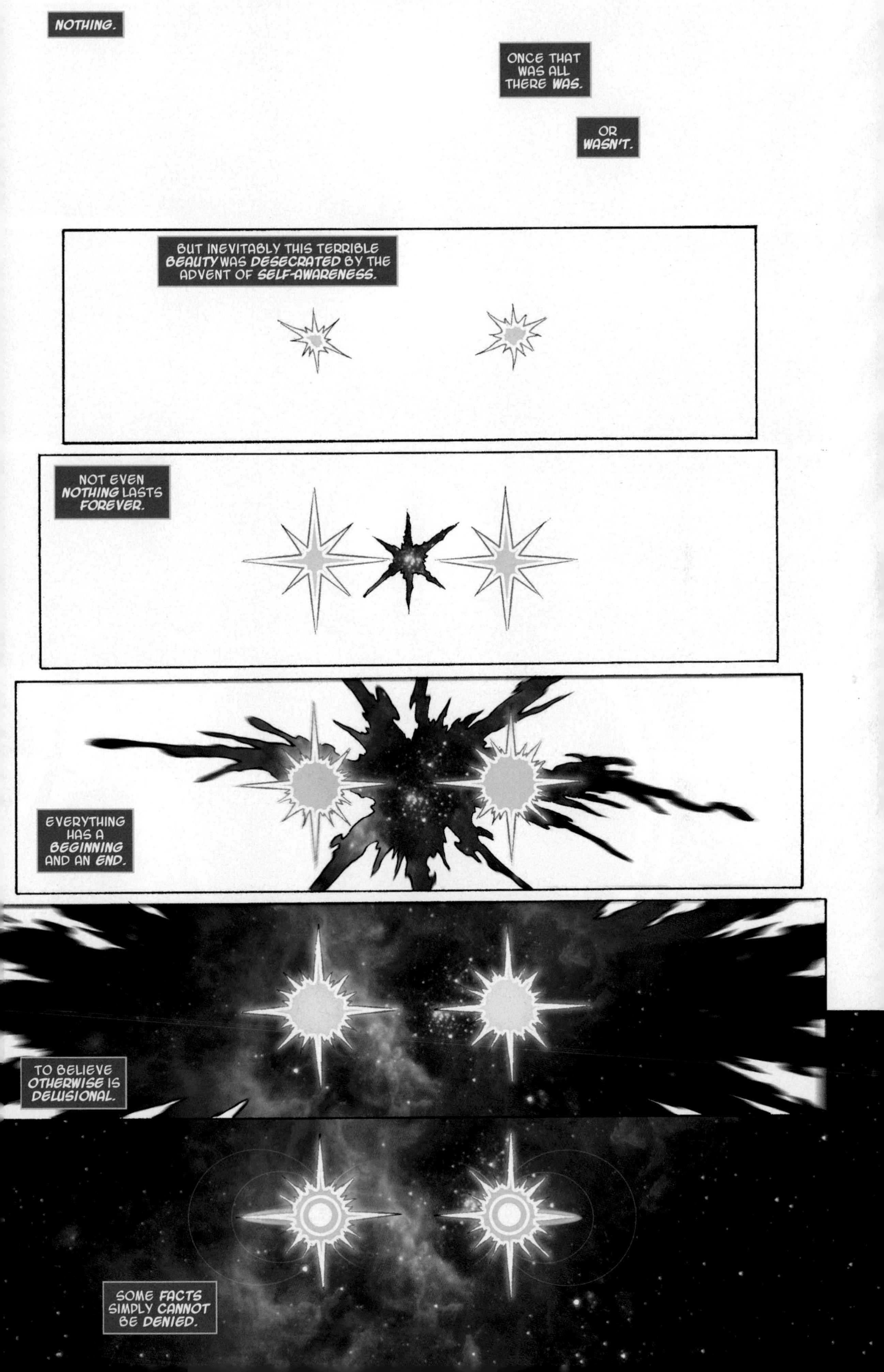

NOTHING.

ONCE THAT WAS ALL THERE *WAS*.

OR *WASN'T*.

BUT INEVITABLY THIS TERRIBLE *BEAUTY* WAS *DESECRATED* BY THE ADVENT OF *SELF-AWARENESS*.

NOT EVEN *NOTHING* LASTS FOREVER.

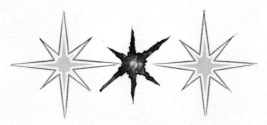

EVERYTHING HAS A *BEGINNING* AND AN *END*.

TO BELIEVE *OTHERWISE* IS DELUSIONAL.

SOME *FACTS* SIMPLY *CANNOT* BE DENIED.

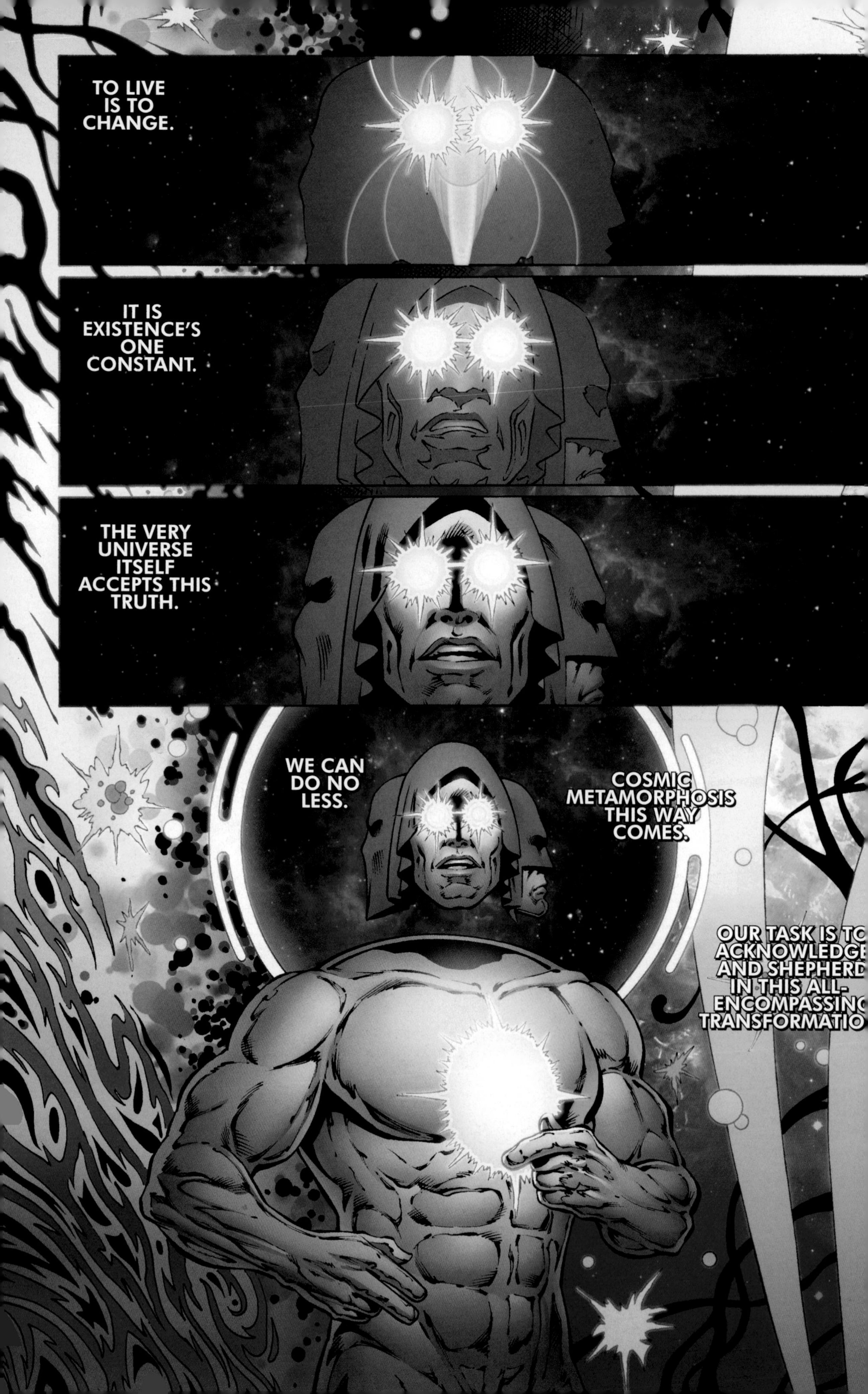

TO LIVE IS TO CHANGE.
IT IS EXISTENCE'S ONE CONSTANT.
THE VERY UNIVERSE ITSELF ACCEPTS THIS TRUTH.
WE CAN DO NO LESS.
COSMIC METAMORPHOSIS THIS WAY COMES.
OUR TASK IS TO ACKNOWLEDG AND SHEPHERD IN THIS ALL-ENCOMPASSIN TRANSFORMATIO

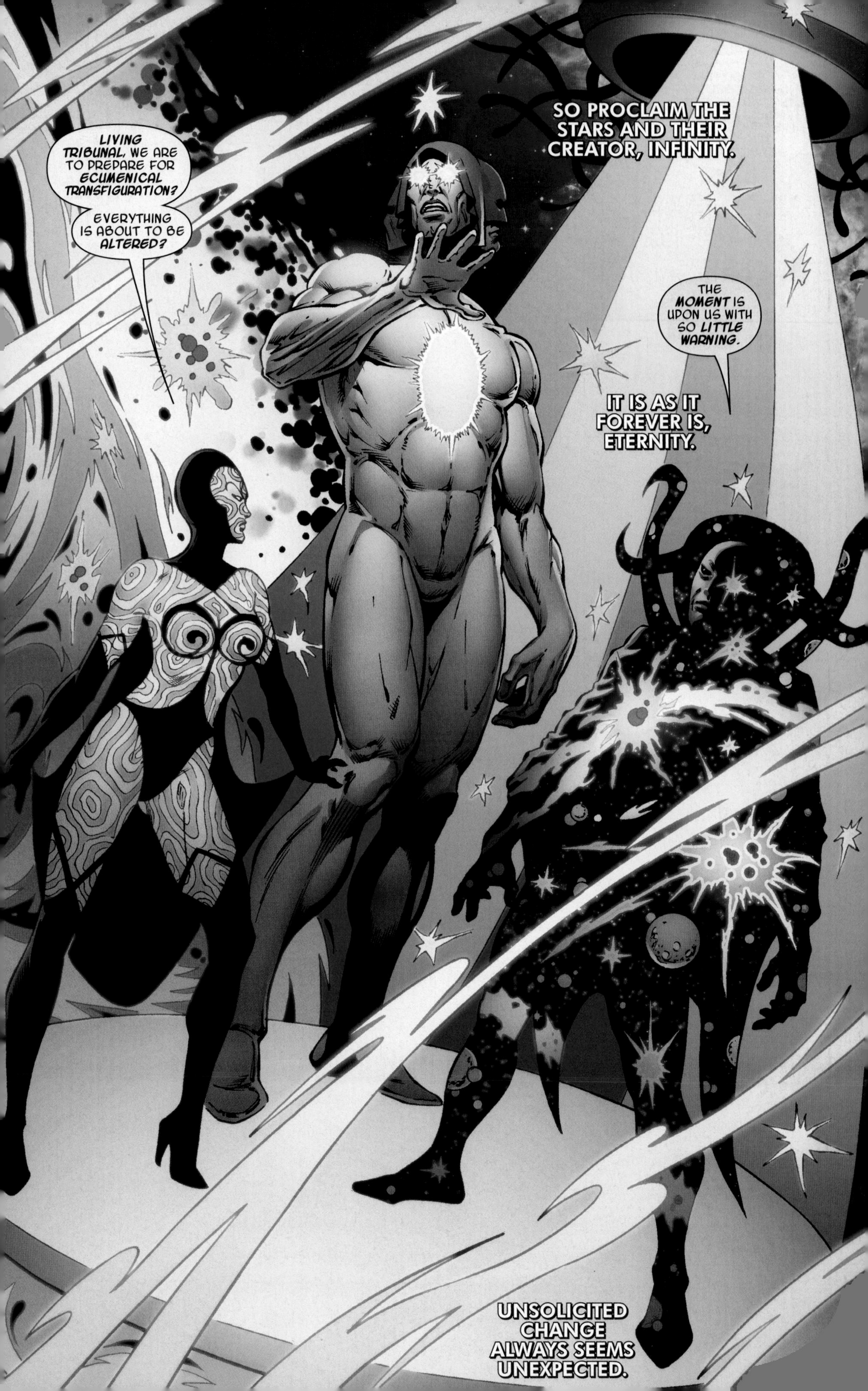
SO PROCLAIM THE STARS AND THEIR CREATOR, INFINITY.
LIVING TRIBUNAL, WE ARE TO PREPARE FOR ECUMENICAL TRANSFIGURATION?
EVERYTHING IS ABOUT TO BE ALTERED?
THE MOMENT IS UPON US WITH SO LITTLE WARNING.
IT IS AS IT FOREVER IS, ETERNITY.
UNSOLICITED CHANGE ALWAYS SEEMS UNEXPECTED.

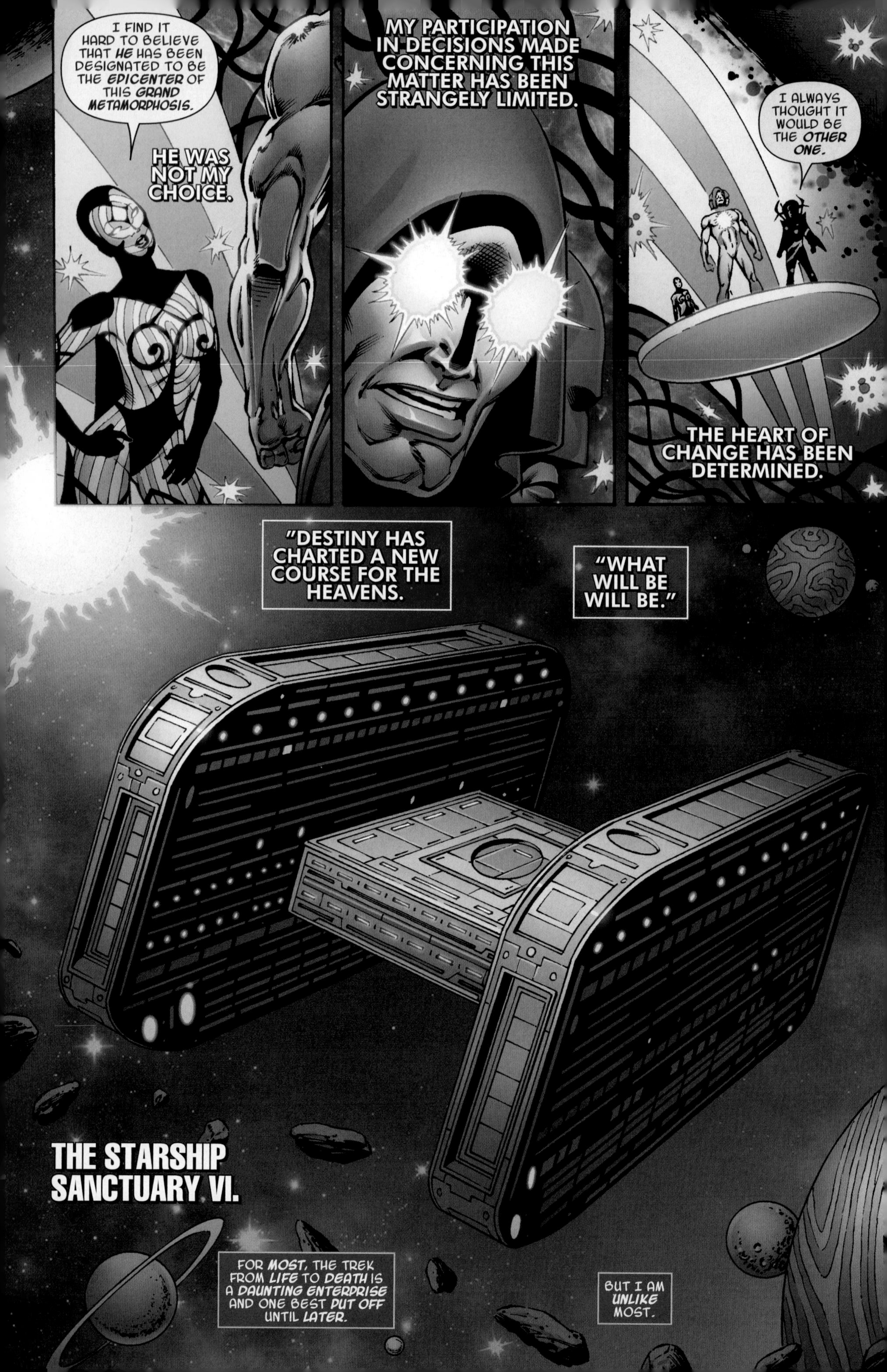
I FIND IT HARD TO BELIEVE THAT *HE* HAS BEEN DESIGNATED TO BE THE *EPICENTER* OF THIS *GRAND METAMORPHOSIS*.
HE WAS NOT MY CHOICE.
MY PARTICIPATION IN DECISIONS MADE CONCERNING THIS MATTER HAS BEEN STRANGELY LIMITED.
I ALWAYS THOUGHT IT WOULD BE THE *OTHER ONE*.
THE HEART OF CHANGE HAS BEEN DETERMINED.
"DESTINY HAS CHARTED A NEW COURSE FOR THE HEAVENS.
"WHAT WILL BE WILL BE."
THE STARSHIP SANCTUARY VI.
FOR *MOST*, THE TREK FROM *LIFE* TO *DEATH* IS A *DAUNTING ENTERPRISE* AND ONE BEST *PUT OFF* UNTIL *LATER*.
BUT I AM *UNLIKE* MOST.

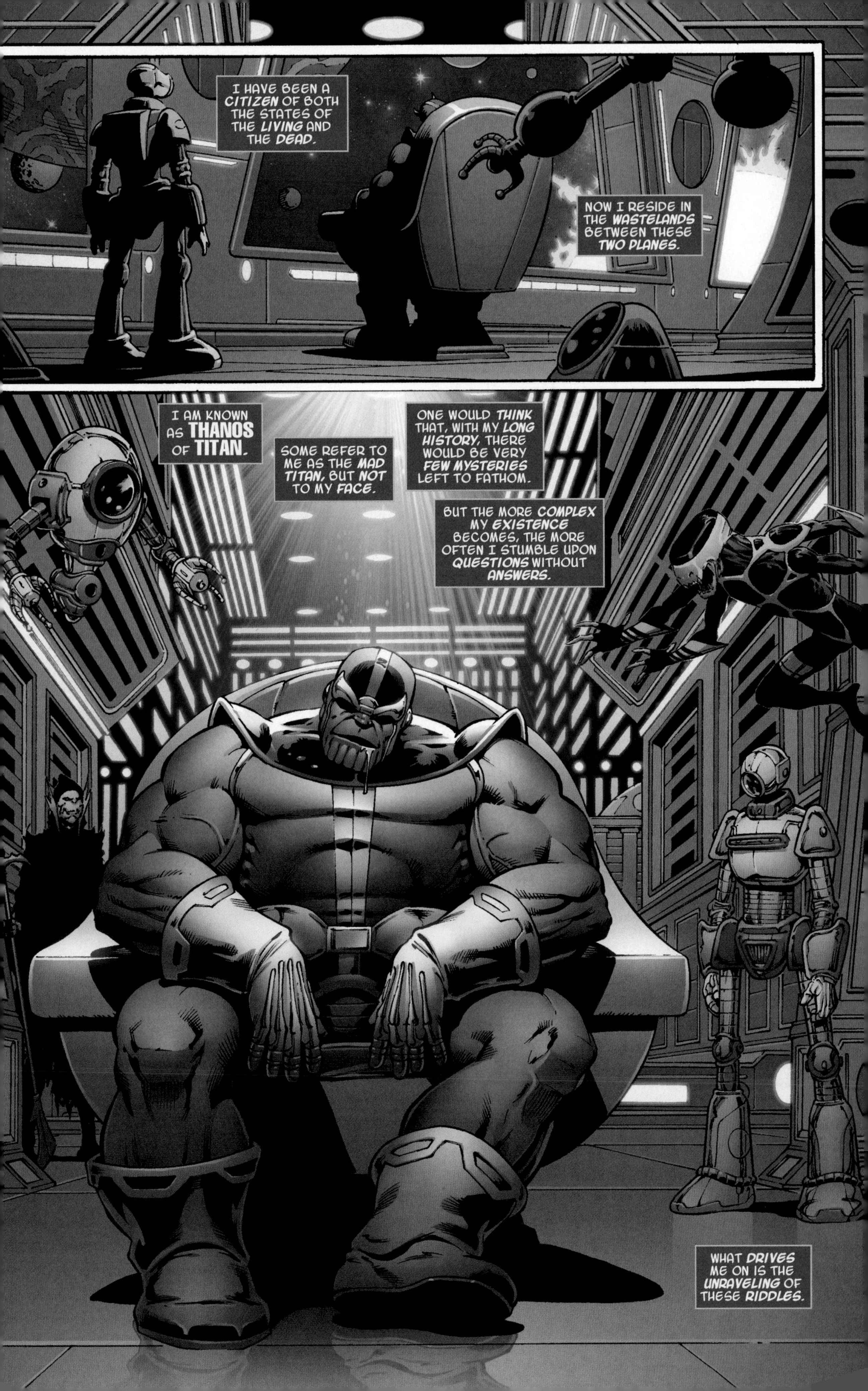
I HAVE BEEN A CITIZEN OF BOTH THE STATES OF THE LIVING AND THE DEAD.
NOW I RESIDE IN THE WASTELANDS BETWEEN THESE TWO PLANES.
I AM KNOWN AS THANOS OF TITAN.
SOME REFER TO ME AS THE MAD TITAN, BUT NOT TO MY FACE.
ONE WOULD THINK THAT, WITH MY LONG HISTORY, THERE WOULD BE VERY FEW MYSTERIES LEFT TO FATHOM.
BUT THE MORE COMPLEX MY EXISTENCE BECOMES, THE MORE OFTEN I STUMBLE UPON QUESTIONS WITHOUT ANSWERS.
WHAT DRIVES ME ON IS THE UNRAVELING OF THESE RIDDLES.

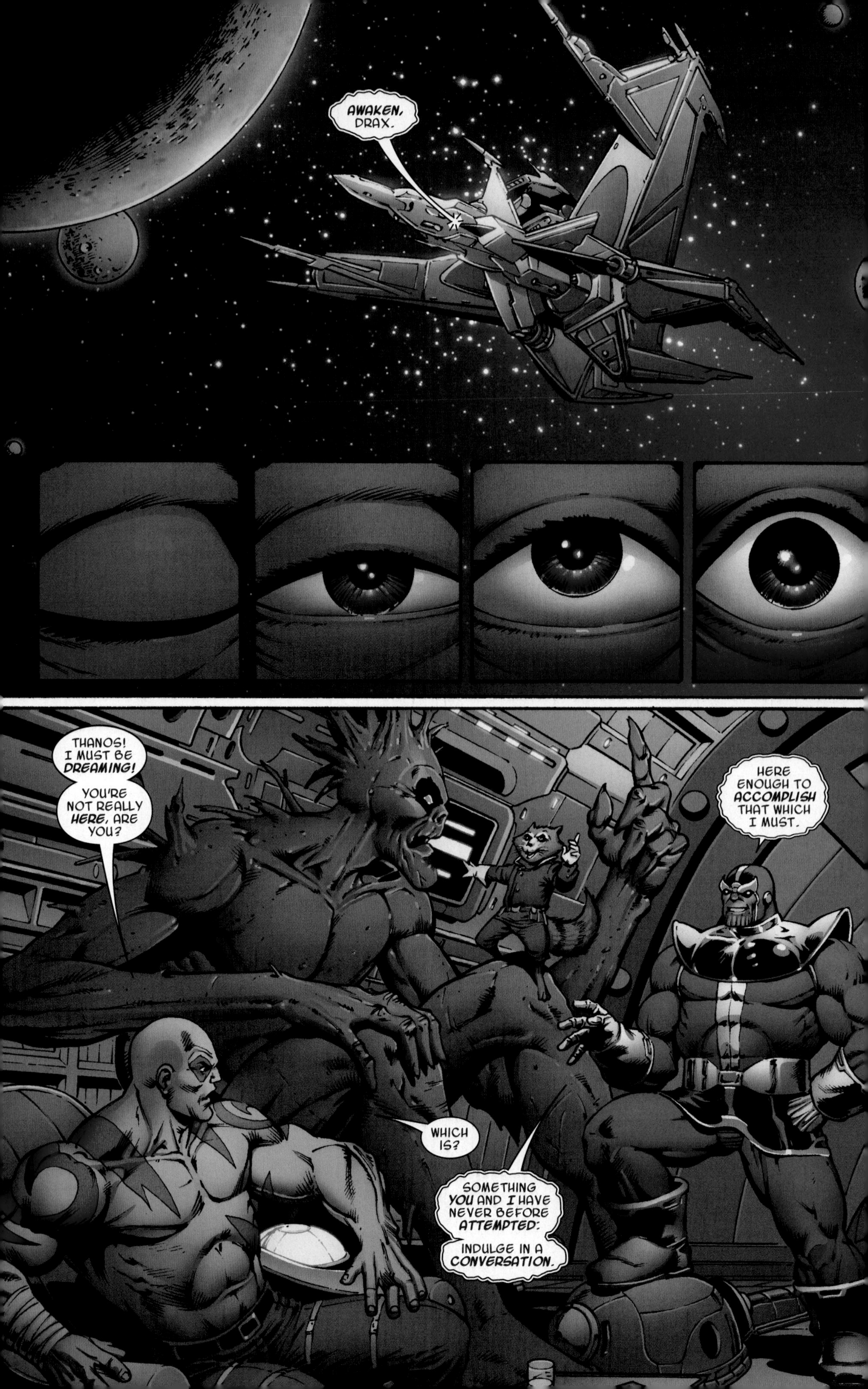

AWAKEN, DRAX.
THANOS! I MUST BE DREAMING!
YOU'RE NOT REALLY HERE, ARE YOU?
HERE ENOUGH TO ACCOMPLISH THAT WHICH I MUST.
WHICH IS?
SOMETHING YOU AND I HAVE NEVER BEFORE ATTEMPTED:
INDULGE IN A CONVERSATION.

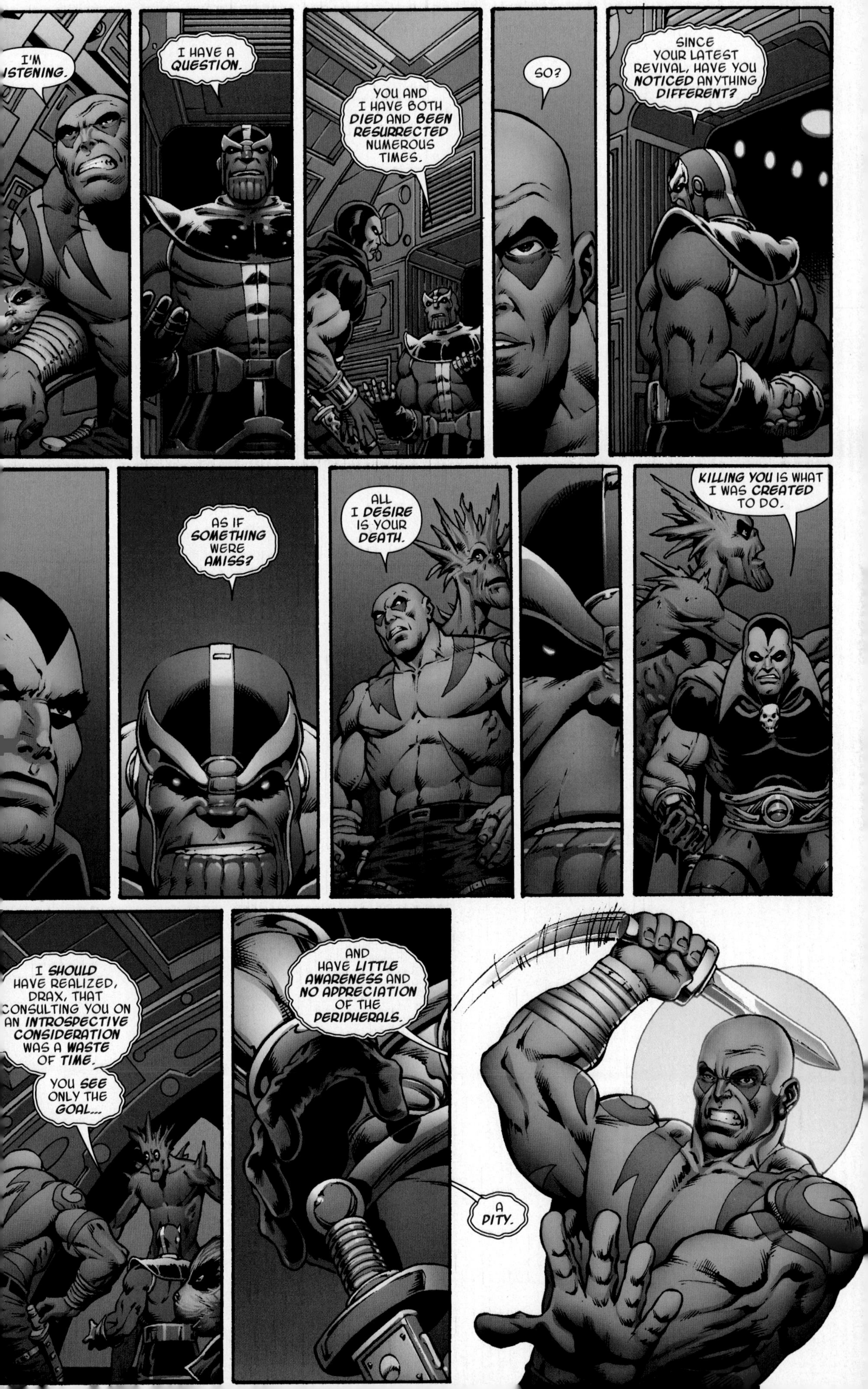

I'M LISTENING.
I HAVE A QUESTION.
YOU AND I HAVE BOTH DIED AND BEEN RESURRECTED NUMEROUS TIMES.
SO?
SINCE YOUR LATEST REVIVAL, HAVE YOU NOTICED ANYTHING DIFFERENT?
AS IF SOMETHING WERE AMISS?
ALL I DESIRE IS YOUR DEATH.
KILLING YOU IS WHAT I WAS CREATED TO DO.
I SHOULD HAVE REALIZED, DRAX, THAT CONSULTING YOU ON AN INTROSPECTIVE CONSIDERATION WAS A WASTE OF TIME.
YOU SEE ONLY THE GOAL...
AND HAVE LITTLE AWARENESS AND NO APPRECIATION OF THE PERIPHERALS.
A PITY.

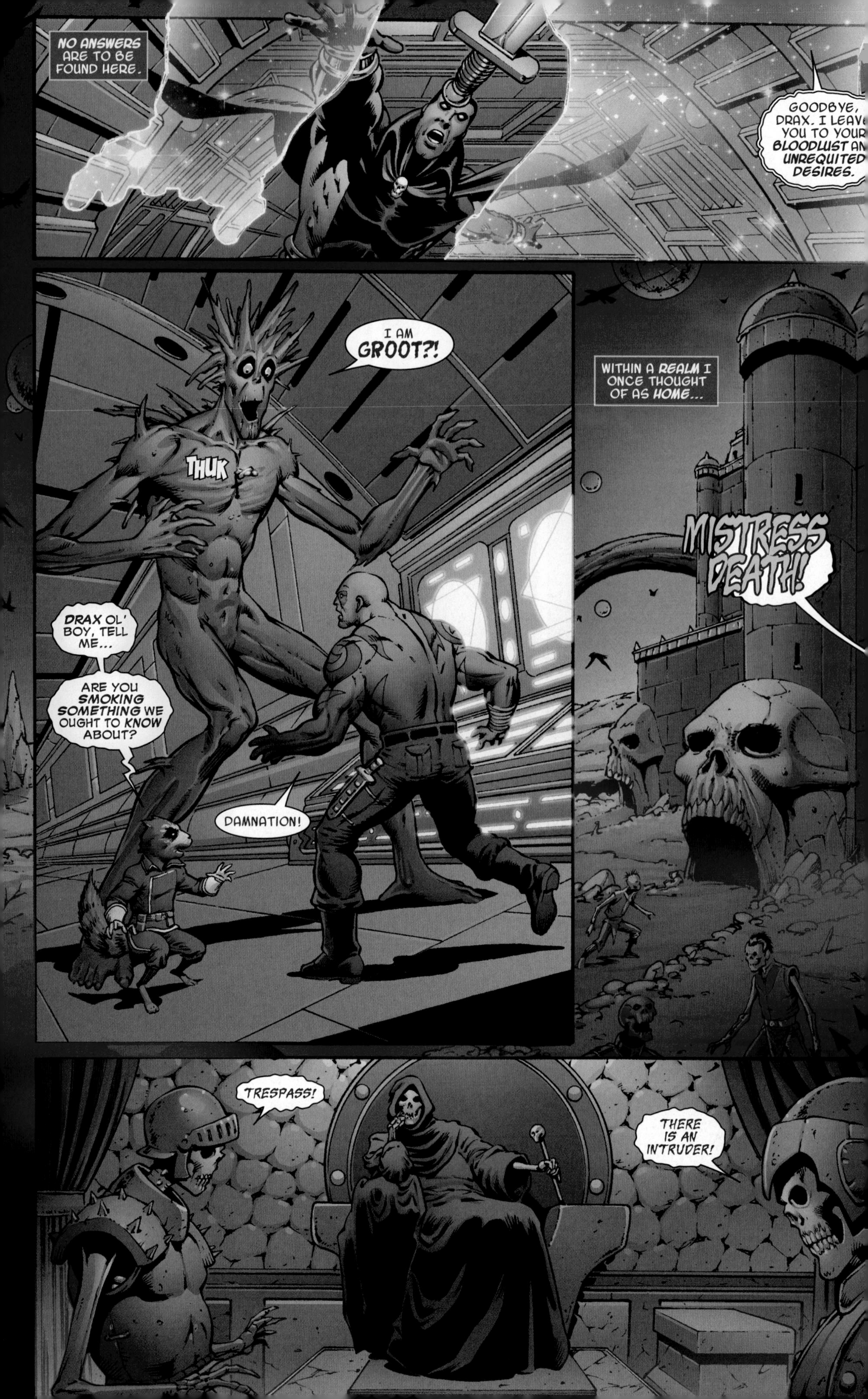
NO ANSWERS ARE TO BE FOUND HERE.
GOODBYE, DRAX. I LEAVE YOU TO YOUR BLOODLUST AND UNREQUITED DESIRES.
I AM GROOT?!
THUK
DRAX OL' BOY, TELL ME...
ARE YOU SMOKING SOMETHING WE OUGHT TO KNOW ABOUT?
DAMNATION!
WITHIN A REALM I ONCE THOUGHT OF AS HOME...
MISTRESS DEATH!
TRESPASS!
THERE IS AN INTRUDER!

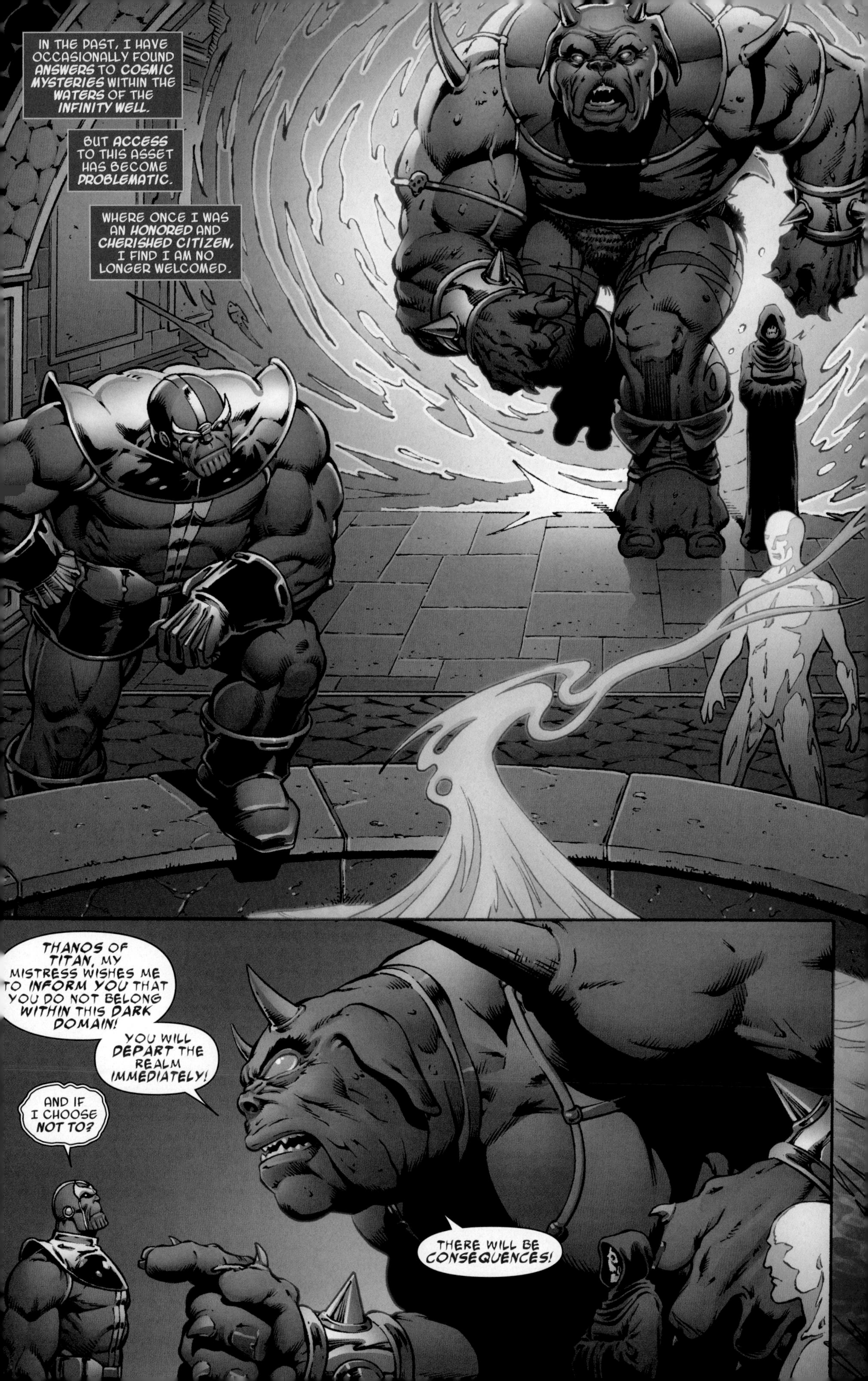
IN THE PAST, I HAVE OCCASIONALLY FOUND ANSWERS TO COSMIC MYSTERIES WITHIN THE WATERS OF THE INFINITY WELL.
BUT ACCESS TO THIS ASSET HAS BECOME PROBLEMATIC.
WHERE ONCE I WAS AN HONORED AND CHERISHED CITIZEN, I FIND I AM NO LONGER WELCOMED.
THANOS OF TITAN, MY MISTRESS WISHES ME TO INFORM YOU THAT YOU DO NOT BELONG WITHIN THIS DARK DOMAIN!
YOU WILL DEPART THE REALM IMMEDIATELY!
AND IF I CHOOSE NOT TO?
THERE WILL BE CONSEQUENCES!

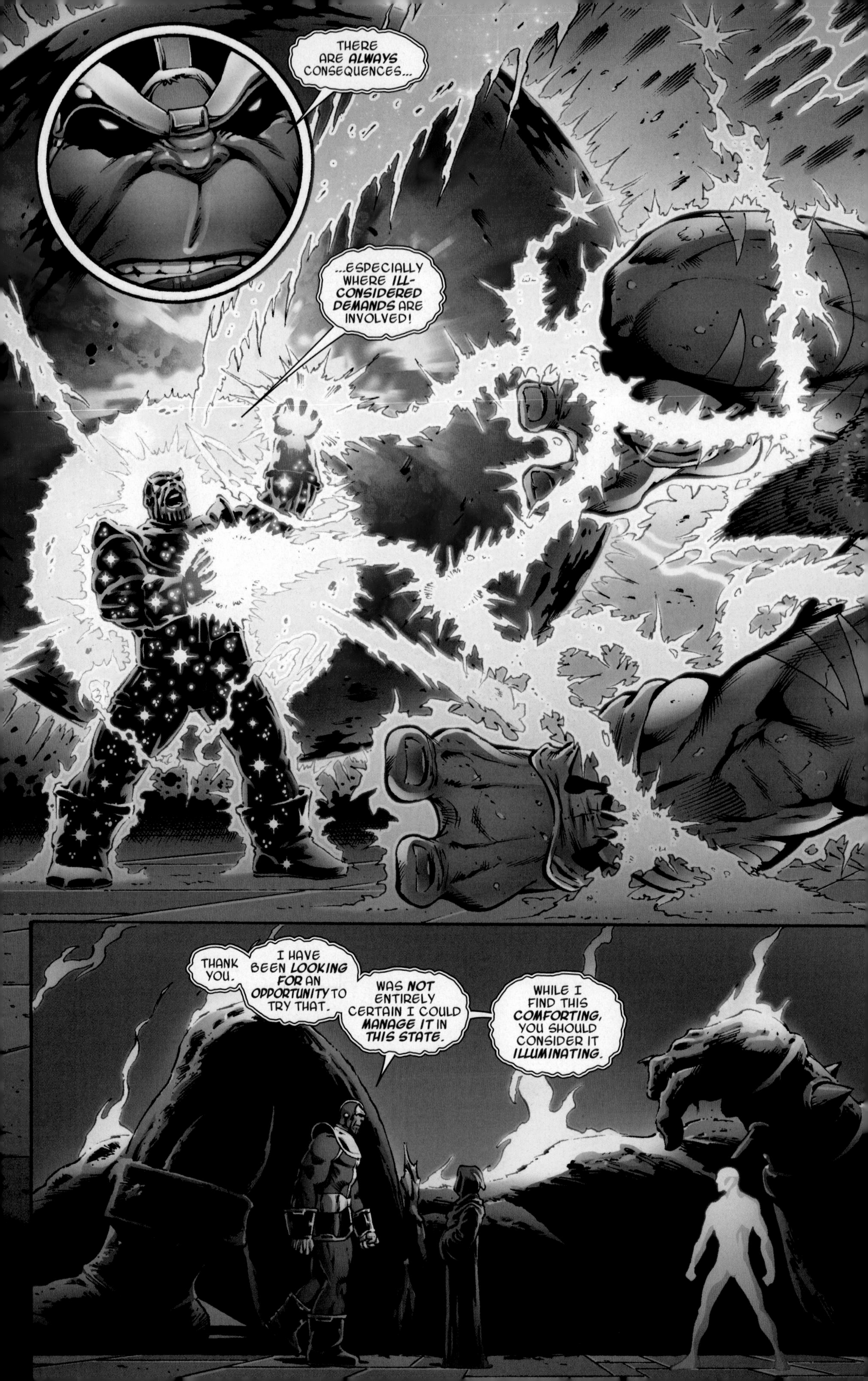
THERE ARE ALWAYS CONSEQUENCES...
...ESPECIALLY WHERE ILL-CONSIDERED DEMANDS ARE INVOLVED!
THANK YOU.
I HAVE BEEN LOOKING FOR AN OPPORTUNITY TO TRY THAT.
WAS NOT ENTIRELY CERTAIN I COULD MANAGE IT IN THIS STATE.
WHILE I FIND THIS COMFORTING, YOU SHOULD CONSIDER IT ILLUMINATING.

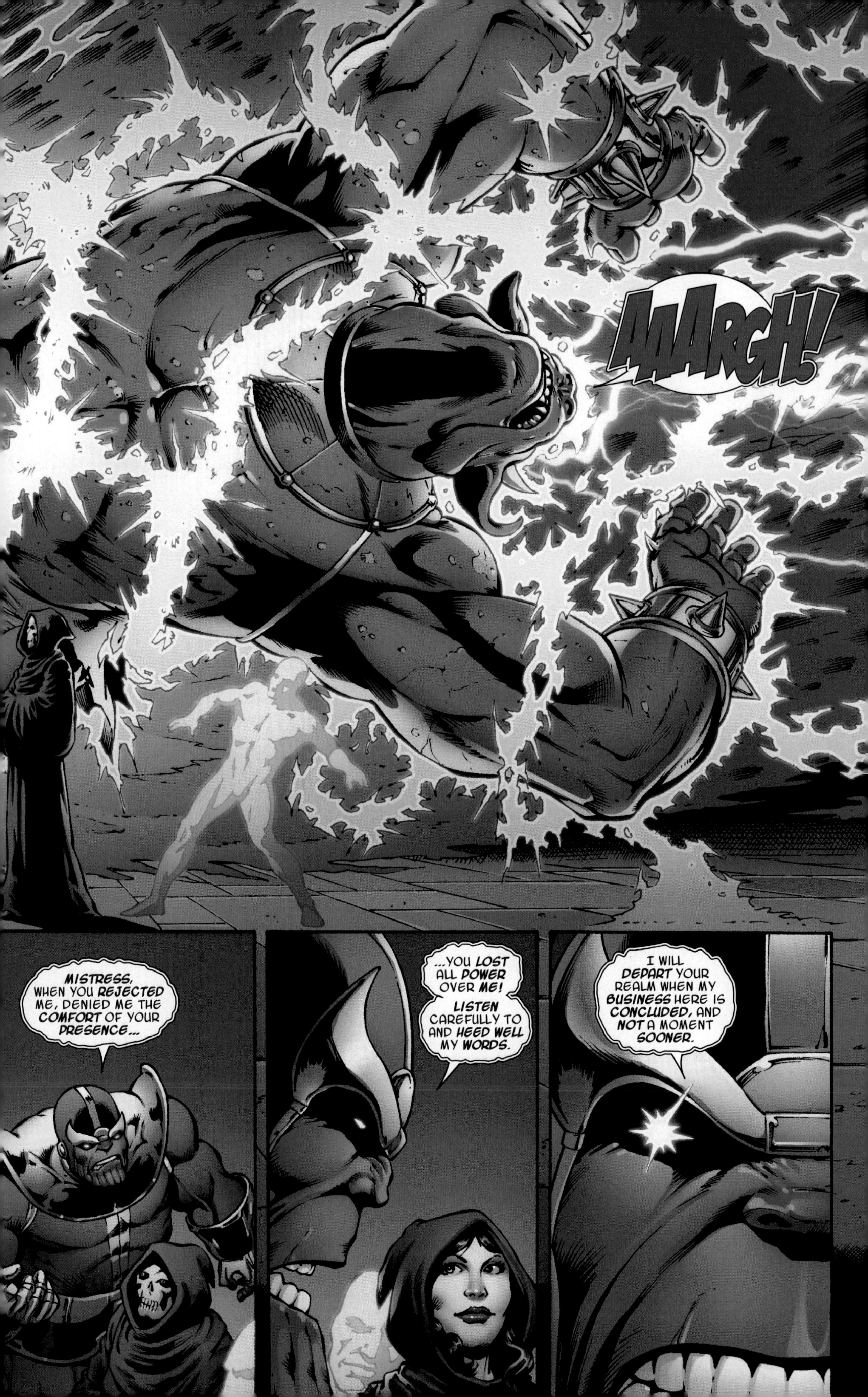

AAARGH!
MISTRESS, WHEN YOU REJECTED ME, DENIED ME THE COMFORT OF YOUR PRESENCE...
...YOU LOST ALL POWER OVER ME!
LISTEN CAREFULLY TO AND HEED WELL MY WORDS.
I WILL DEPART YOUR REALM WHEN MY BUSINESS HERE IS CONCLUDED, AND NOT A MOMENT SOONER.

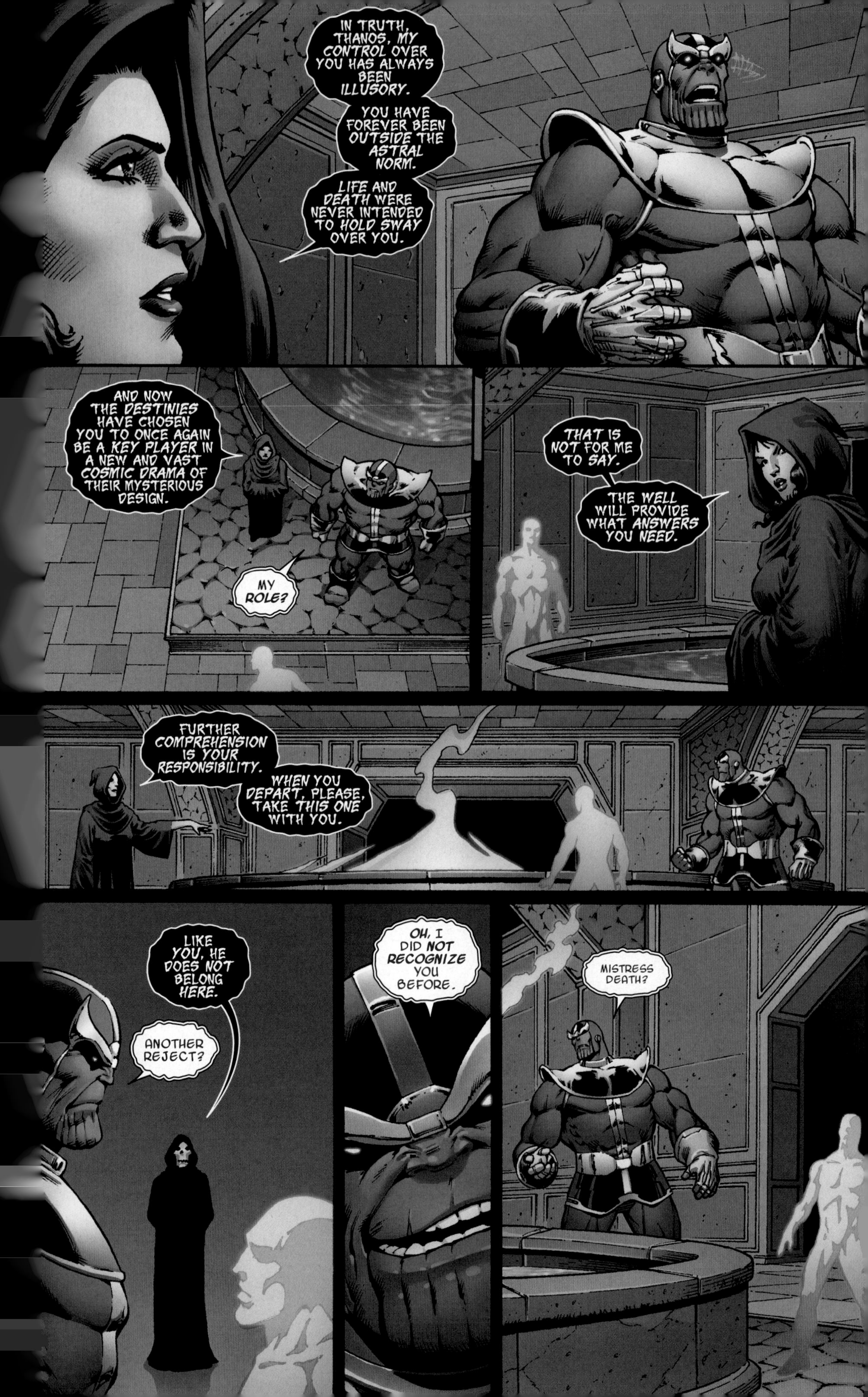
IN TRUTH, THANOS, MY CONTROL OVER YOU HAS ALWAYS BEEN ILLUSORY.
YOU HAVE FOREVER BEEN OUTSIDE THE ASTRAL NORM.
LIFE AND DEATH WERE NEVER INTENDED TO HOLD SWAY OVER YOU.
AND NOW THE DESTINIES HAVE CHOSEN YOU TO ONCE AGAIN BE A KEY PLAYER IN A NEW AND VAST COSMIC DRAMA OF THEIR MYSTERIOUS DESIGN.
MY ROLE?
THAT IS NOT FOR ME TO SAY.
THE WELL WILL PROVIDE WHAT ANSWERS YOU NEED.
FURTHER COMPREHENSION IS YOUR RESPONSIBILITY.
WHEN YOU DEPART, PLEASE, TAKE THIS ONE WITH YOU.
LIKE YOU, HE DOES NOT BELONG HERE.
ANOTHER REJECT?
OH, I DID NOT RECOGNIZE YOU BEFORE.
MISTRESS DEATH?

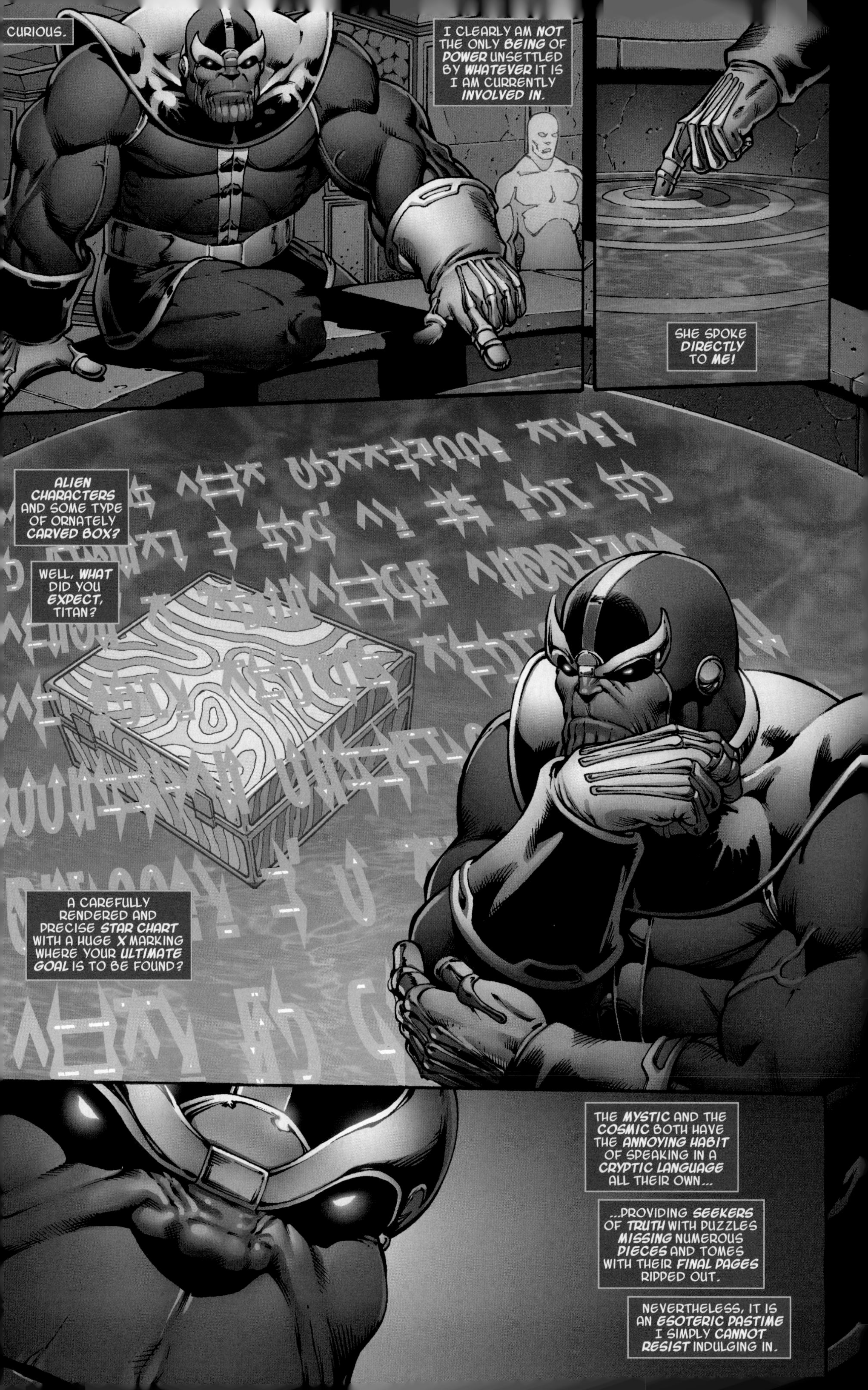
CURIOUS.
I CLEARLY AM NOT THE ONLY BEING OF POWER UNSETTLED BY WHATEVER IT IS I AM CURRENTLY INVOLVED IN.
SHE SPOKE DIRECTLY TO ME!
ALIEN CHARACTERS AND SOME TYPE OF ORNATELY CARVED BOX?
WELL, WHAT DID YOU EXPECT, TITAN?
A CAREFULLY RENDERED AND PRECISE STAR CHART WITH A HUGE X MARKING WHERE YOUR ULTIMATE GOAL IS TO BE FOUND?
THE MYSTIC AND THE COSMIC BOTH HAVE THE ANNOYING HABIT OF SPEAKING IN A CRYPTIC LANGUAGE ALL THEIR OWN...
...PROVIDING SEEKERS OF TRUTH WITH PUZZLES MISSING NUMEROUS PIECES AND TOMES WITH THEIR FINAL PAGES RIPPED OUT.
NEVERTHELESS, IT IS AN ESOTERIC PASTIME I SIMPLY CANNOT RESIST INDULGING IN.

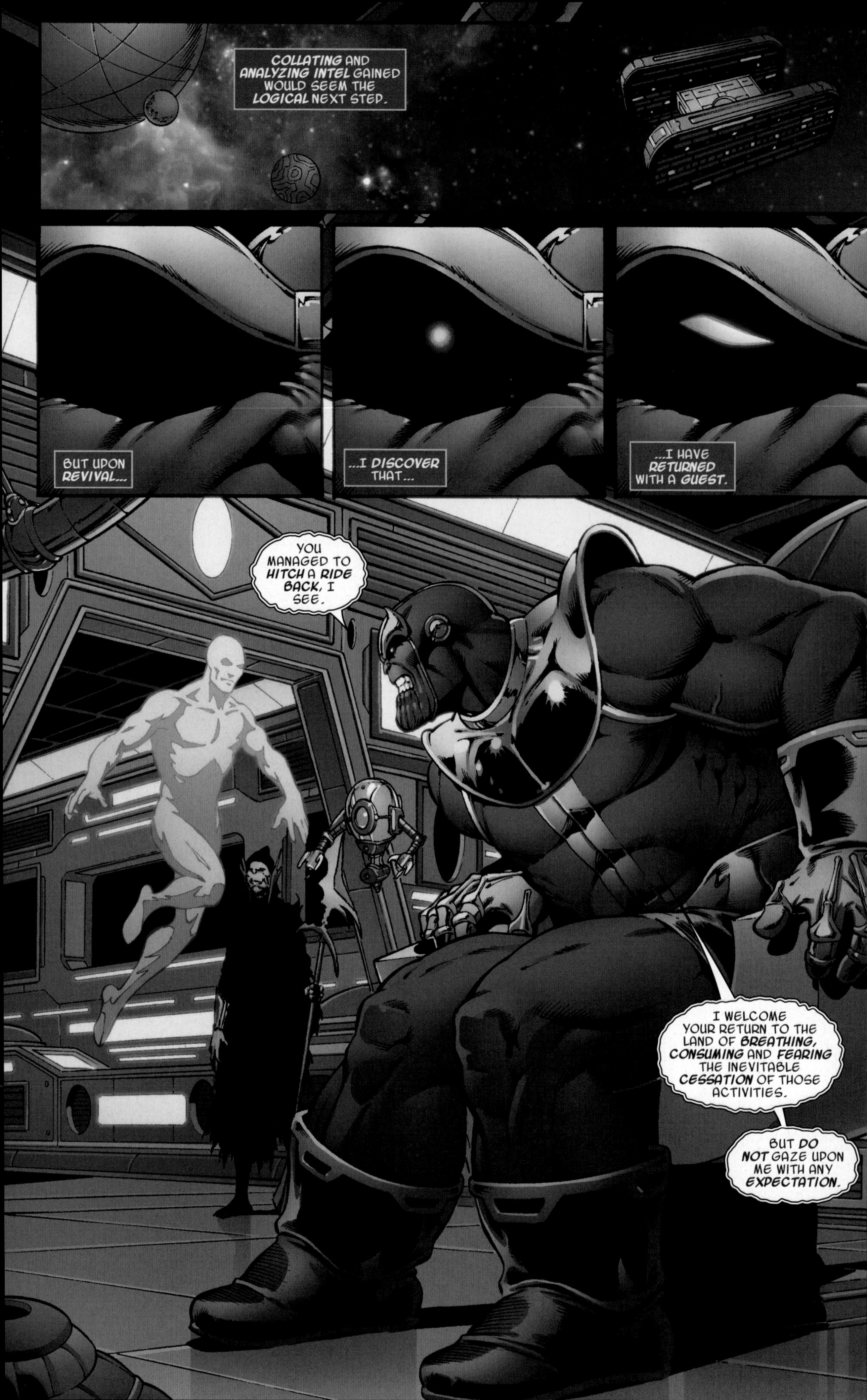

COLLATING AND ANALYZING INTEL GAINED WOULD SEEM THE LOGICAL NEXT STEP.
BUT UPON REVIVAL...
...I DISCOVER THAT...
...I HAVE RETURNED WITH A GUEST.
YOU MANAGED TO HITCH A RIDE BACK, I SEE.
I WELCOME YOUR RETURN TO THE LAND OF BREATHING, CONSUMING AND FEARING THE INEVITABLE CESSATION OF THOSE ACTIVITIES.
BUT DO NOT GAZE UPON ME WITH ANY EXPECTATION.

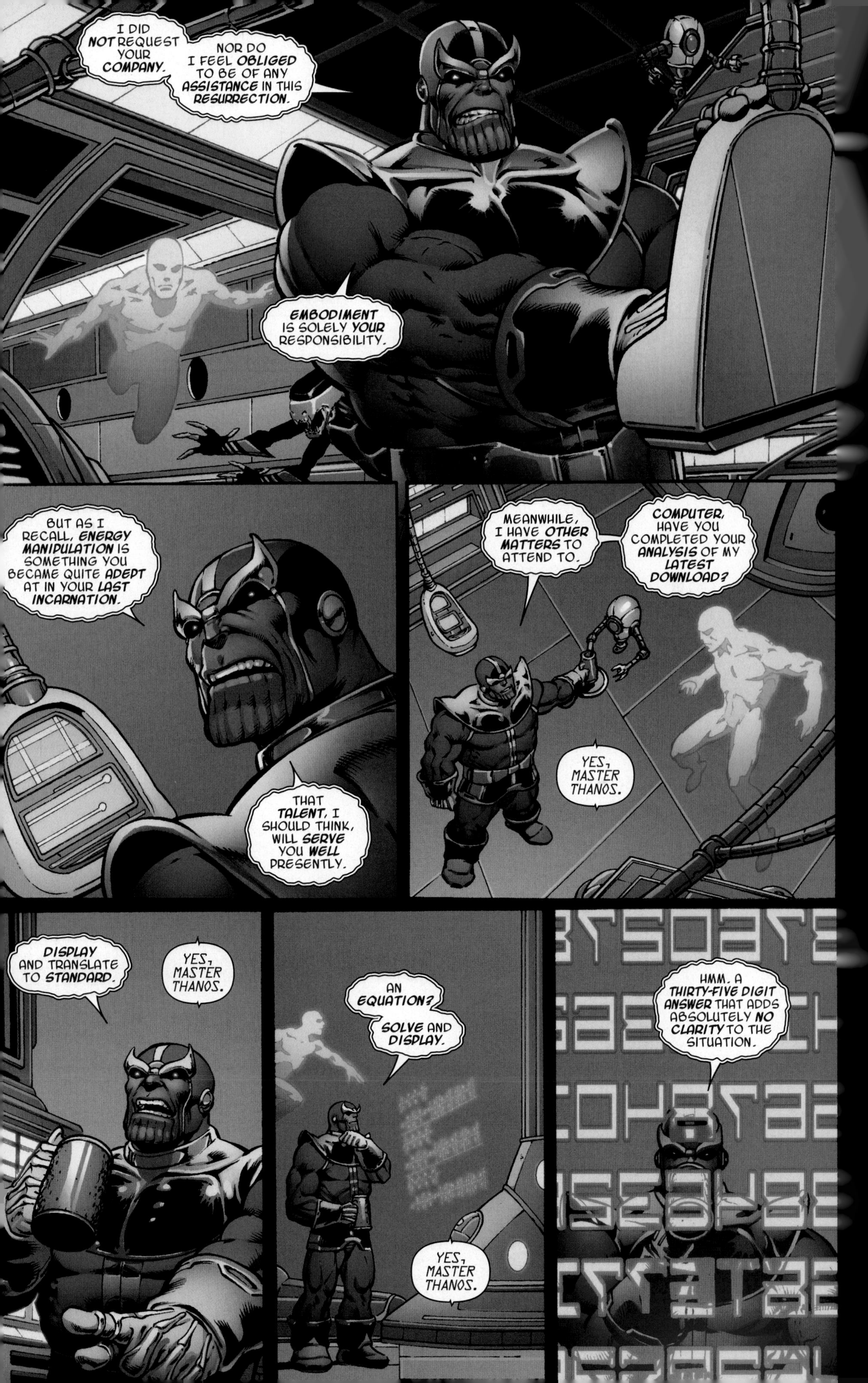

I DID NOT REQUEST YOUR COMPANY.
NOR DO I FEEL OBLIGED TO BE OF ANY ASSISTANCE IN THIS RESURRECTION.
EMBODIMENT IS SOLELY YOUR RESPONSIBILITY.
BUT AS I RECALL, ENERGY MANIPULATION IS SOMETHING YOU BECAME QUITE ADEPT AT IN YOUR LAST INCARNATION.
THAT TALENT, I SHOULD THINK, WILL SERVE YOU WELL PRESENTLY.
MEANWHILE, I HAVE OTHER MATTERS TO ATTEND TO.
COMPUTER, HAVE YOU COMPLETED YOUR ANALYSIS OF MY LATEST DOWNLOAD?
YES, MASTER THANOS.
DISPLAY AND TRANSLATE TO STANDARD.
YES, MASTER THANOS.
AN EQUATION?
SOLVE AND DISPLAY.
YES, MASTER THANOS.
HMM. A THIRTY-FIVE DIGIT ANSWER THAT ADDS ABSOLUTELY NO CLARITY TO THE SITUATION.

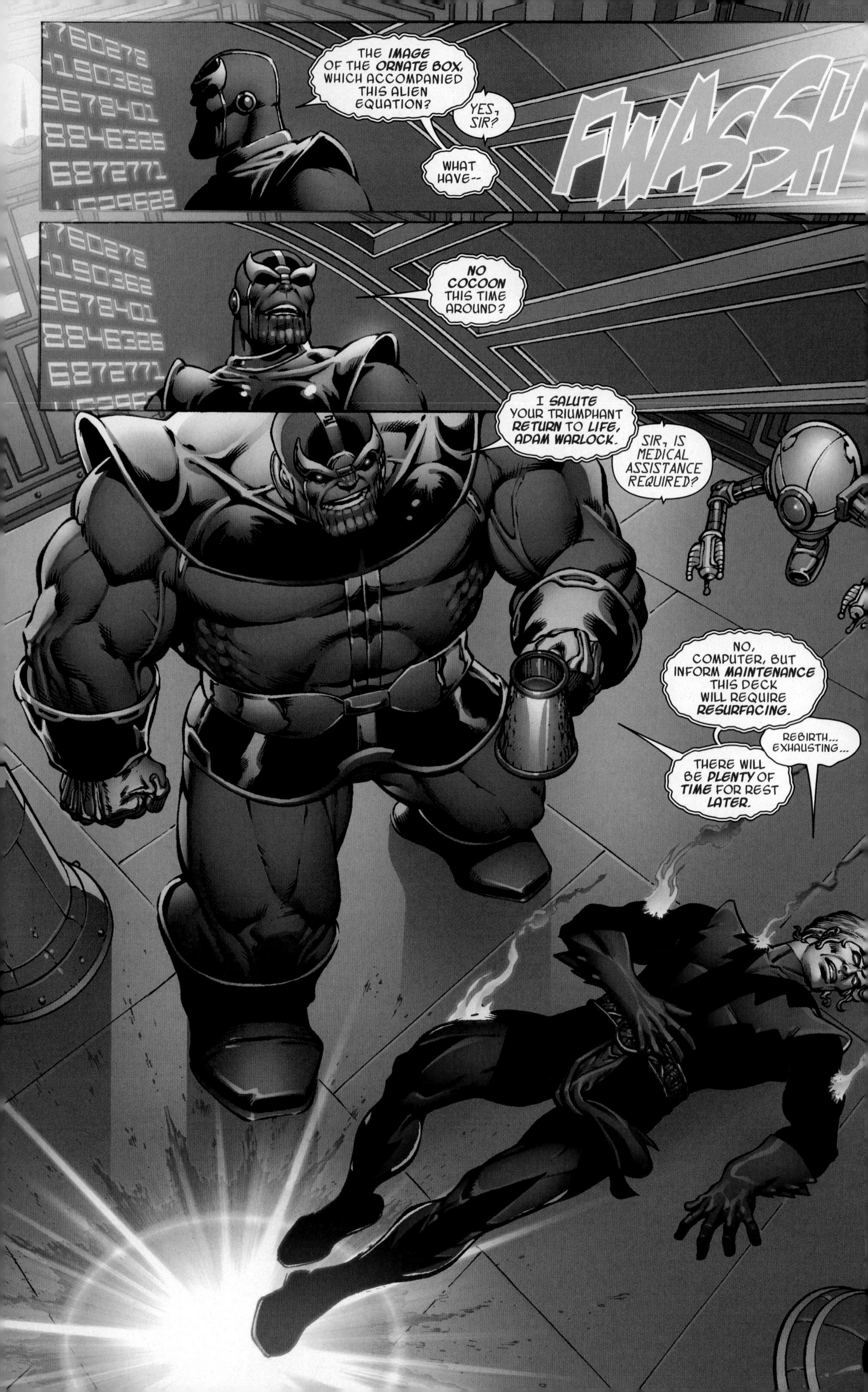
THE IMAGE OF THE ORNATE BOX, WHICH ACCOMPANIED THIS ALIEN EQUATION?
YES, SIR?
WHAT HAVE--
FWASSH
NO COCOON THIS TIME AROUND?
I SALUTE YOUR TRIUMPHANT RETURN TO LIFE, ADAM WARLOCK.
SIR, IS MEDICAL ASSISTANCE REQUIRED?
NO, COMPUTER, BUT INFORM MAINTENANCE THIS DECK WILL REQUIRE RESURFACING.
REBIRTH... EXHAUSTING...
THERE WILL BE PLENTY OF TIME FOR REST LATER.

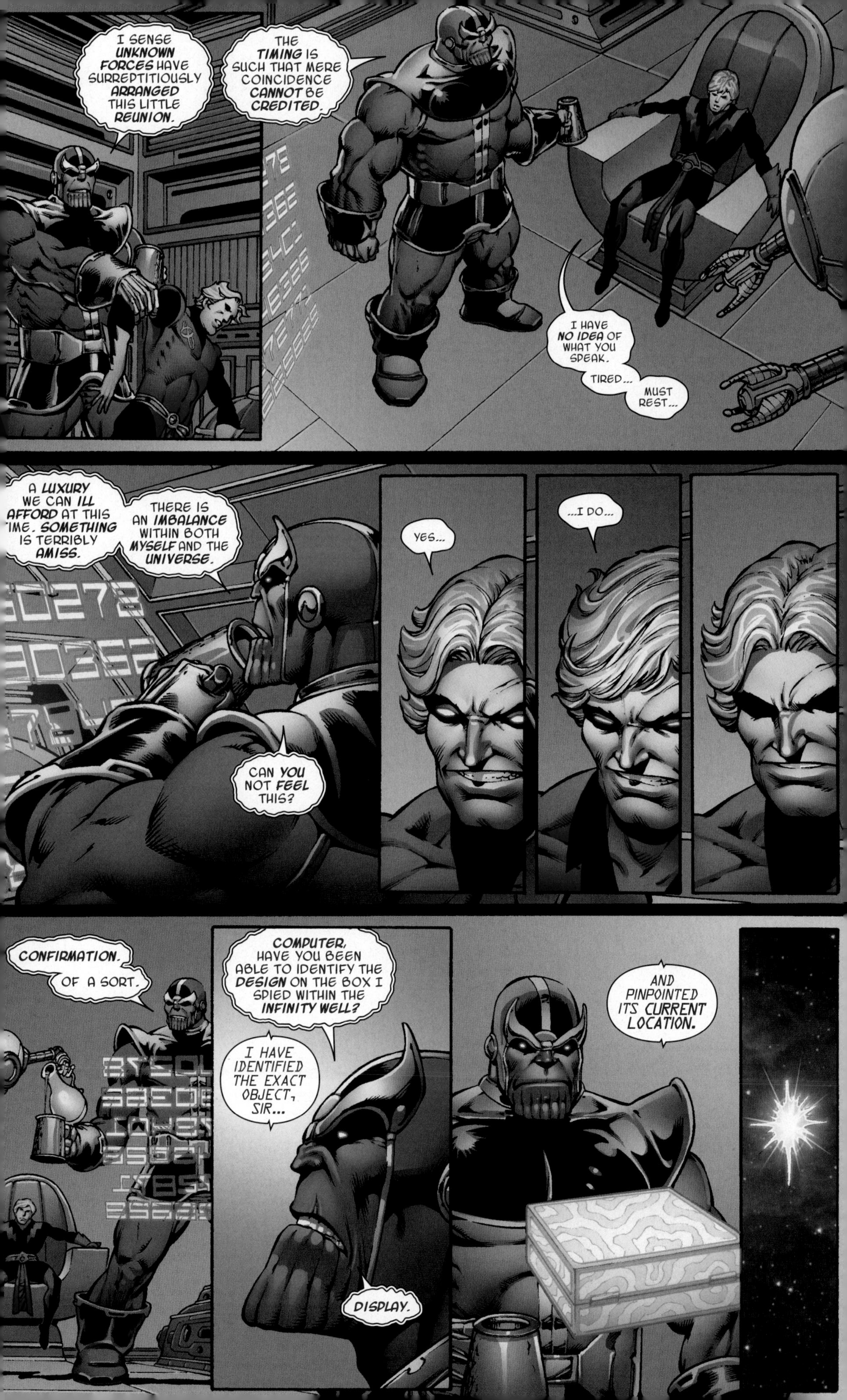
I SENSE UNKNOWN FORCES HAVE SURREPTITIOUSLY ARRANGED THIS LITTLE REUNION.
THE TIMING IS SUCH THAT MERE COINCIDENCE CANNOT BE CREDITED.
I HAVE NO IDEA OF WHAT YOU SPEAK.
TIRED...
MUST REST...
A LUXURY WE CAN ILL AFFORD AT THIS TIME. SOMETHING IS TERRIBLY AMISS.
THERE IS AN IMBALANCE WITHIN BOTH MYSELF AND THE UNIVERSE.
CAN YOU NOT FEEL THIS?
YES...
...I DO...
CONFIRMATION.
OF A SORT.
COMPUTER, HAVE YOU BEEN ABLE TO IDENTIFY THE DESIGN ON THE BOX I SPIED WITHIN THE INFINITY WELL?
I HAVE IDENTIFIED THE EXACT OBJECT, SIR...
AND PINPOINTED ITS CURRENT LOCATION.
DISPLAY.

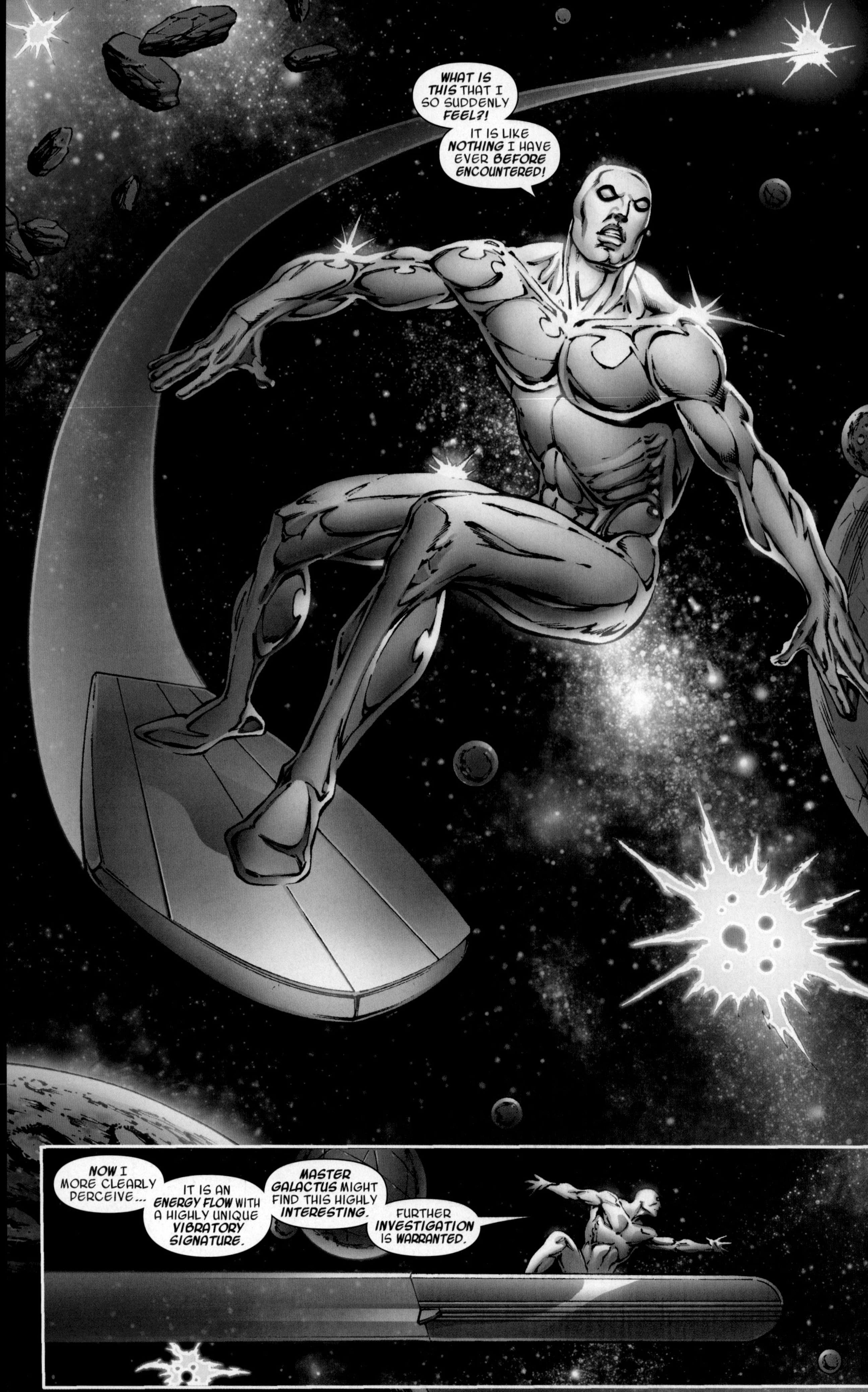
WHAT IS THIS THAT I SO SUDDENLY FEEL?!
IT IS LIKE NOTHING I HAVE EVER BEFORE ENCOUNTERED!
NOW I MORE CLEARLY PERCEIVE...
IT IS AN ENERGY FLOW WITH A HIGHLY UNIQUE VIBRATORY SIGNATURE.
MASTER GALACTUS MIGHT FIND THIS HIGHLY INTERESTING.
FURTHER INVESTIGATION IS WARRANTED.

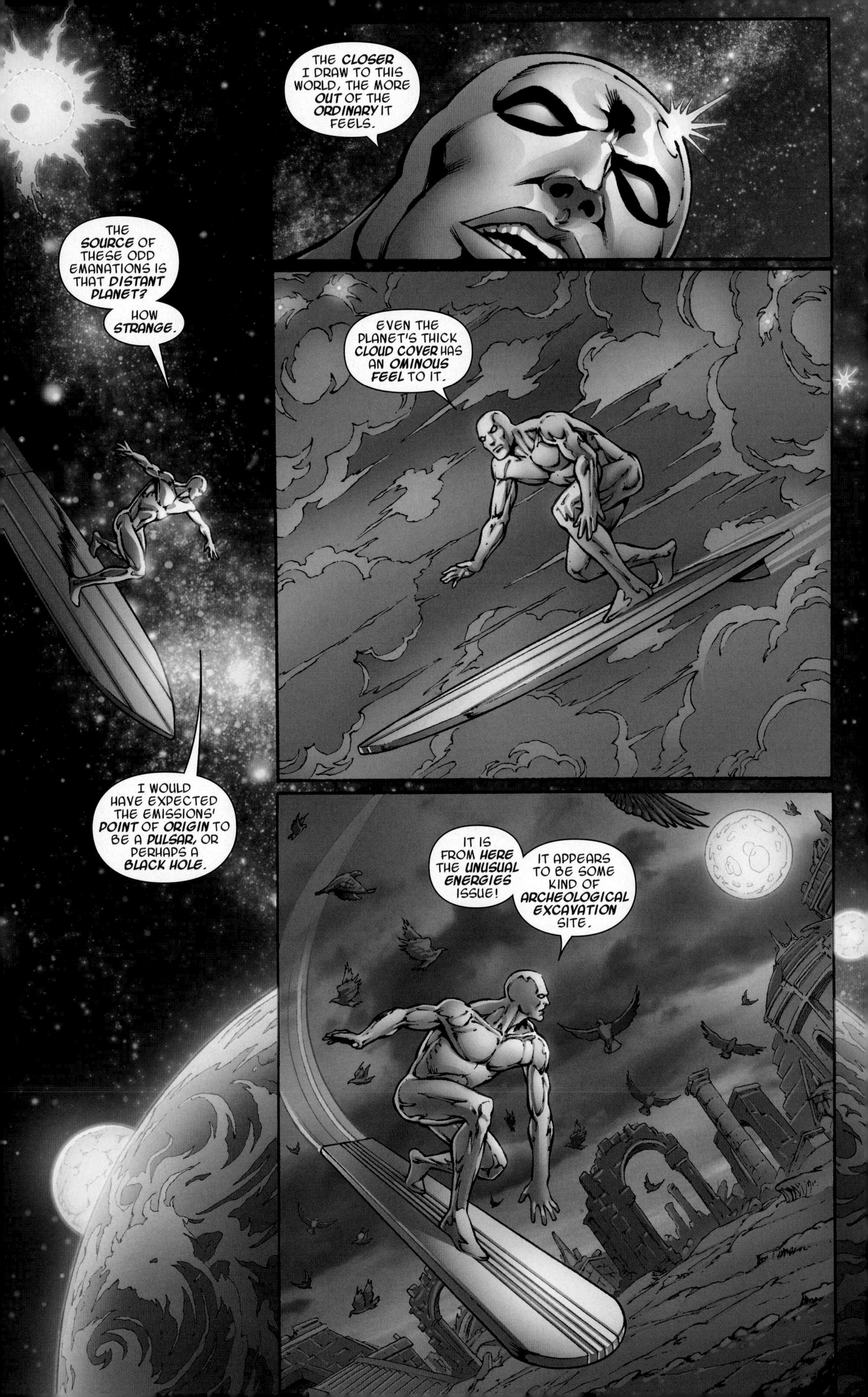
THE CLOSER I DRAW TO THIS WORLD, THE MORE OUT OF THE ORDINARY IT FEELS.
THE SOURCE OF THESE ODD EMANATIONS IS THAT DISTANT PLANET?
HOW STRANGE.
I WOULD HAVE EXPECTED THE EMISSIONS' POINT OF ORIGIN TO BE A PULSAR, OR PERHAPS A BLACK HOLE.
EVEN THE PLANET'S THICK CLOUD COVER HAS AN OMINOUS FEEL TO IT.
IT IS FROM HERE THE UNUSUAL ENERGIES ISSUE!
IT APPEARS TO BE SOME KIND OF ARCHEOLOGICAL EXCAVATION SITE.

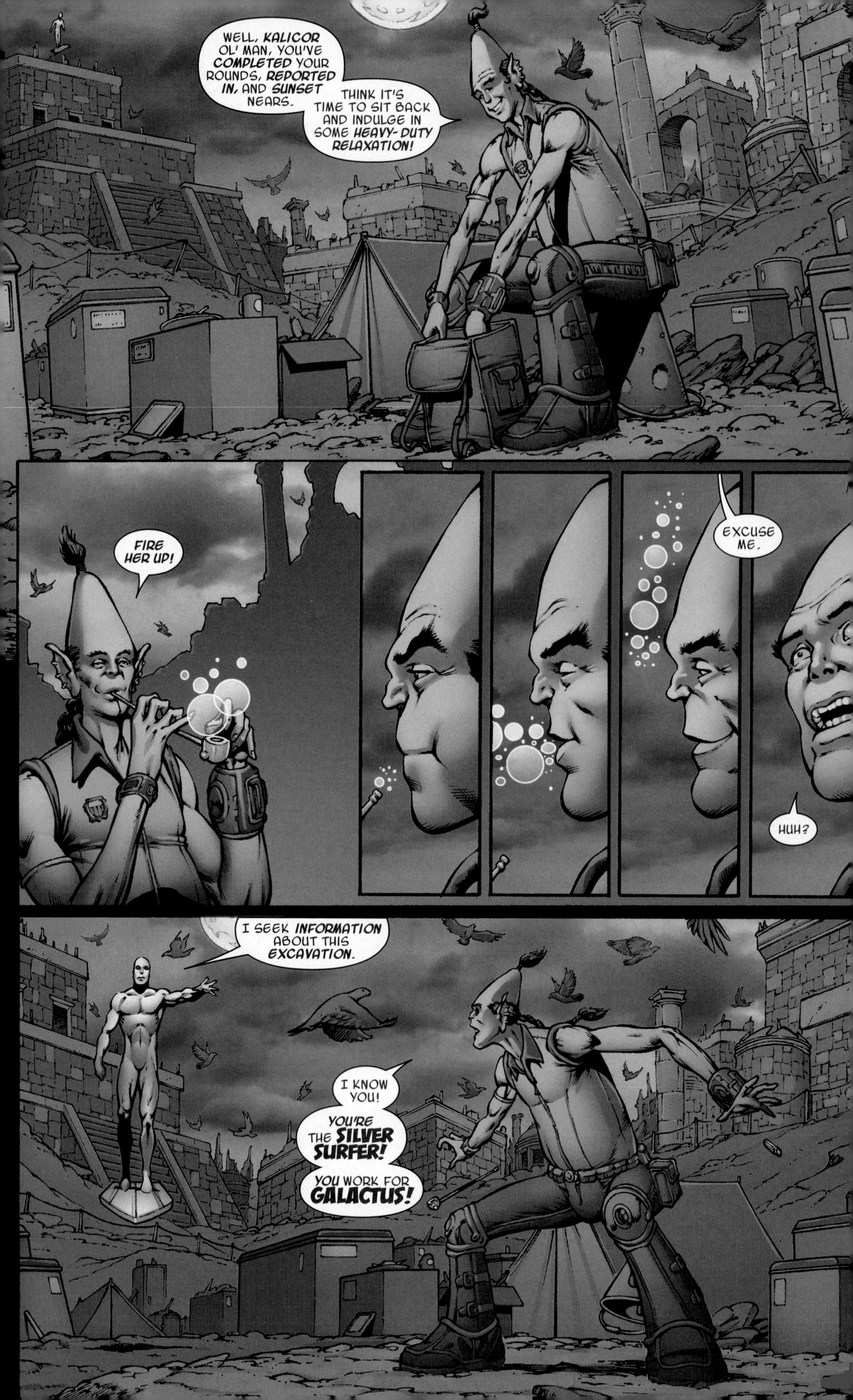
WELL, KALICOR OL' MAN, YOU'VE COMPLETED YOUR ROUNDS, REPORTED IN, AND SUNSET NEARS.
THINK IT'S TIME TO SIT BACK AND INDULGE IN SOME HEAVY-DUTY RELAXATION!
FIRE HER UP!
EXCUSE ME.
HUH?
I SEEK INFORMATION ABOUT THIS EXCAVATION.
I KNOW YOU!
YOU'RE THE SILVER SURFER!
YOU WORK FOR GALACTUS!

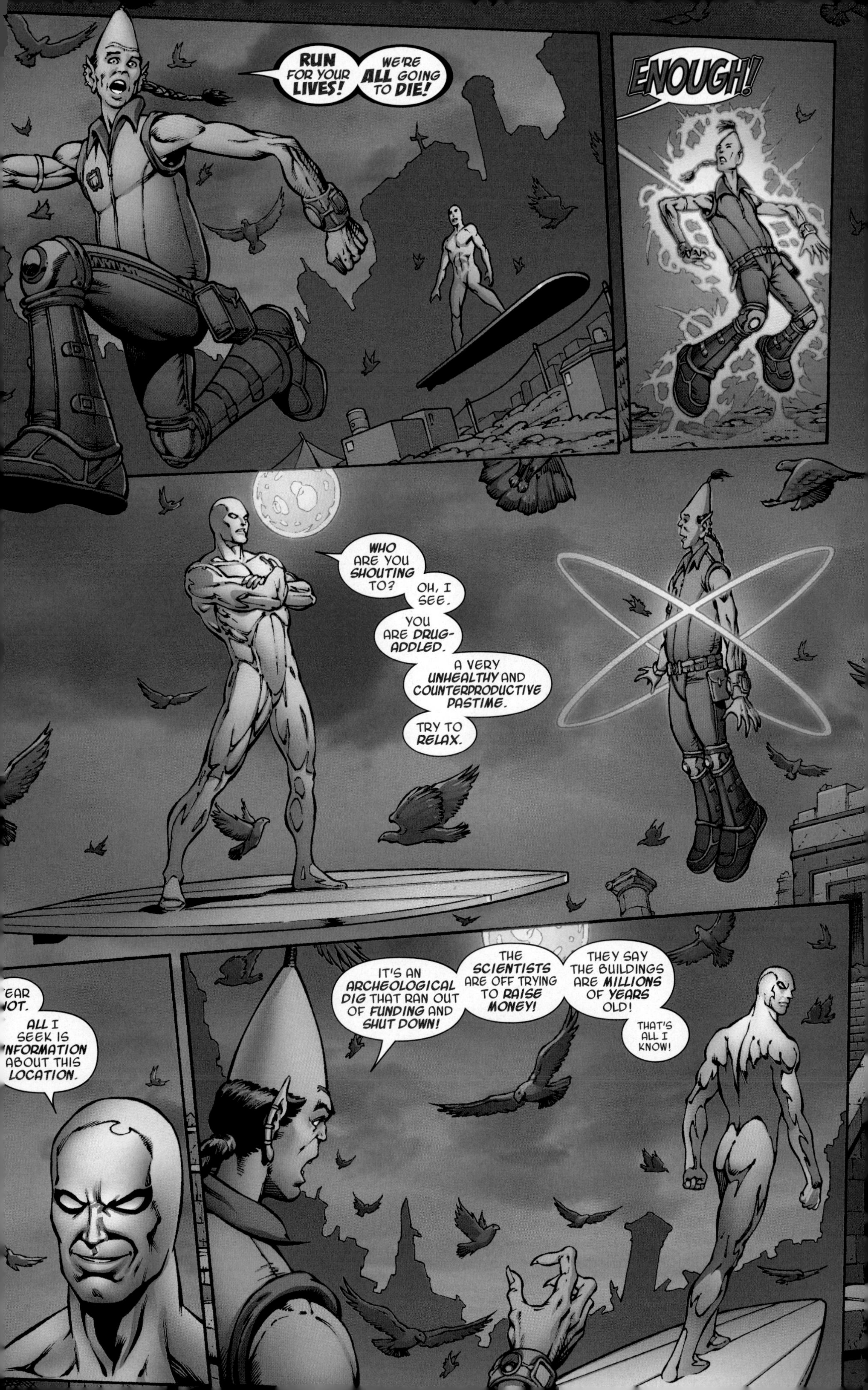

RUN FOR YOUR LIVES!
WE'RE ALL GOING TO DIE!
ENOUGH!
WHO ARE YOU SHOUTING TO?
OH, I SEE.
YOU ARE DRUG-ADDLED.
A VERY UNHEALTHY AND COUNTERPRODUCTIVE PASTIME.
TRY TO RELAX.
EAR NOT.
ALL I SEEK IS NFORMATION ABOUT THIS LOCATION.
IT'S AN ARCHEOLOGICAL DIG THAT RAN OUT OF FUNDING AND SHUT DOWN!
THE SCIENTISTS ARE OFF TRYING TO RAISE MONEY!
THEY SAY THE BUILDINGS ARE MILLIONS OF YEARS OLD!
THAT'S ALL I KNOW!

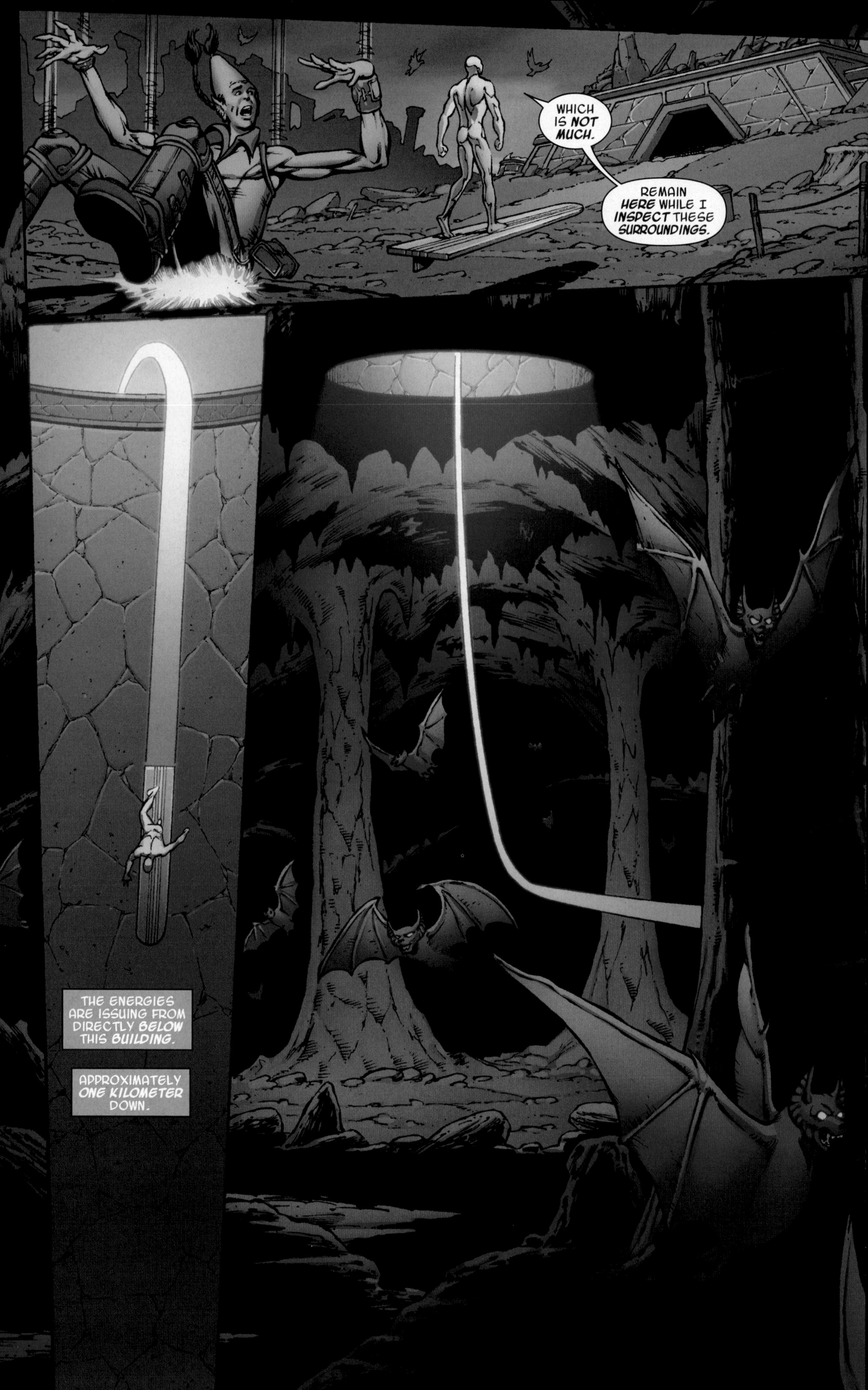
WHICH IS NOT MUCH.
REMAIN HERE WHILE I INSPECT THESE SURROUNDINGS.
THE ENERGIES ARE ISSUING FROM DIRECTLY BELOW THIS BUILDING.
APPROXIMATELY ONE KILOMETER DOWN.

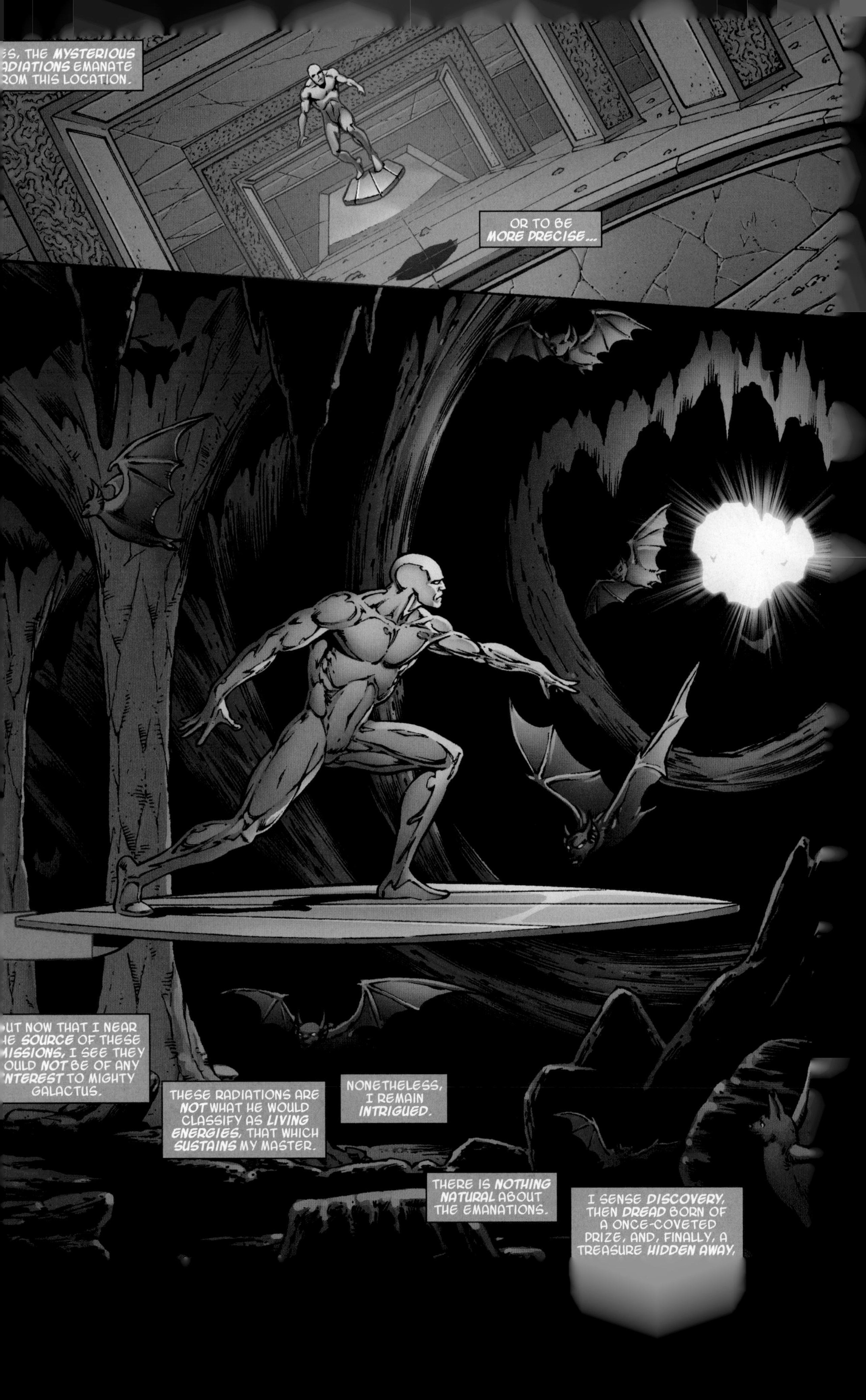

ES, THE MYSTERIOUS ADIATIONS EMANATE ROM THIS LOCATION.
OR TO BE MORE PRECISE...
UT NOW THAT I NEAR HE SOURCE OF THESE MISSIONS, I SEE THEY OULD NOT BE OF ANY NTEREST TO MIGHTY GALACTUS.
THESE RADIATIONS ARE NOT WHAT HE WOULD CLASSIFY AS LIVING ENERGIES, THAT WHICH SUSTAINS MY MASTER.
NONETHELESS, I REMAIN INTRIGUED.
THERE IS NOTHING NATURAL ABOUT THE EMANATIONS.
I SENSE DISCOVERY, THEN DREAD BORN OF A ONCE-COVETED PRIZE, AND, FINALLY, A TREASURE HIDDEN AWAY.

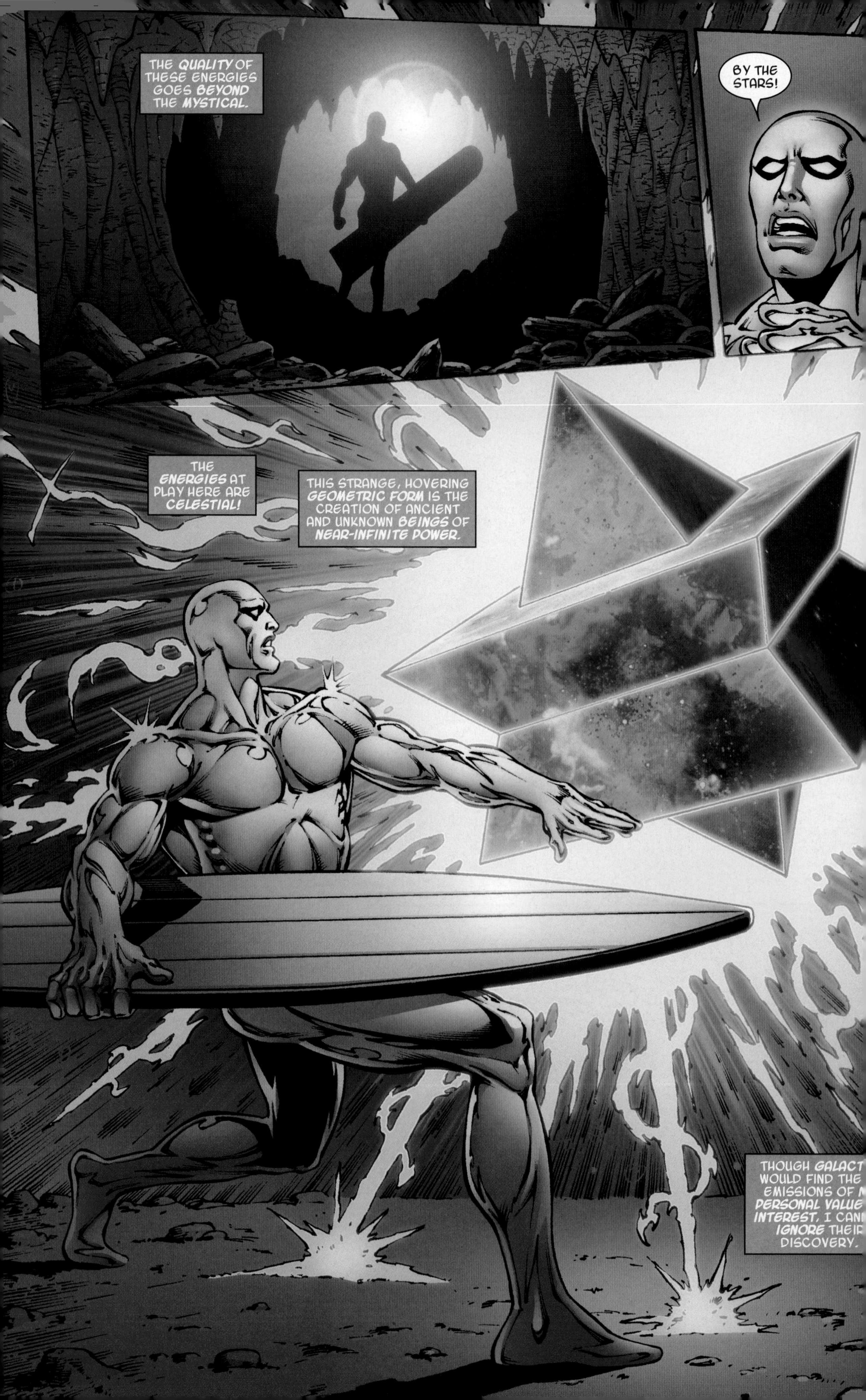
THE QUALITY OF THESE ENERGIES GOES BEYOND THE MYSTICAL.
BY THE STARS!
THE ENERGIES AT PLAY HERE ARE CELESTIAL!
THIS STRANGE, HOVERING GEOMETRIC FORM IS THE CREATION OF ANCIENT AND UNKNOWN BEINGS OF NEAR-INFINITE POWER.
THOUGH GALACT WOULD FIND THE EMISSIONS OF PERSONAL VALUE INTEREST, I CAN IGNORE THEI DISCOVERY.

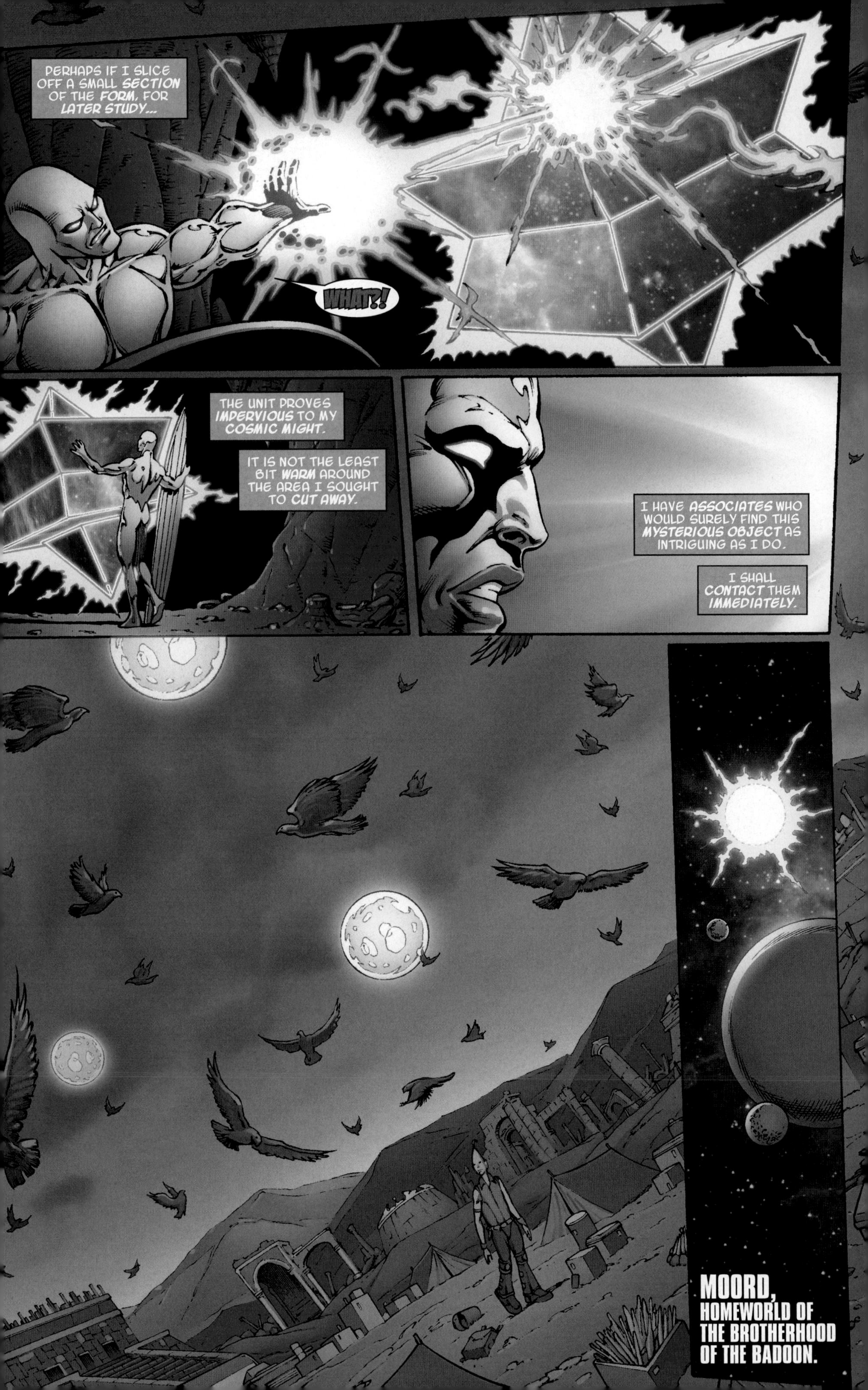

PERHAPS IF I SLICE OFF A SMALL SECTION OF THE FORM, FOR LATER STUDY...
WHAT?!
THE UNIT PROVES IMPERVIOUS TO MY COSMIC MIGHT.
IT IS NOT THE LEAST BIT WARM AROUND THE AREA I SOUGHT TO CUT AWAY.
I HAVE ASSOCIATES WHO WOULD SURELY FIND THIS MYSTERIOUS OBJECT AS INTRIGUING AS I DO.
I SHALL CONTACT THEM IMMEDIATELY.
MOORD, HOMEWORLD OF THE BROTHERHOOD OF THE BADOON.

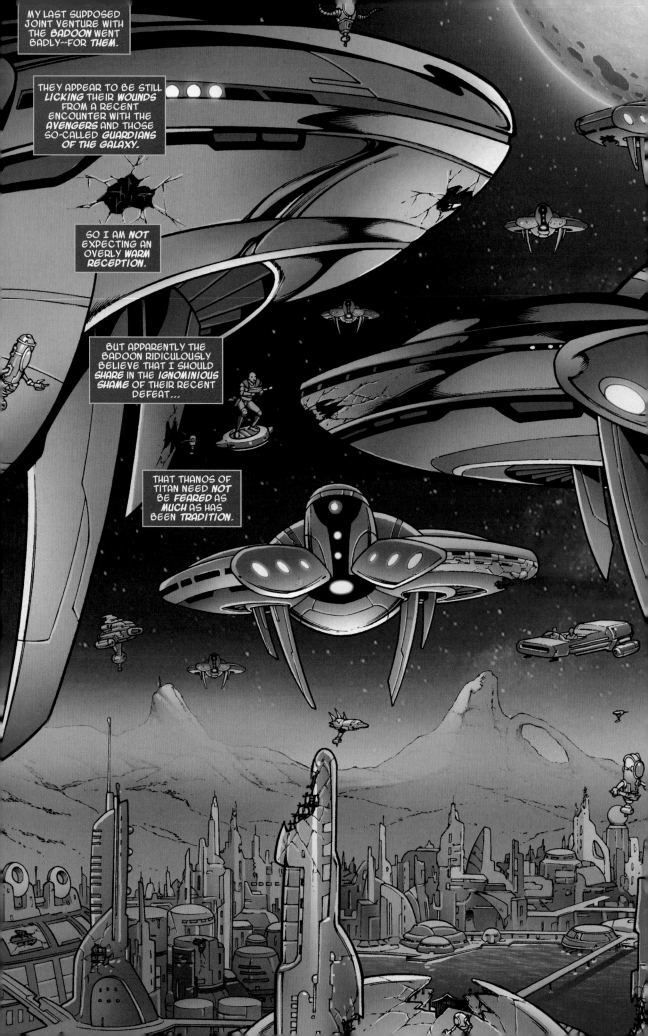

MY LAST SUPPOSED JOINT VENTURE WITH THE *BADOON* WENT BADLY--FOR *THEM.*

THEY APPEAR TO BE STILL *LICKING* THEIR *WOUNDS* FROM A RECENT ENCOUNTER WITH THE *AVENGERS* AND THOSE SO-CALLED *GUARDIANS OF THE GALAXY.*

SO I AM *NOT* EXPECTING AN OVERLY *WARM* RECEPTION.

BUT APPARENTLY THE BADOON *RIDICULOUSLY* BELIEVE THAT I SHOULD *SHARE* IN THE *IGNOMINIOUS SHAME* OF THEIR *RECENT DEFEAT...*

THAT THANOS OF TITAN NEED *NOT* BE *FEARED* AS *MUCH* AS HAS BEEN *TRADITION.*

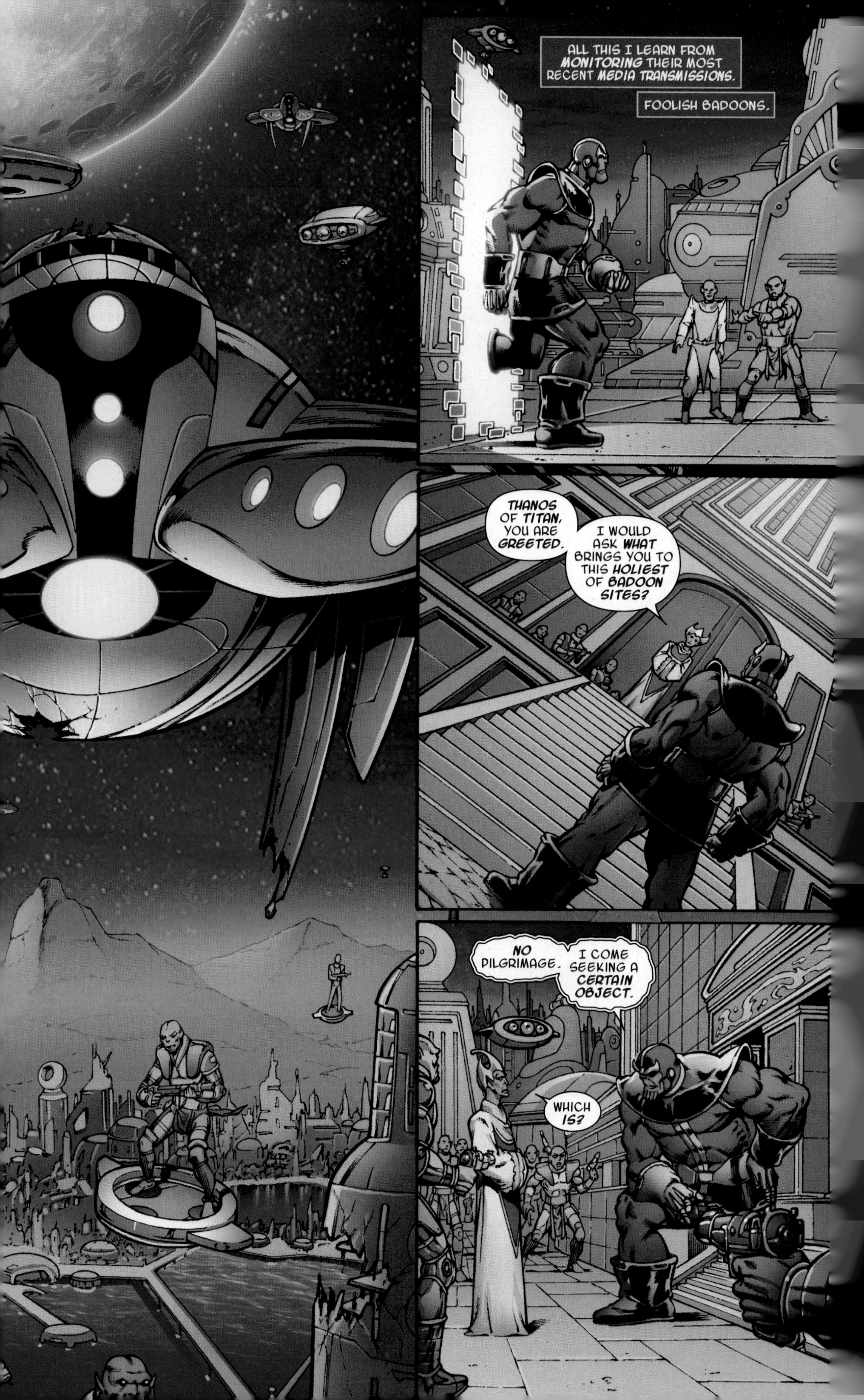
ALL THIS I LEARN FROM MONITORING THEIR MOST RECENT MEDIA TRANSMISSIONS.
FOOLISH BADOONS.
THANOS OF TITAN, YOU ARE GREETED.
I WOULD ASK WHAT BRINGS YOU TO THIS HOLIEST OF BADOON SITES?
NO PILGRIMAGE.
I COME SEEKING A CERTAIN OBJECT.
WHICH IS?

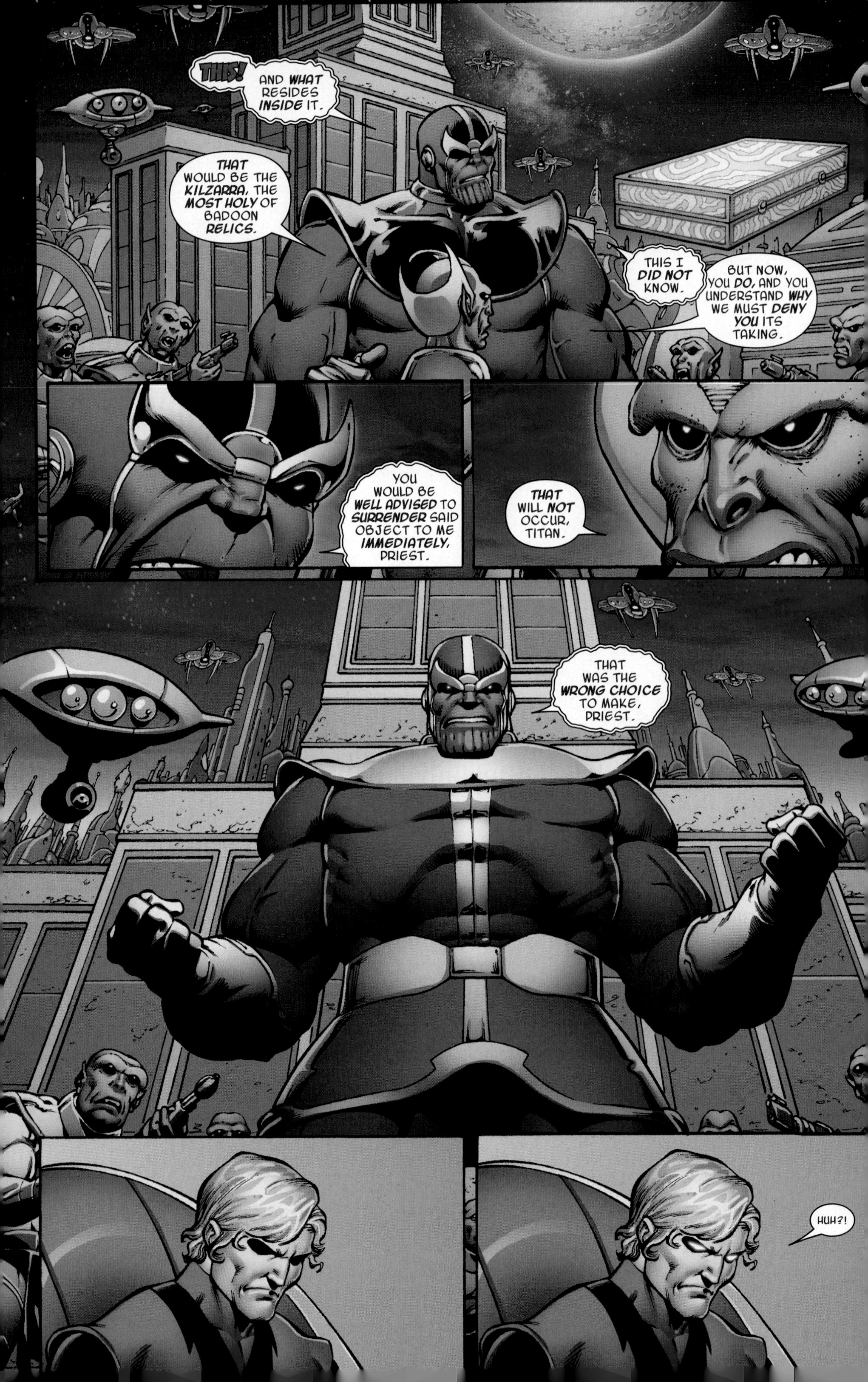
THIS!
AND WHAT RESIDES INSIDE IT.
THAT WOULD BE THE KILZARRA, THE MOST HOLY OF BADOON RELICS.
THIS I DID NOT KNOW.
BUT NOW, YOU DO, AND YOU UNDERSTAND WHY WE MUST DENY YOU ITS TAKING.
YOU WOULD BE WELL ADVISED TO SURRENDER SAID OBJECT TO ME IMMEDIATELY, PRIEST.
THAT WILL NOT OCCUR, TITAN.
THAT WAS THE WRONG CHOICE TO MAKE, PRIEST.
HUH?!

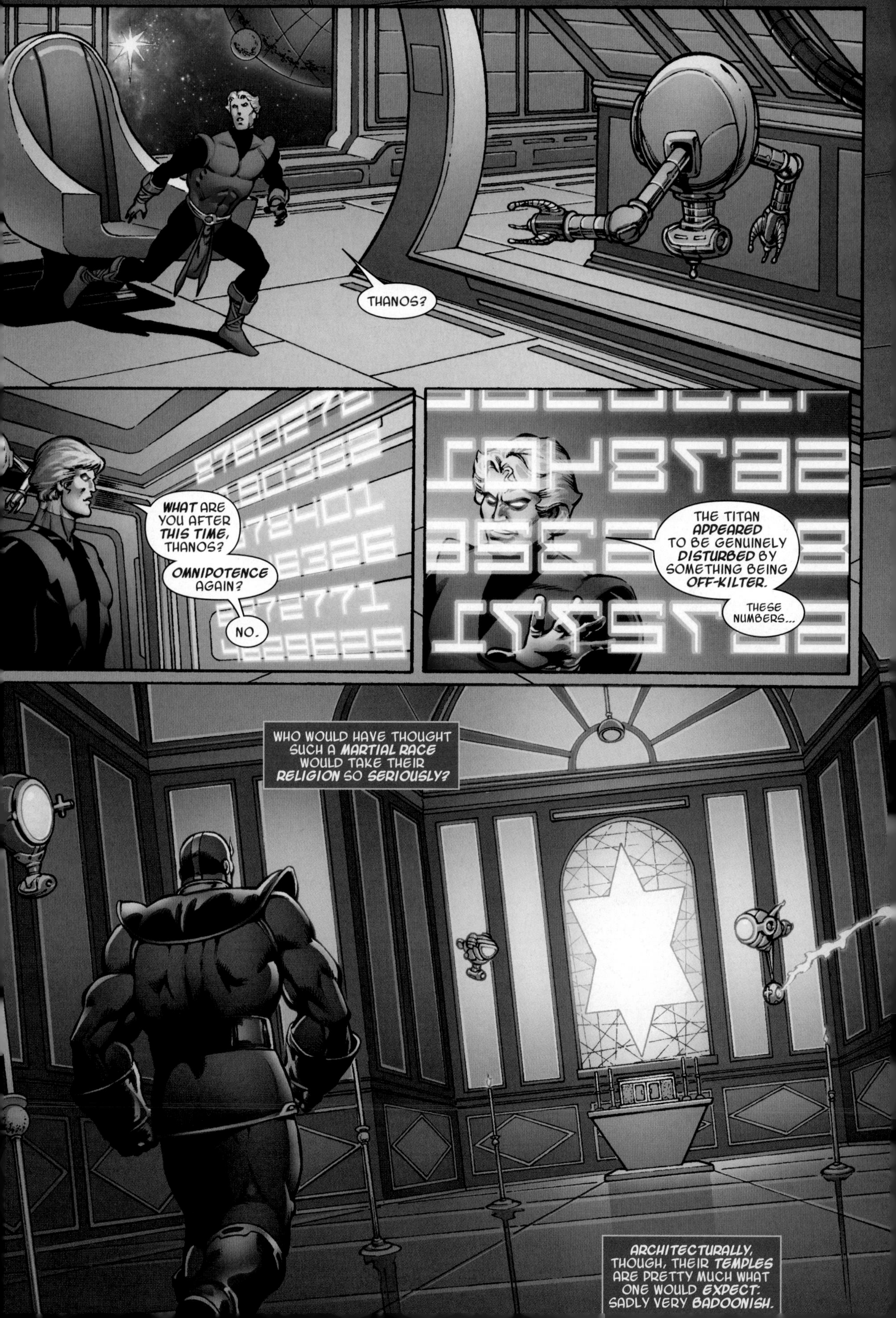
THANOS?
WHAT ARE YOU AFTER THIS TIME, THANOS?
OMNIPOTENCE AGAIN?
NO.
THE TITAN APPEARED TO BE GENUINELY DISTURBED BY SOMETHING BEING OFF-KILTER.
THESE NUMBERS...
WHO WOULD HAVE THOUGHT SUCH A MARTIAL RACE WOULD TAKE THEIR RELIGION SO SERIOUSLY?
ARCHITECTURALLY, THOUGH, THEIR TEMPLES ARE PRETTY MUCH WHAT ONE WOULD EXPECT: SADLY VERY BADOONISH.

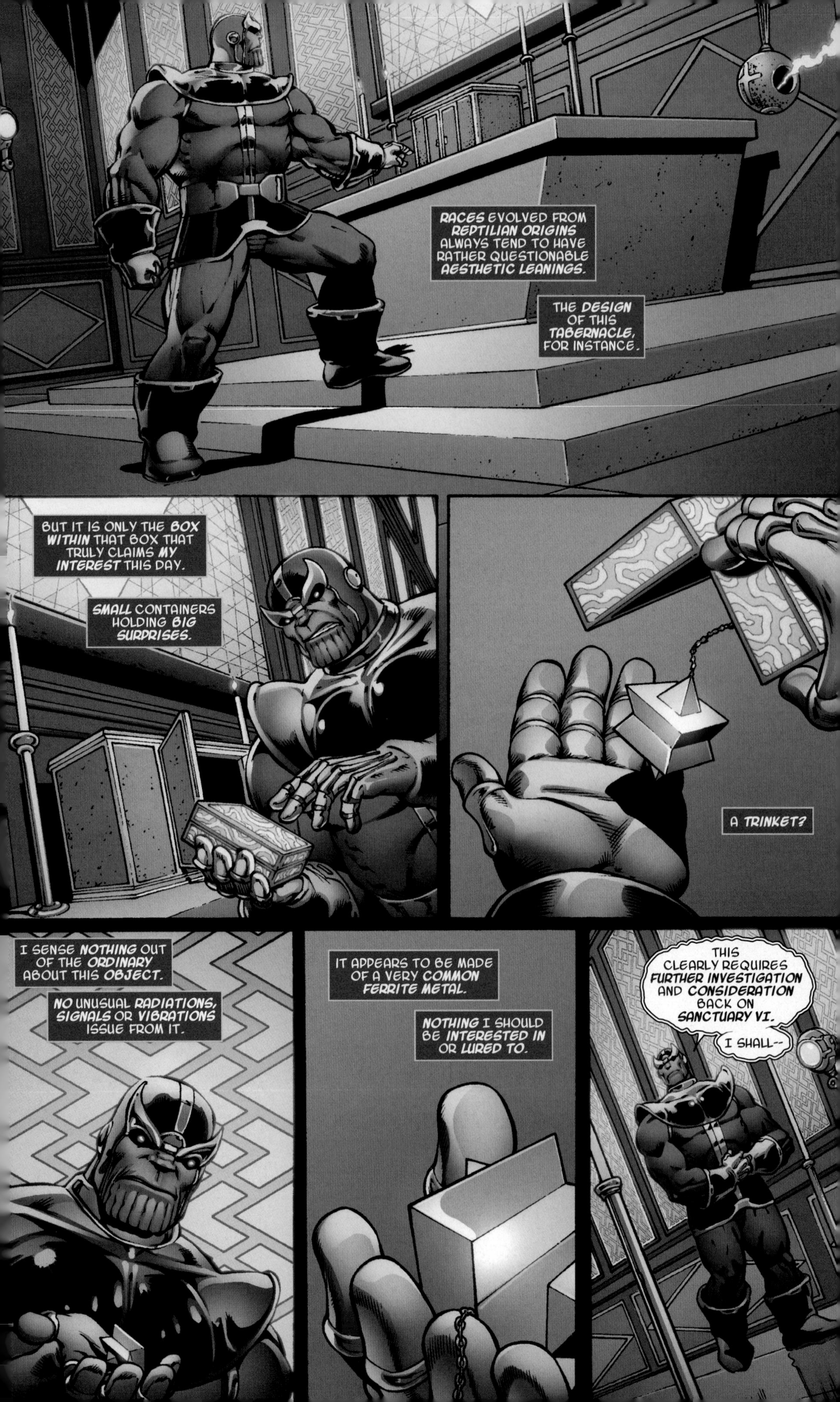
RACES EVOLVED FROM REPTILIAN ORIGINS ALWAYS TEND TO HAVE RATHER QUESTIONABLE AESTHETIC LEANINGS.
THE DESIGN OF THIS TABERNACLE, FOR INSTANCE.
BUT IT IS ONLY THE BOX WITHIN THAT BOX THAT TRULY CLAIMS MY INTEREST THIS DAY.
SMALL CONTAINERS HOLDING BIG SURPRISES.
A TRINKET?
I SENSE NOTHING OUT OF THE ORDINARY ABOUT THIS OBJECT.
NO UNUSUAL RADIATIONS, SIGNALS OR VIBRATIONS ISSUE FROM IT.
IT APPEARS TO BE MADE OF A VERY COMMON FERRITE METAL.
NOTHING I SHOULD BE INTERESTED IN OR LURED TO.
THIS CLEARLY REQUIRES FURTHER INVESTIGATION AND CONSIDERATION BACK ON SANCTUARY VI.
I SHALL--

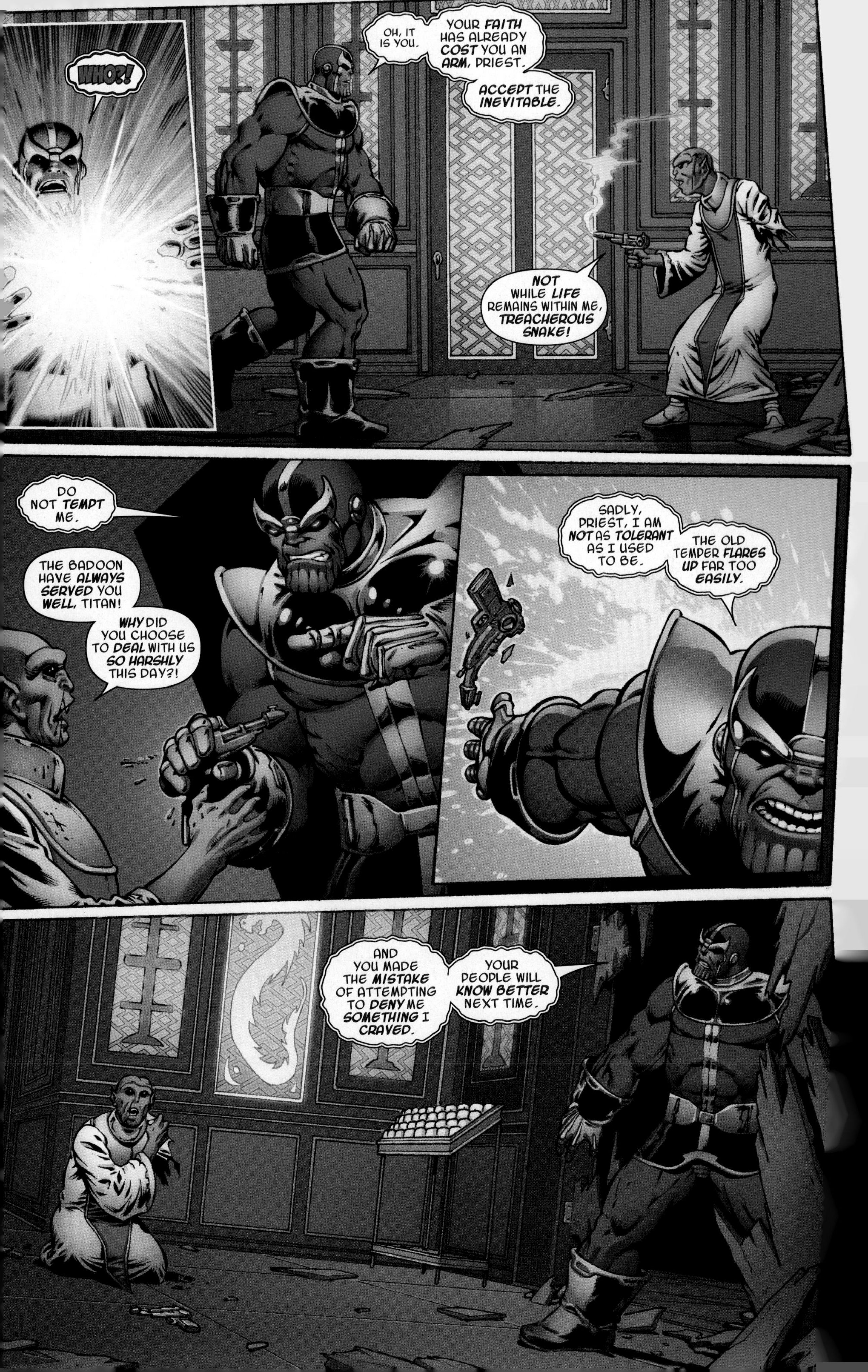
WHO?!
OH, IT IS YOU.
YOUR FAITH HAS ALREADY COST YOU AN ARM, PRIEST.
ACCEPT THE INEVITABLE.
NOT WHILE LIFE REMAINS WITHIN ME, TREACHEROUS SNAKE!
DO NOT TEMPT ME.
THE BADOON HAVE ALWAYS SERVED YOU WELL, TITAN!
WHY DID YOU CHOOSE TO DEAL WITH US SO HARSHLY THIS DAY?!
SADLY, PRIEST, I AM NOT AS TOLERANT AS I USED TO BE.
THE OLD TEMPER FLARES UP FAR TOO EASILY.
AND YOU MADE THE MISTAKE OF ATTEMPTING TO DENY ME SOMETHING I CRAVED.
YOUR PEOPLE WILL KNOW BETTER NEXT TIME.

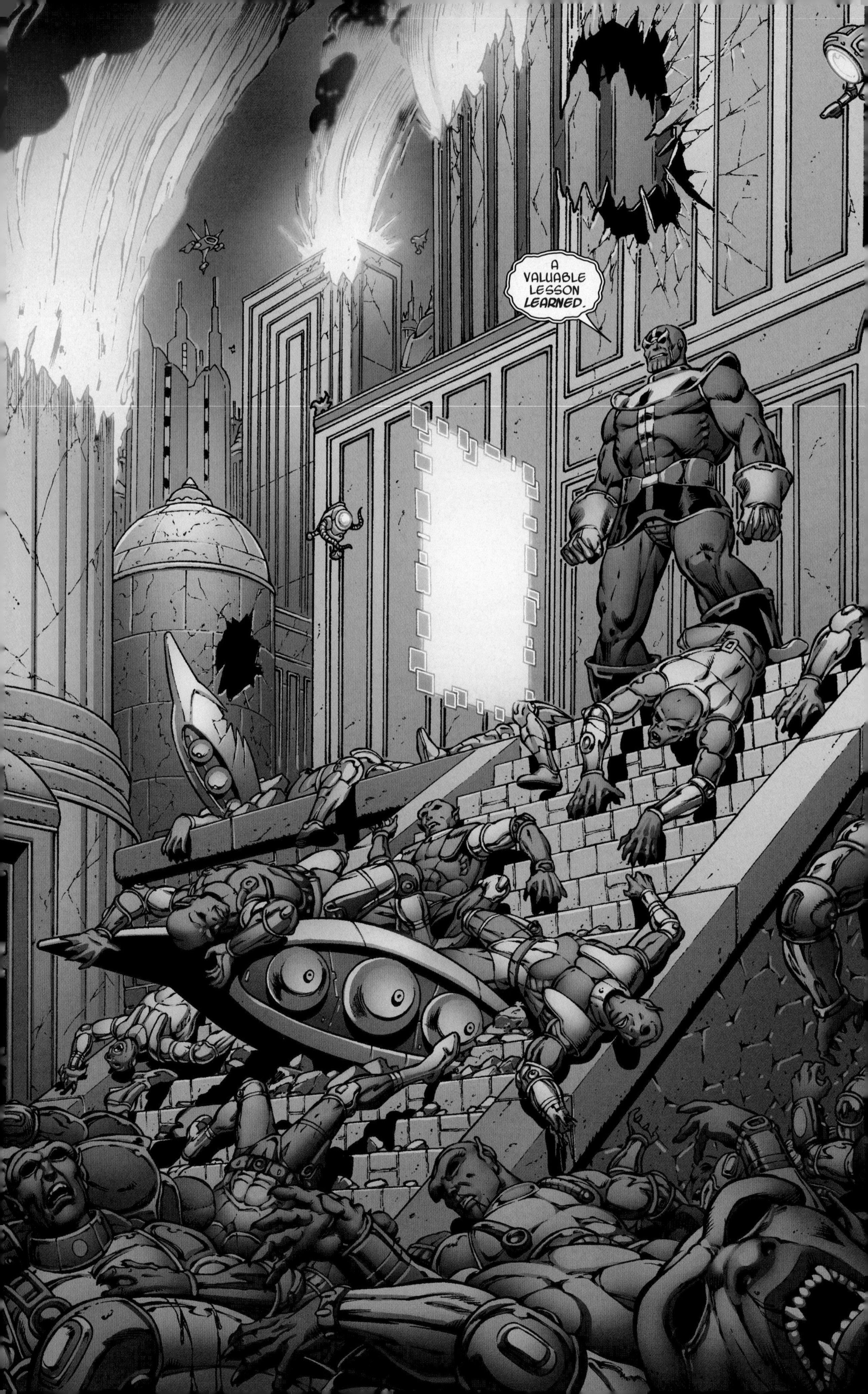
A VALUABLE LESSON LEARNED.

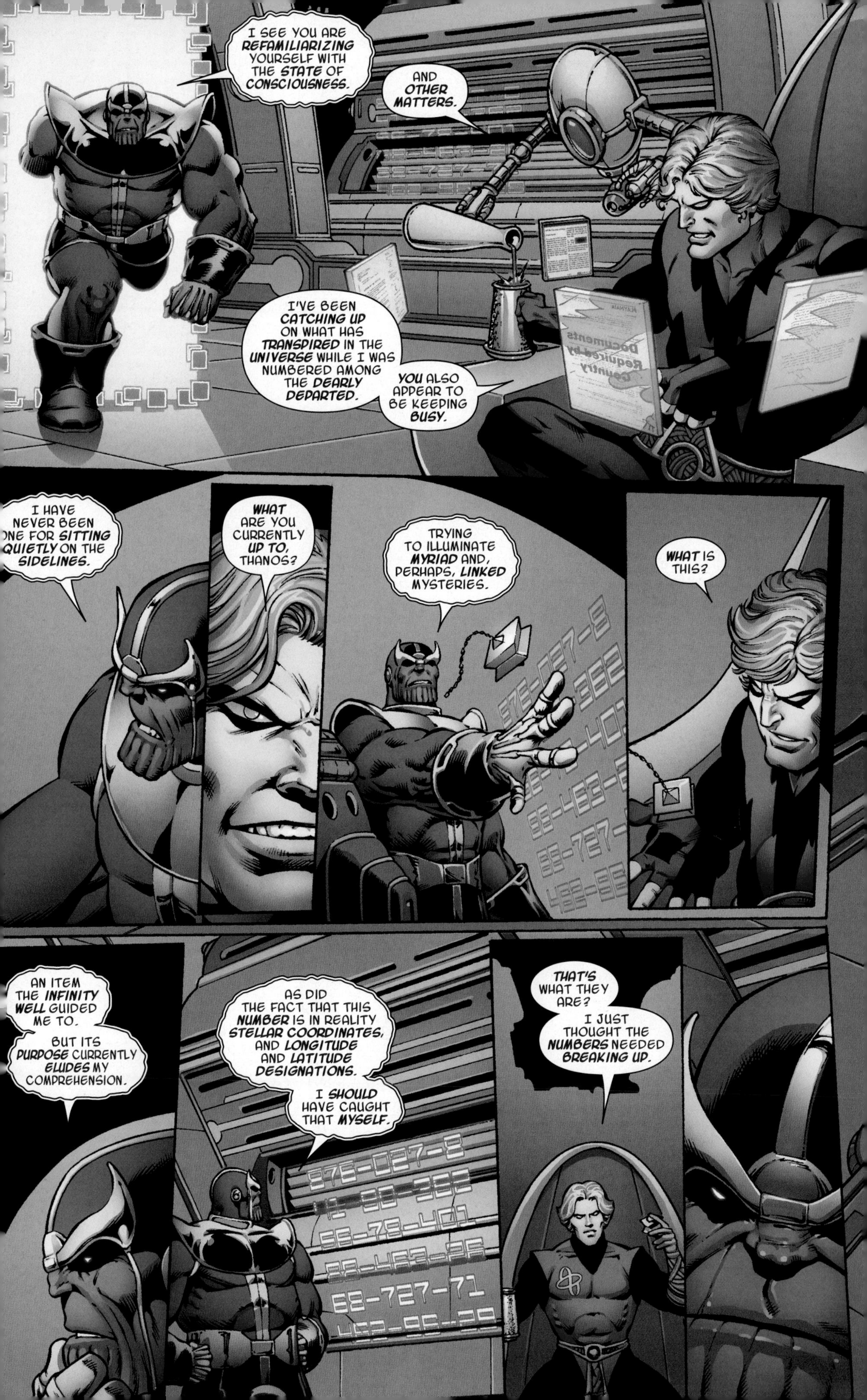
I SEE YOU ARE REFAMILIARIZING YOURSELF WITH THE STATE OF CONSCIOUSNESS.
AND OTHER MATTERS.
I'VE BEEN CATCHING UP ON WHAT HAS TRANSPIRED IN THE UNIVERSE WHILE I WAS NUMBERED AMONG THE DEARLY DEPARTED.
YOU ALSO APPEAR TO BE KEEPING BUSY.
I HAVE NEVER BEEN ONE FOR SITTING QUIETLY ON THE SIDELINES.
WHAT ARE YOU CURRENTLY UP TO, THANOS?
TRYING TO ILLUMINATE MYRIAD AND, PERHAPS, LINKED MYSTERIES.
WHAT IS THIS?
AN ITEM THE INFINITY WELL GUIDED ME TO.
BUT ITS PURPOSE CURRENTLY ELUDES MY COMPREHENSION.
AS DID THE FACT THAT THIS NUMBER IS IN REALITY STELLAR COORDINATES, AND LONGITUDE AND LATITUDE DESIGNATIONS.
I SHOULD HAVE CAUGHT THAT MYSELF.
THAT'S WHAT THEY ARE?
I JUST THOUGHT THE NUMBERS NEEDED BREAKING UP.
875-027-8
88-727-71

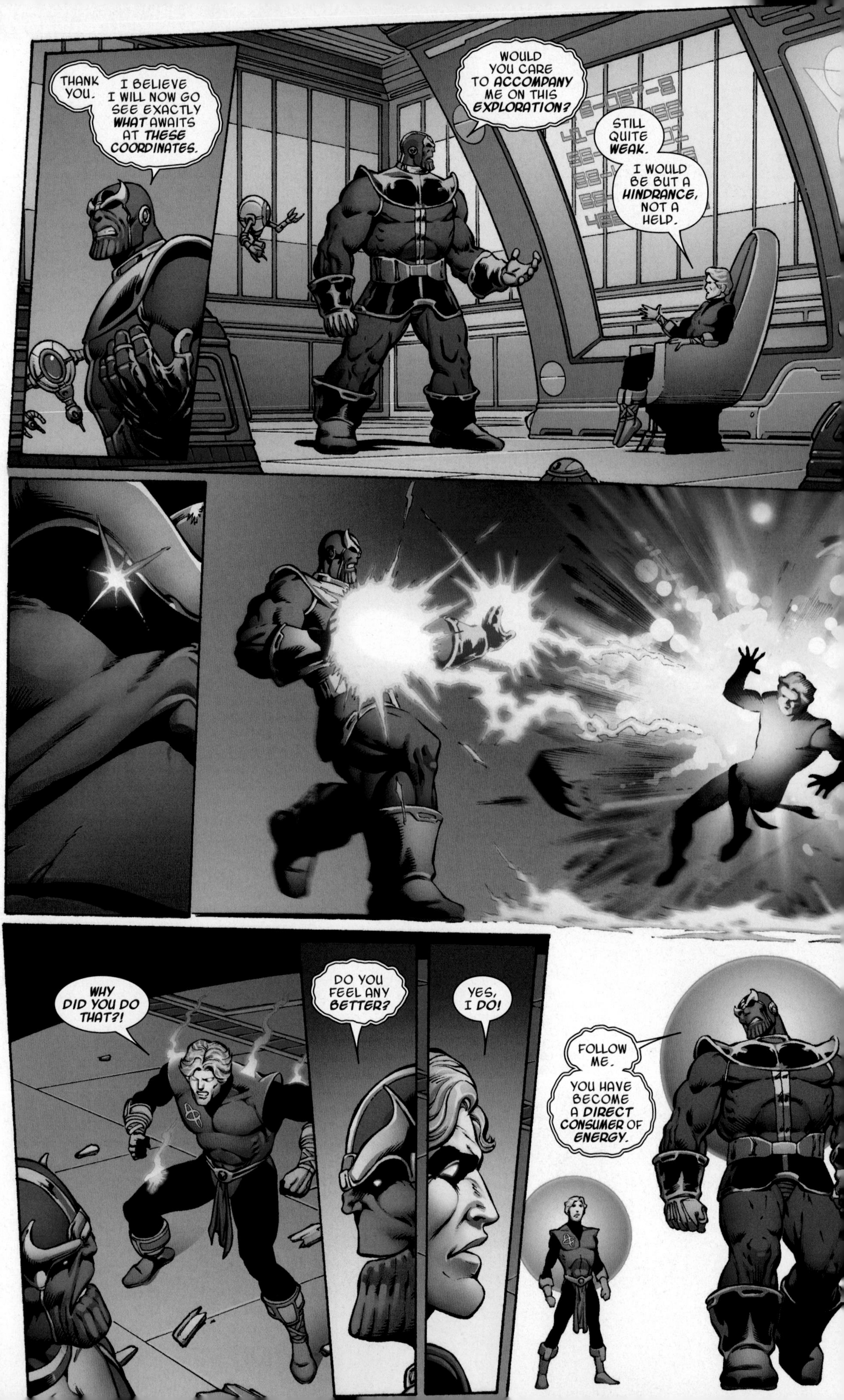
THANK YOU.
I BELIEVE I WILL NOW GO SEE EXACTLY WHAT AWAITS AT THESE COORDINATES.
WOULD YOU CARE TO ACCOMPANY ME ON THIS EXPLORATION?
STILL QUITE WEAK.
I WOULD BE BUT A HINDRANCE, NOT A HELP.
WHY DID YOU DO THAT?!
DO YOU FEEL ANY BETTER?
YES, I DO!
FOLLOW ME.
YOU HAVE BECOME A DIRECT CONSUMER OF ENERGY.

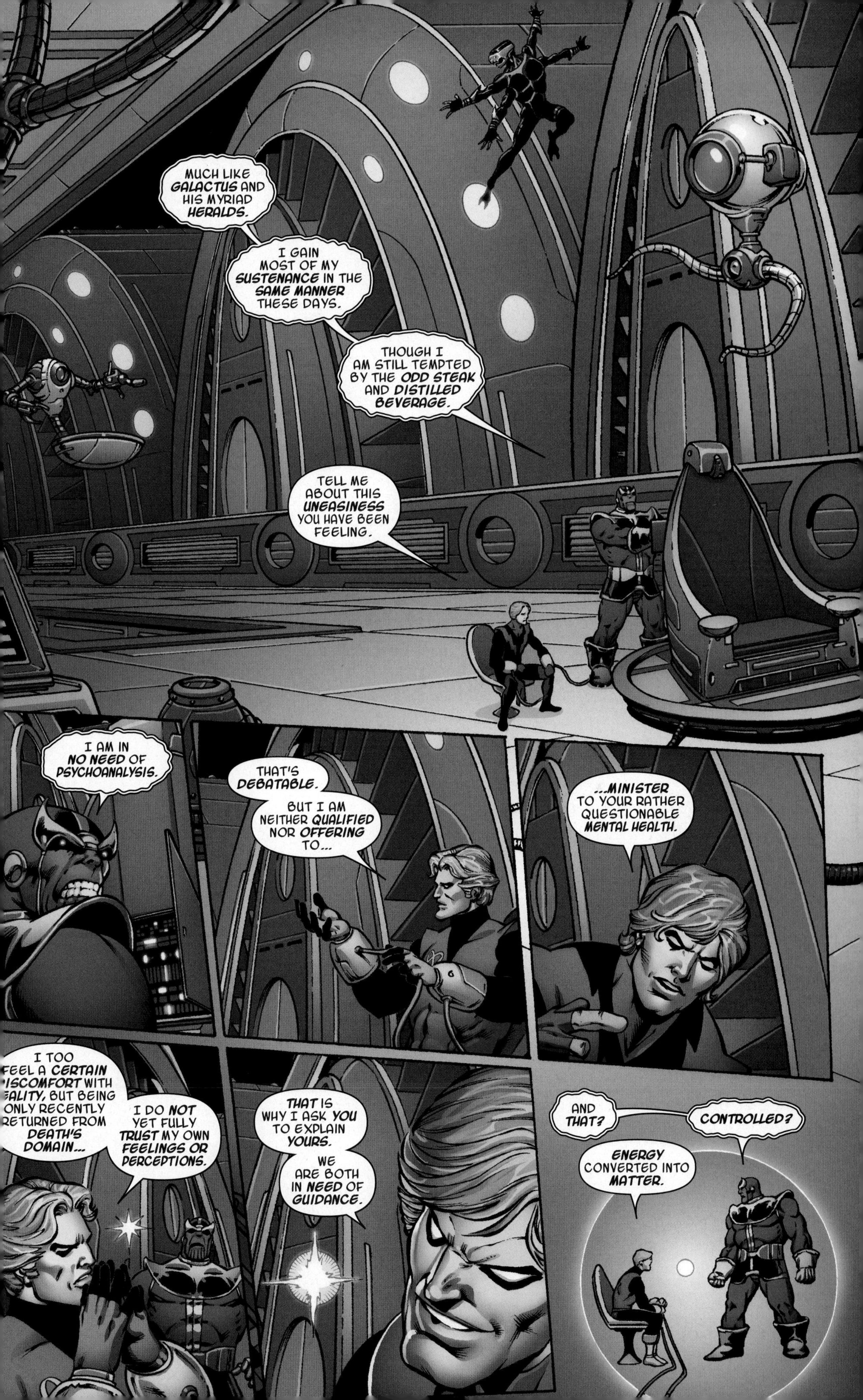

MUCH LIKE GALACTUS AND HIS MYRIAD HERALDS.
I GAIN MOST OF MY SUSTENANCE IN THE SAME MANNER THESE DAYS.
THOUGH I AM STILL TEMPTED BY THE ODD STEAK AND DISTILLED BEVERAGE.
TELL ME ABOUT THIS UNEASINESS YOU HAVE BEEN FEELING.
I AM IN NO NEED OF PSYCHOANALYSIS.
THAT'S DEBATABLE.
BUT I AM NEITHER QUALIFIED NOR OFFERING TO...
...MINISTER TO YOUR RATHER QUESTIONABLE MENTAL HEALTH.
I TOO FEEL A CERTAIN ISCOMFORT WITH EALITY, BUT BEING ONLY RECENTLY RETURNED FROM DEATH'S DOMAIN...
I DO NOT YET FULLY TRUST MY OWN FEELINGS OR PERCEPTIONS.
THAT IS WHY I ASK YOU TO EXPLAIN YOURS.
WE ARE BOTH IN NEED OF GUIDANCE.
AND THAT?
ENERGY CONVERTED INTO MATTER.
CONTROLLED?

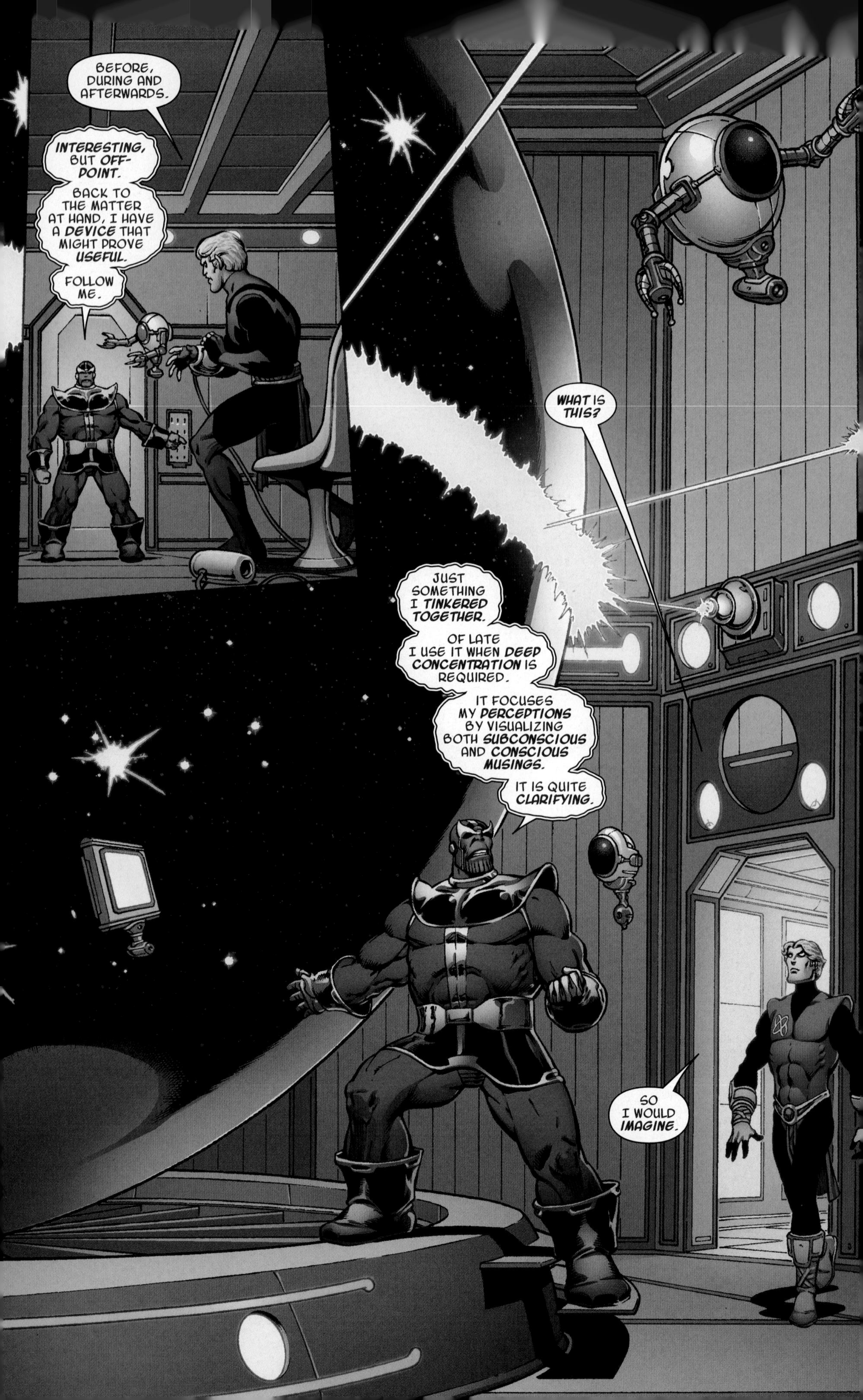
BEFORE, DURING AND AFTERWARDS.
INTERESTING, BUT OFF-POINT.
BACK TO THE MATTER AT HAND, I HAVE A DEVICE THAT MIGHT PROVE USEFUL.
FOLLOW ME.
WHAT IS THIS?
JUST SOMETHING I TINKERED TOGETHER.
OF LATE I USE IT WHEN DEEP CONCENTRATION IS REQUIRED.
IT FOCUSES MY PERCEPTIONS BY VISUALIZING BOTH SUBCONSCIOUS AND CONSCIOUS MUSINGS.
IT IS QUITE CLARIFYING.
SO I WOULD IMAGINE.

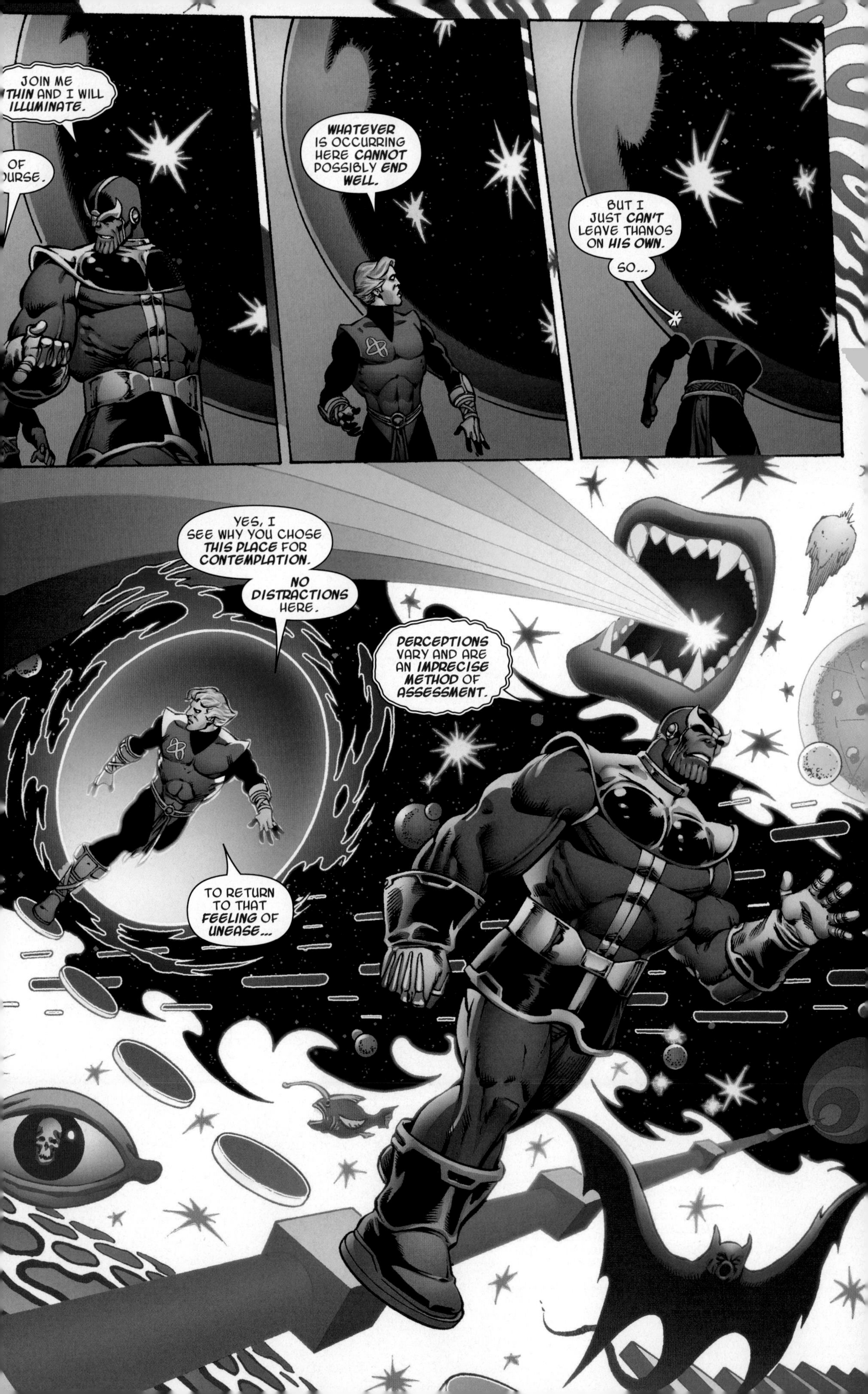
JOIN ME
THIN AND I WILL ILLUMINATE.
OF
URSE.
WHATEVER IS OCCURRING HERE CANNOT POSSIBLY END WELL.
BUT I JUST CAN'T LEAVE THANOS ON HIS OWN.
SO...
YES, I SEE WHY YOU CHOSE THIS PLACE FOR CONTEMPLATION.
NO DISTRACTIONS HERE.
PERCEPTIONS VARY AND ARE AN IMPRECISE METHOD OF ASSESSMENT.
TO RETURN TO THAT FEELING OF UNEASE...

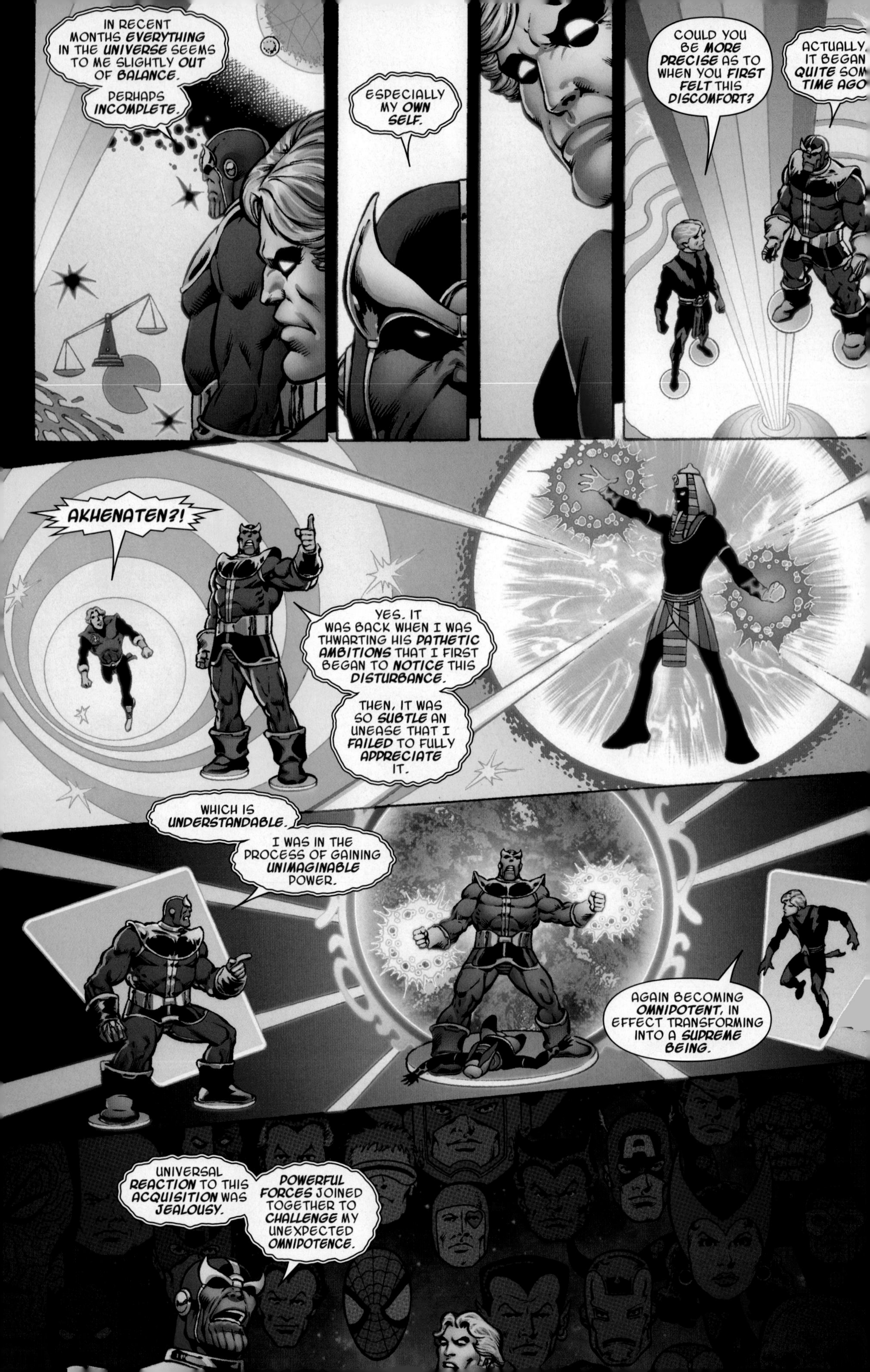

IN RECENT MONTHS EVERYTHING IN THE UNIVERSE SEEMS TO ME SLIGHTLY OUT OF BALANCE.
PERHAPS INCOMPLETE.
ESPECIALLY MY OWN SELF.
COULD YOU BE MORE PRECISE AS TO WHEN YOU FIRST FELT THIS DISCOMFORT?
ACTUALLY, IT BEGAN QUITE SOM TIME AGO
AKHENATEN?!
YES. IT WAS BACK WHEN I WAS THWARTING HIS PATHETIC AMBITIONS THAT I FIRST BEGAN TO NOTICE THIS DISTURBANCE.
THEN, IT WAS SO SUBTLE AN UNEASE THAT I FAILED TO FULLY APPRECIATE IT.
WHICH IS UNDERSTANDABLE.
I WAS IN THE PROCESS OF GAINING UNIMAGINABLE POWER.
AGAIN BECOMING OMNIPOTENT, IN EFFECT TRANSFORMING INTO A SUPREME BEING.
UNIVERSAL REACTION TO THIS ACQUISITION WAS JEALOUSY.
POWERFUL FORCES JOINED TOGETHER TO CHALLENGE MY UNEXPECTED OMNIPOTENCE.

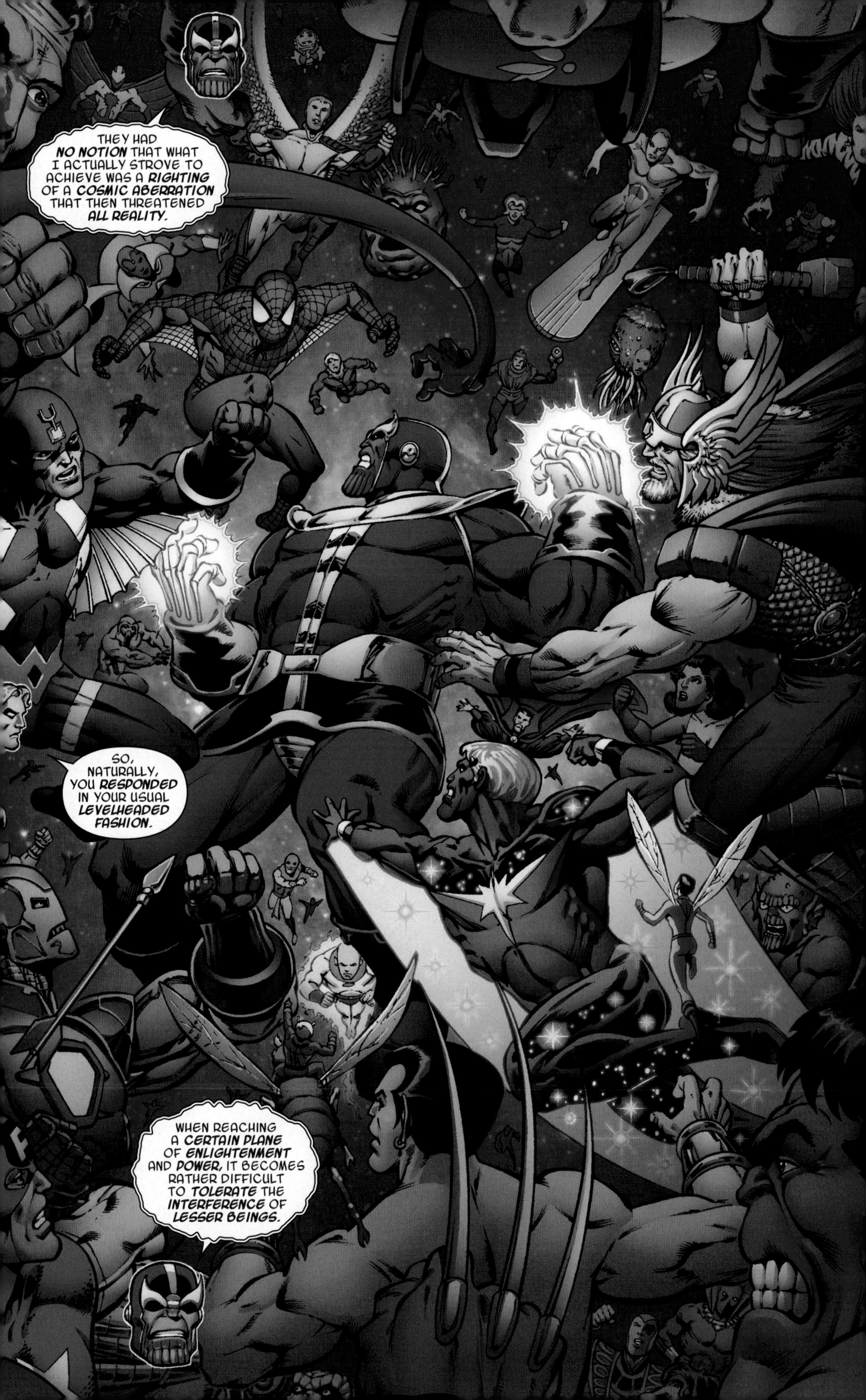
THEY HAD NO NOTION THAT WHAT I ACTUALLY STROVE TO ACHIEVE WAS A RIGHTING OF A COSMIC ABERRATION THAT THEN THREATENED ALL REALITY.
SO, NATURALLY, YOU RESPONDED IN YOUR USUAL LEVELHEADED FASHION.
WHEN REACHING A CERTAIN PLANE OF ENLIGHTENMENT AND POWER, IT BECOMES RATHER DIFFICULT TO TOLERATE THE INTERFERENCE OF LESSER BEINGS.

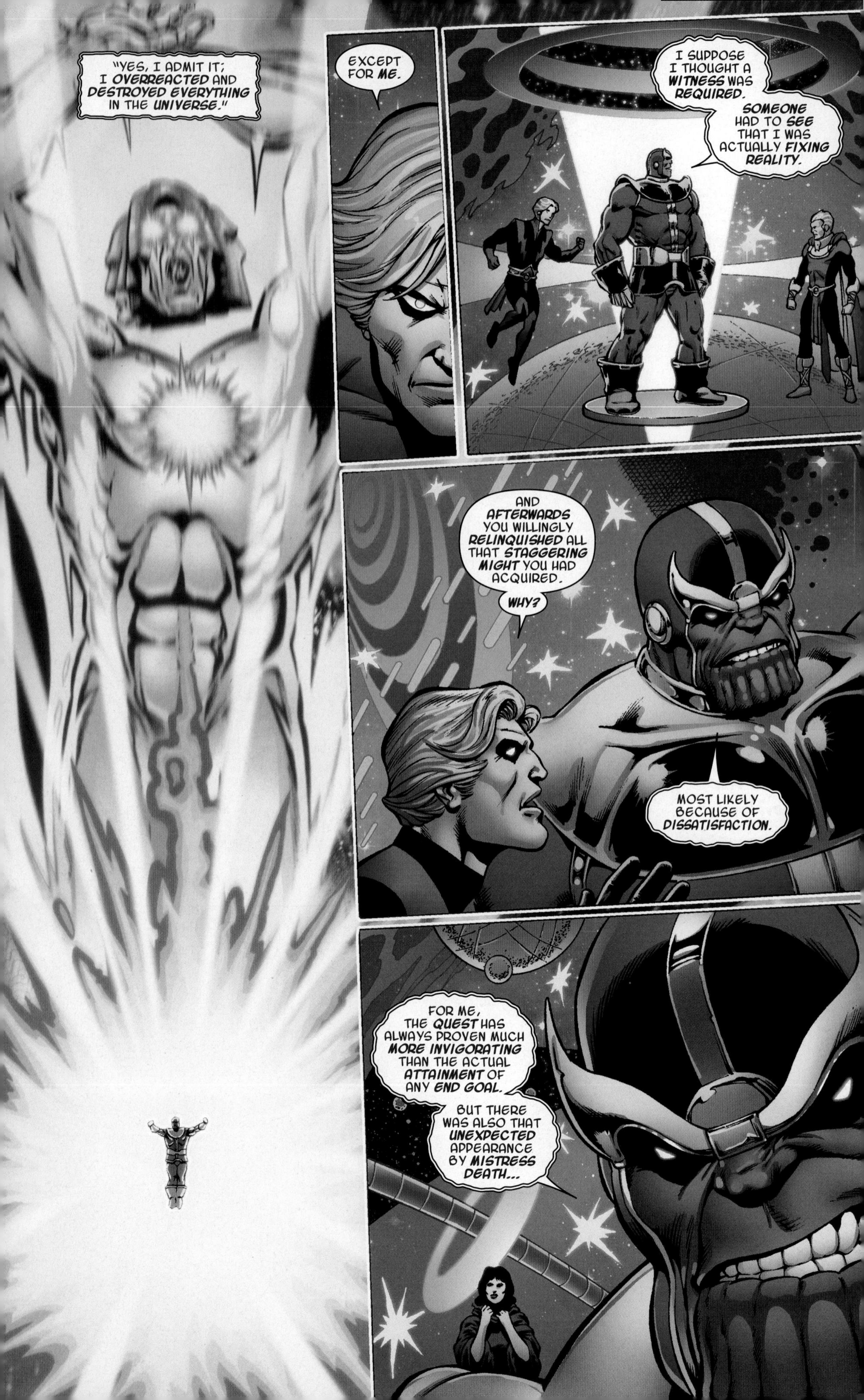
"YES, I ADMIT IT; I OVERREACTED AND DESTROYED EVERYTHING IN THE UNIVERSE."
EXCEPT FOR ME.
I SUPPOSE I THOUGHT A WITNESS WAS REQUIRED.
SOMEONE HAD TO SEE THAT I WAS ACTUALLY FIXING REALITY.
AND AFTERWARDS YOU WILLINGLY RELINQUISHED ALL THAT STAGGERING MIGHT YOU HAD ACQUIRED.
WHY?
MOST LIKELY BECAUSE OF DISSATISFACTION.
FOR ME, THE QUEST HAS ALWAYS PROVEN MUCH MORE INVIGORATING THAN THE ACTUAL ATTAINMENT OF ANY END GOAL.
BUT THERE WAS ALSO THAT UNEXPECTED APPEARANCE BY MISTRESS DEATH...

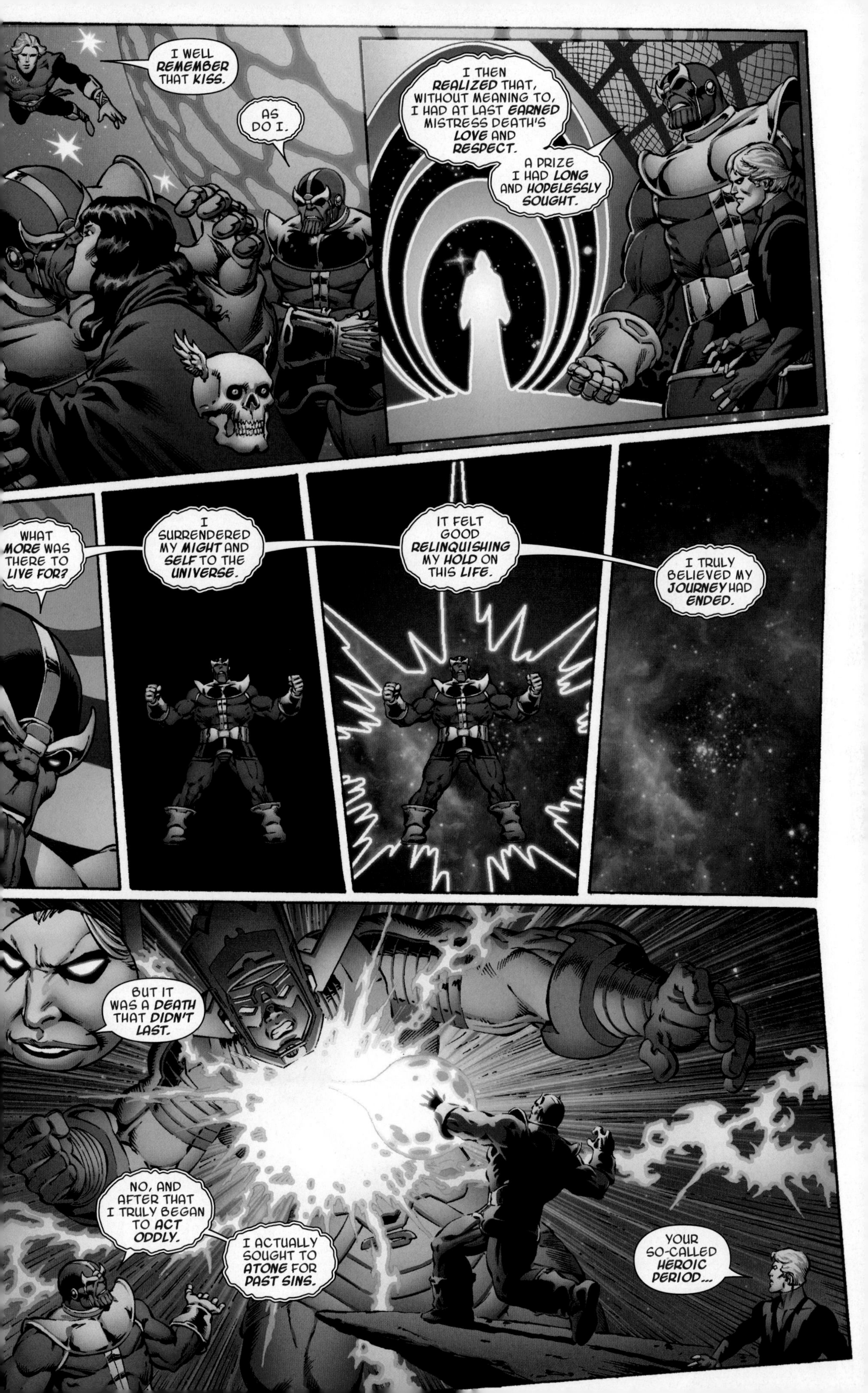
I WELL REMEMBER THAT KISS.
AS DO I.
I THEN REALIZED THAT, WITHOUT MEANING TO, I HAD AT LAST EARNED MISTRESS DEATH'S LOVE AND RESPECT.
A PRIZE I HAD LONG AND HOPELESSLY SOUGHT.
WHAT MORE WAS THERE TO LIVE FOR?
I SURRENDERED MY MIGHT AND SELF TO THE UNIVERSE.
IT FELT GOOD RELINQUISHING MY HOLD ON THIS LIFE.
I TRULY BELIEVED MY JOURNEY HAD ENDED.
BUT IT WAS A DEATH THAT DIDN'T LAST.
NO, AND AFTER THAT I TRULY BEGAN TO ACT ODDLY.
I ACTUALLY SOUGHT TO ATONE FOR PAST SINS.
YOUR SO-CALLED HEROIC PERIOD...

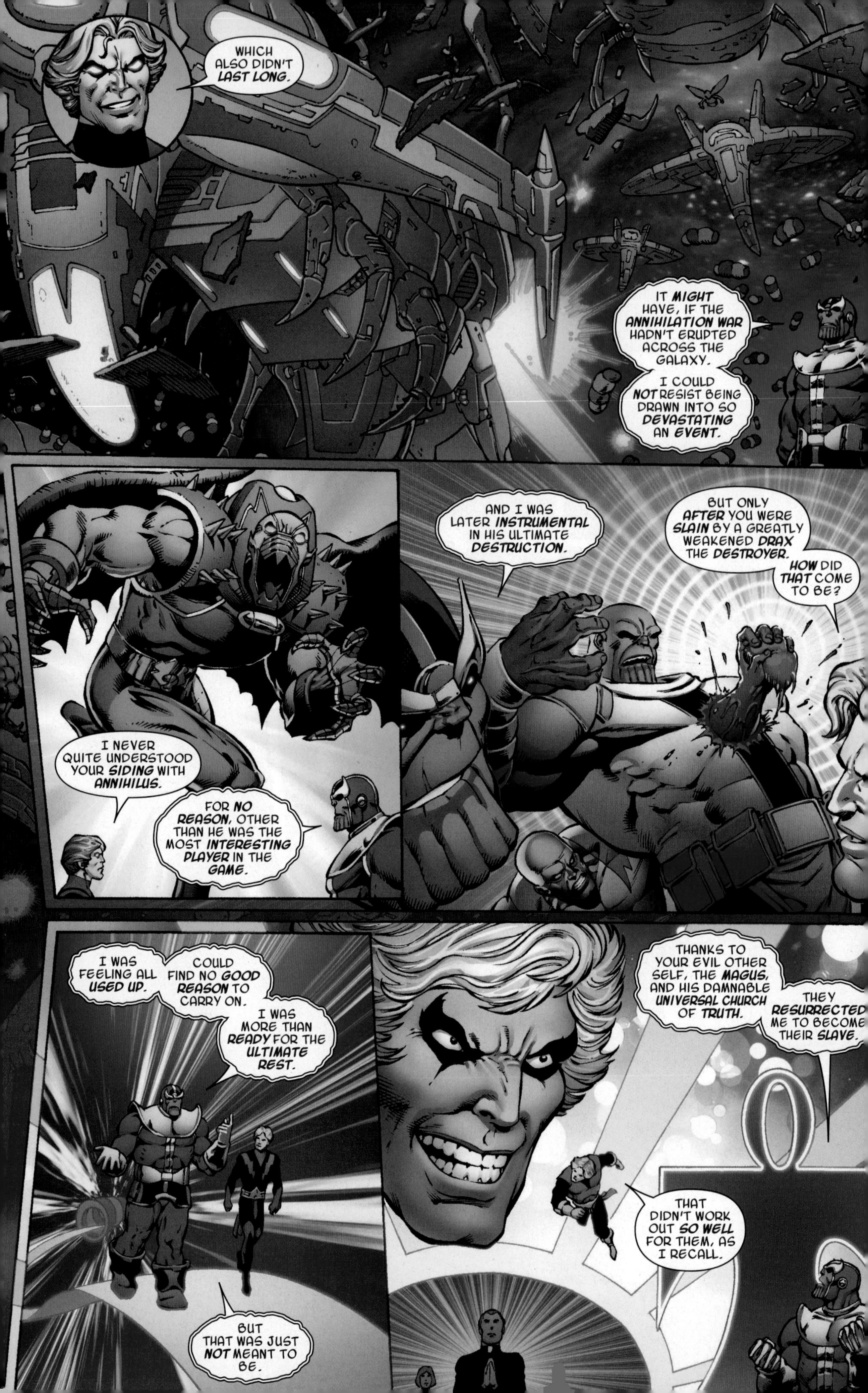
WHICH ALSO DIDN'T LAST LONG.
IT MIGHT HAVE, IF THE ANNIHILATION WAR HADN'T ERUPTED ACROSS THE GALAXY.
I COULD NOT RESIST BEING DRAWN INTO SO DEVASTATING AN EVENT.
I NEVER QUITE UNDERSTOOD YOUR SIDING WITH ANNIHILUS.
FOR NO REASON, OTHER THAN HE WAS THE MOST INTERESTING PLAYER IN THE GAME.
AND I WAS LATER INSTRUMENTAL IN HIS ULTIMATE DESTRUCTION.
BUT ONLY AFTER YOU WERE SLAIN BY A GREATLY WEAKENED DRAX THE DESTROYER.
HOW DID THAT COME TO BE?
I WAS FEELING ALL USED UP.
COULD FIND NO GOOD REASON TO CARRY ON.
I WAS MORE THAN READY FOR THE ULTIMATE REST.
BUT THAT WAS JUST NOT MEANT TO BE.
THANKS TO YOUR EVIL OTHER SELF, THE MAGUS, AND HIS DAMNABLE UNIVERSAL CHURCH OF TRUTH.
THEY RESURRECTED ME TO BECOME THEIR SLAVE.
THAT DIDN'T WORK OUT SO WELL FOR THEM, AS I RECALL.

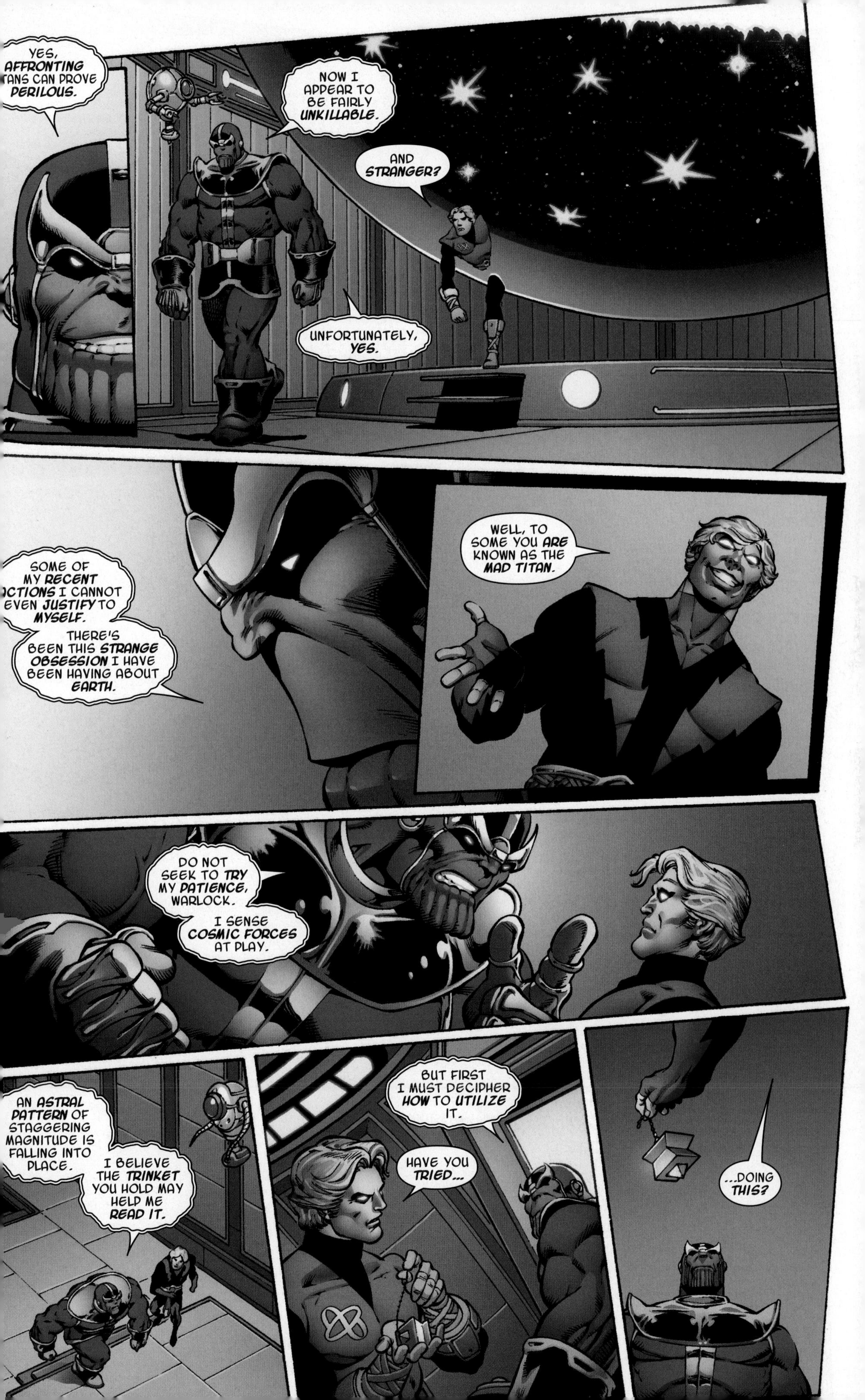
YES, AFFRONTING TITANS CAN PROVE PERILOUS.
NOW I APPEAR TO BE FAIRLY UNKILLABLE.
AND STRANGER?
UNFORTUNATELY, YES.
SOME OF MY RECENT ACTIONS I CANNOT EVEN JUSTIFY TO MYSELF.
THERE'S BEEN THIS STRANGE OBSESSION I HAVE BEEN HAVING ABOUT EARTH.
WELL, TO SOME YOU ARE KNOWN AS THE MAD TITAN.
DO NOT SEEK TO TRY MY PATIENCE, WARLOCK.
I SENSE COSMIC FORCES AT PLAY.
AN ASTRAL PATTERN OF STAGGERING MAGNITUDE IS FALLING INTO PLACE.
I BELIEVE THE TRINKET YOU HOLD MAY HELP ME READ IT.
BUT FIRST I MUST DECIPHER HOW TO UTILIZE IT.
HAVE YOU TRIED...
...DOING THIS?

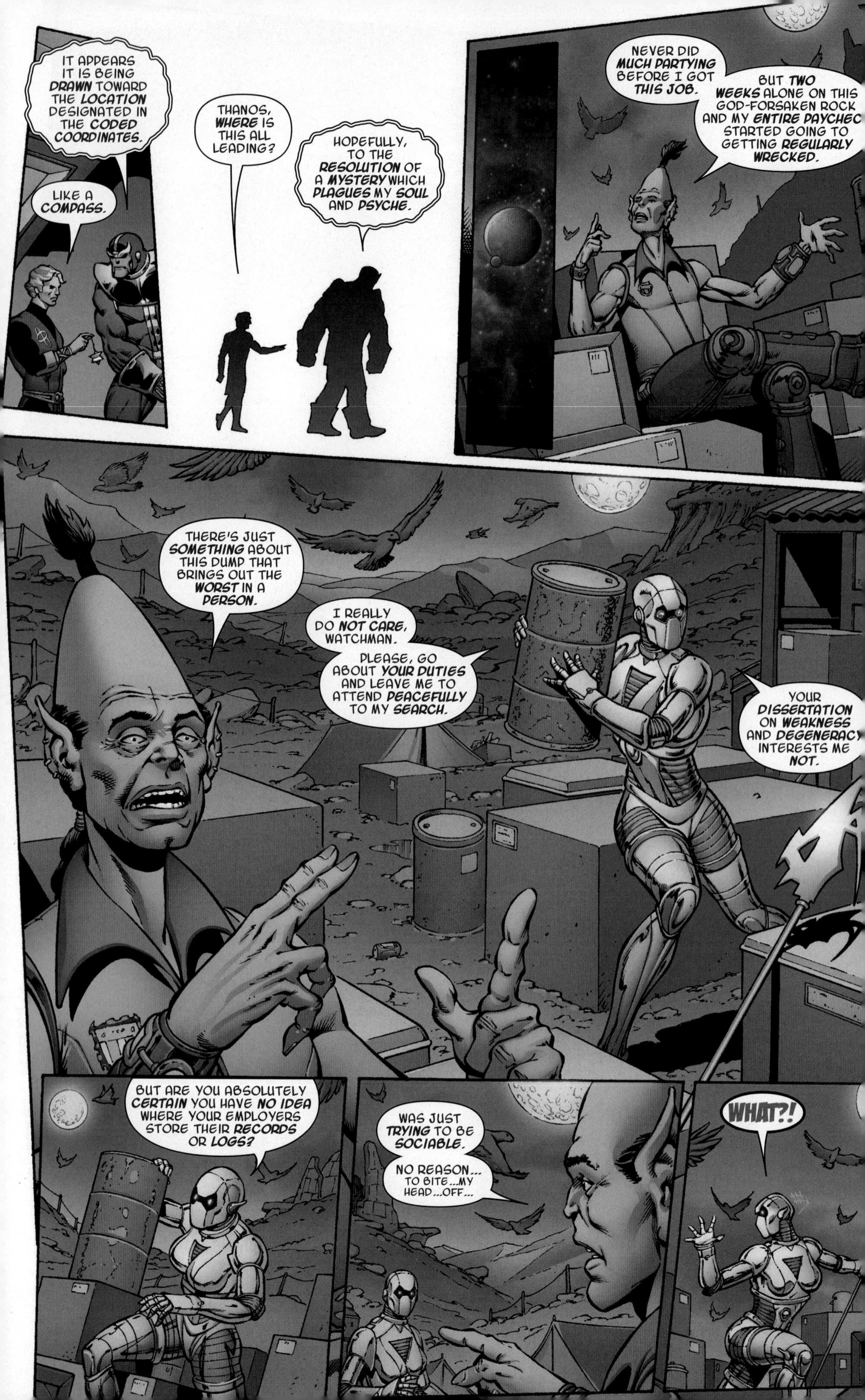
IT APPEARS IT IS BEING DRAWN TOWARD THE LOCATION DESIGNATED IN THE CODED COORDINATES.
LIKE A COMPASS.
THANOS, WHERE IS THIS ALL LEADING?
HOPEFULLY, TO THE RESOLUTION OF A MYSTERY WHICH PLAGUES MY SOUL AND PSYCHE.
NEVER DID MUCH PARTYING BEFORE I GOT THIS JOB.
BUT TWO WEEKS ALONE ON THIS GOD-FORSAKEN ROCK AND MY ENTIRE PAYCHEC STARTED GOING TO GETTING REGULARLY WRECKED.
THERE'S JUST SOMETHING ABOUT THIS DUMP THAT BRINGS OUT THE WORST IN A PERSON.
I REALLY DO NOT CARE, WATCHMAN.
PLEASE, GO ABOUT YOUR DUTIES AND LEAVE ME TO ATTEND PEACEFULLY TO MY SEARCH.
YOUR DISSERTATION ON WEAKNESS AND DEGENERAC INTERESTS ME NOT.
BUT ARE YOU ABSOLUTELY CERTAIN YOU HAVE NO IDEA WHERE YOUR EMPLOYERS STORE THEIR RECORDS OR LOGS?
WAS JUST TRYING TO BE SOCIABLE.
NO REASON... TO BITE...MY HEAD...OFF...
WHAT?!

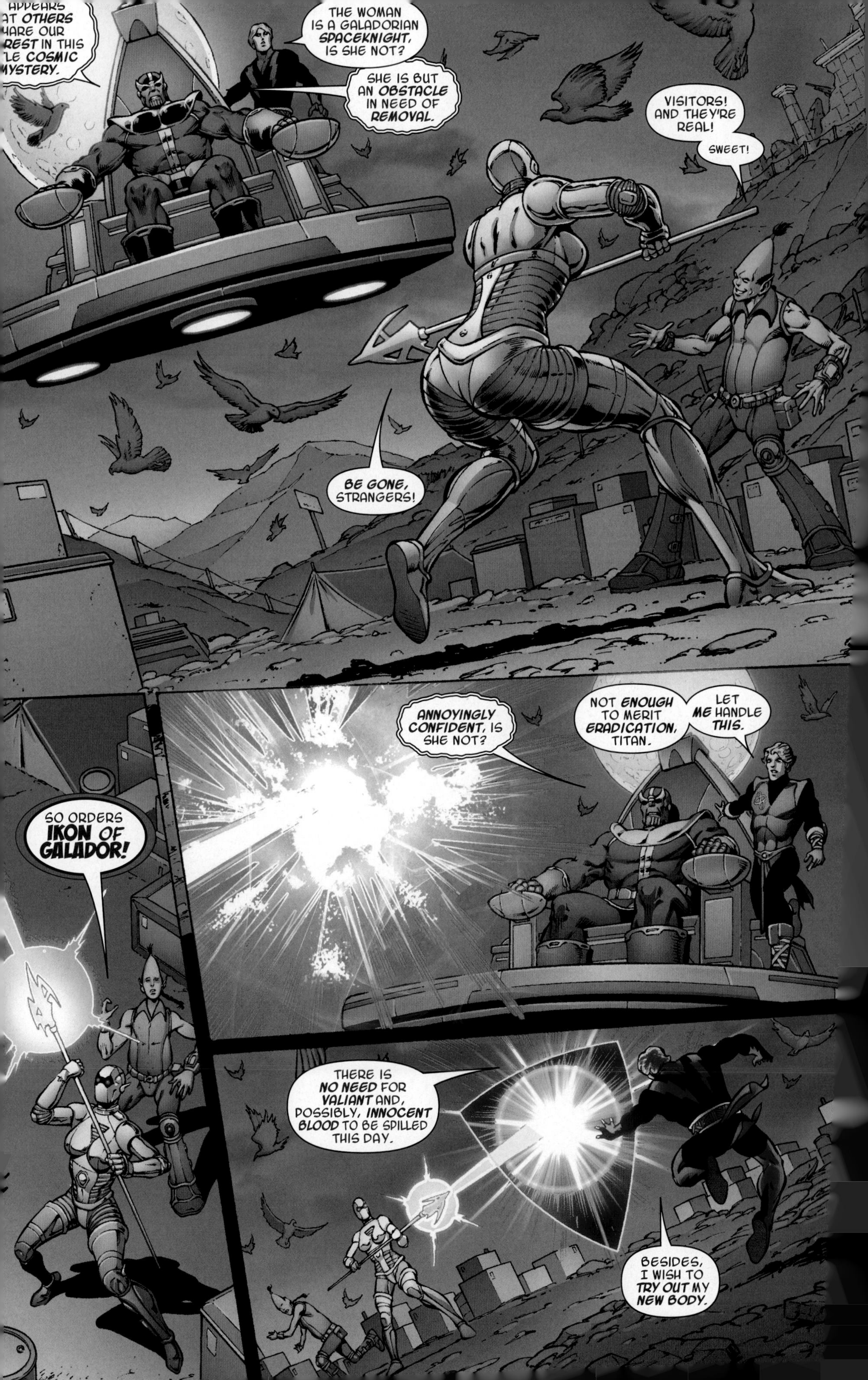
APPEARS AT OTHERS HARE OUR REST IN THIS LE COSMIC MYSTERY.
THE WOMAN IS A GALADORIAN SPACEKNIGHT, IS SHE NOT?
SHE IS BUT AN OBSTACLE IN NEED OF REMOVAL.
VISITORS! AND THEY'RE REAL!
SWEET!
BE GONE, STRANGERS!
SO ORDERS IKON OF GALADOR!
ANNOYINGLY CONFIDENT, IS SHE NOT?
NOT ENOUGH TO MERIT ERADICATION, TITAN.
LET ME HANDLE THIS.
THERE IS NO NEED FOR VALIANT AND, POSSIBLY, INNOCENT BLOOD TO BE SPILLED THIS DAY.
BESIDES, I WISH TO TRY OUT MY NEW BODY.

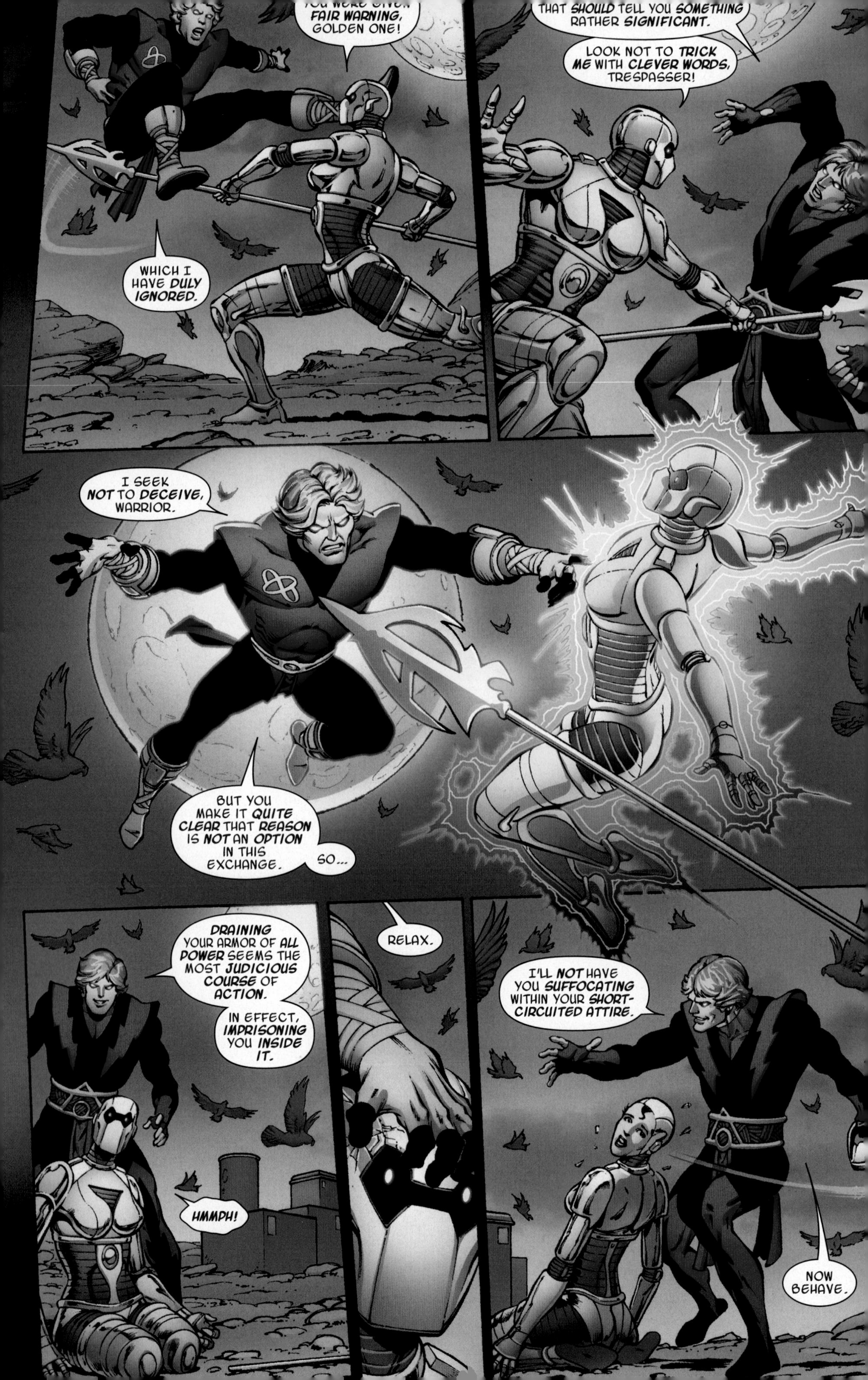
FAIR WARNING, GOLDEN ONE!
WHICH I HAVE DULY IGNORED.
THAT SHOULD TELL YOU SOMETHING RATHER SIGNIFICANT.
LOOK NOT TO TRICK ME WITH CLEVER WORDS, TRESPASSER!
I SEEK NOT TO DECEIVE, WARRIOR.
BUT YOU MAKE IT QUITE CLEAR THAT REASON IS NOT AN OPTION IN THIS EXCHANGE.
SO...
DRAINING YOUR ARMOR OF ALL POWER SEEMS THE MOST JUDICIOUS COURSE OF ACTION.
IN EFFECT, IMPRISONING YOU INSIDE IT.
HMMPH!
RELAX.
I'LL NOT HAVE YOU SUFFOCATING WITHIN YOUR SHORT-CIRCUITED ATTIRE.
NOW BEHAVE.

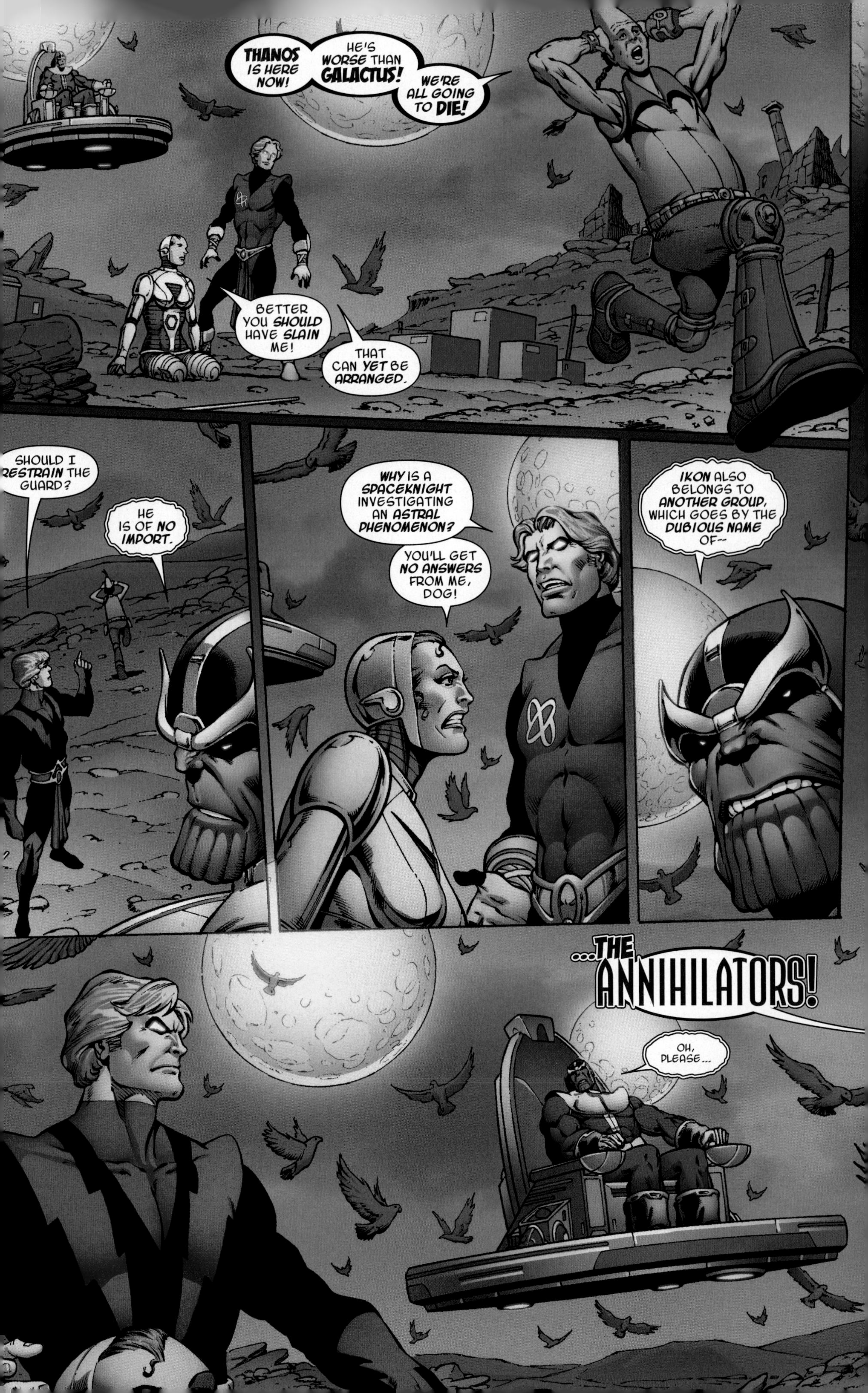
THANOS IS HERE NOW!
HE'S WORSE THAN GALACTUS!
WE'RE ALL GOING TO DIE!
BETTER YOU SHOULD HAVE SLAIN ME!
THAT CAN YET BE ARRANGED.
SHOULD I RESTRAIN THE GUARD?
HE IS OF NO IMPORT.
WHY IS A SPACEKNIGHT INVESTIGATING AN ASTRAL PHENOMENON?
YOU'LL GET NO ANSWERS FROM ME, DOG!
IKON ALSO BELONGS TO ANOTHER GROUP, WHICH GOES BY THE DUBIOUS NAME OF--
...THE ANNIHILATORS!
OH, PLEASE...

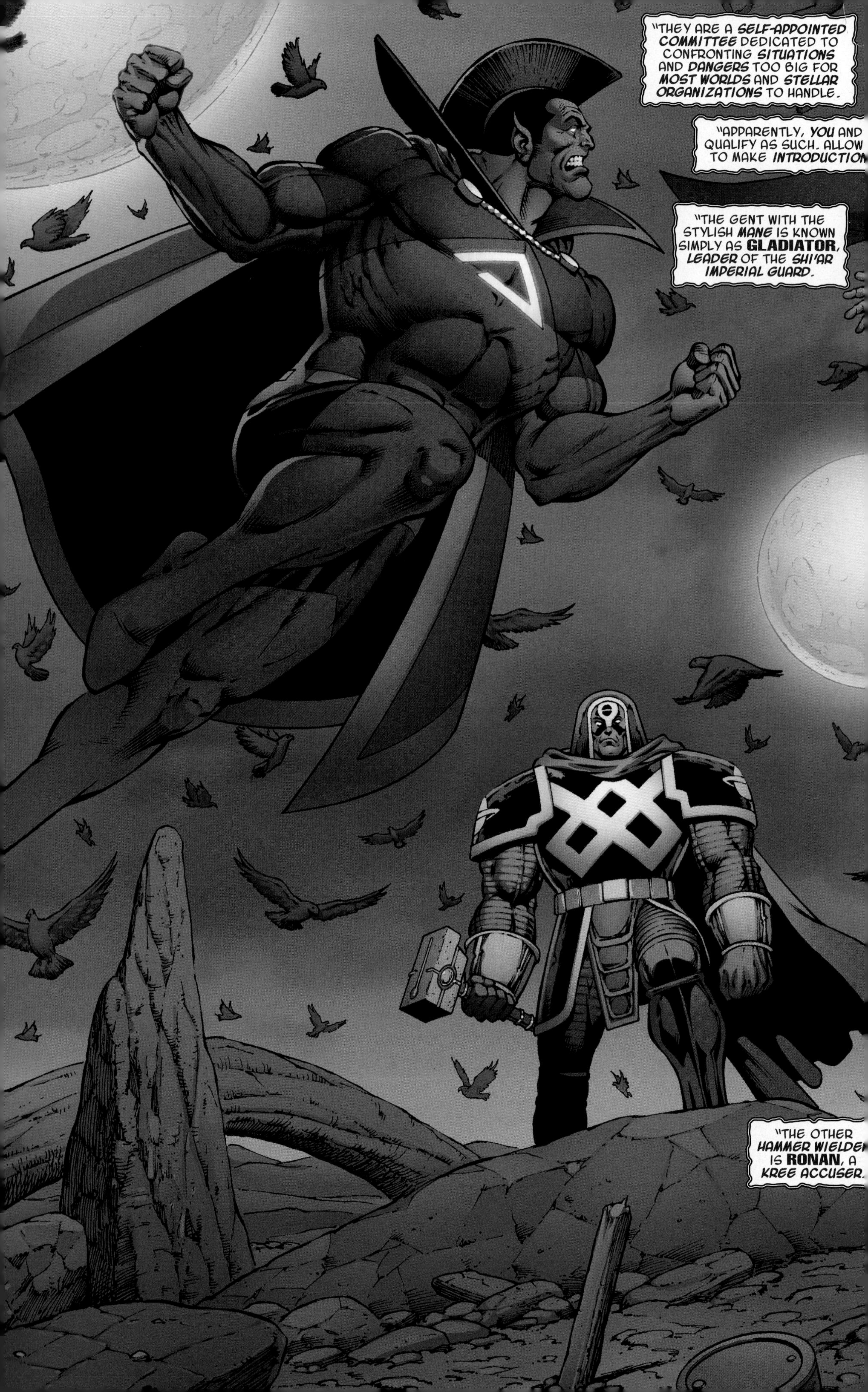
"THEY ARE A SELF-APPOINTED COMMITTEE DEDICATED TO CONFRONTING SITUATIONS AND DANGERS TOO BIG FOR MOST WORLDS AND STELLAR ORGANIZATIONS TO HANDLE.
"APPARENTLY, YOU AND QUALIFY AS SUCH. ALLOW TO MAKE INTRODUCTION
"THE GENT WITH THE STYLISH MANE IS KNOWN SIMPLY AS GLADIATOR, LEADER OF THE SHI'AR IMPERIAL GUARD.
"THE OTHER HAMMER WIELDE IS RONAN, A KREE ACCUSER.

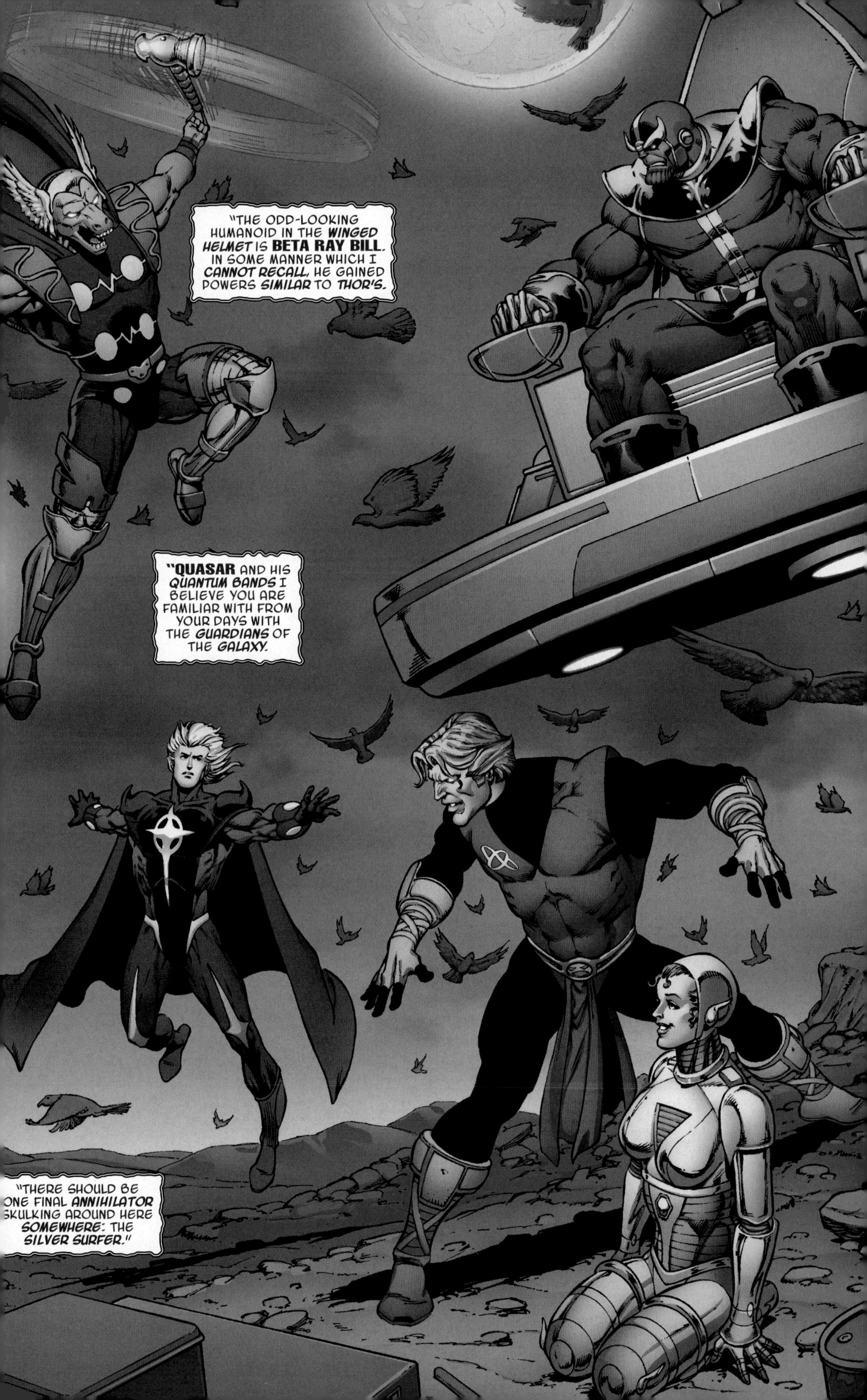
"THE ODD-LOOKING HUMANOID IN THE WINGED HELMET IS BETA RAY BILL. IN SOME MANNER WHICH I CANNOT RECALL, HE GAINED POWERS SIMILAR TO THOR'S.
"QUASAR AND HIS QUANTUM BANDS I BELIEVE YOU ARE FAMILIAR WITH FROM YOUR DAYS WITH THE GUARDIANS OF THE GALAXY.
"THERE SHOULD BE ONE FINAL ANNIHILATOR SKULKING AROUND HERE SOMEWHERE: THE SILVER SURFER."

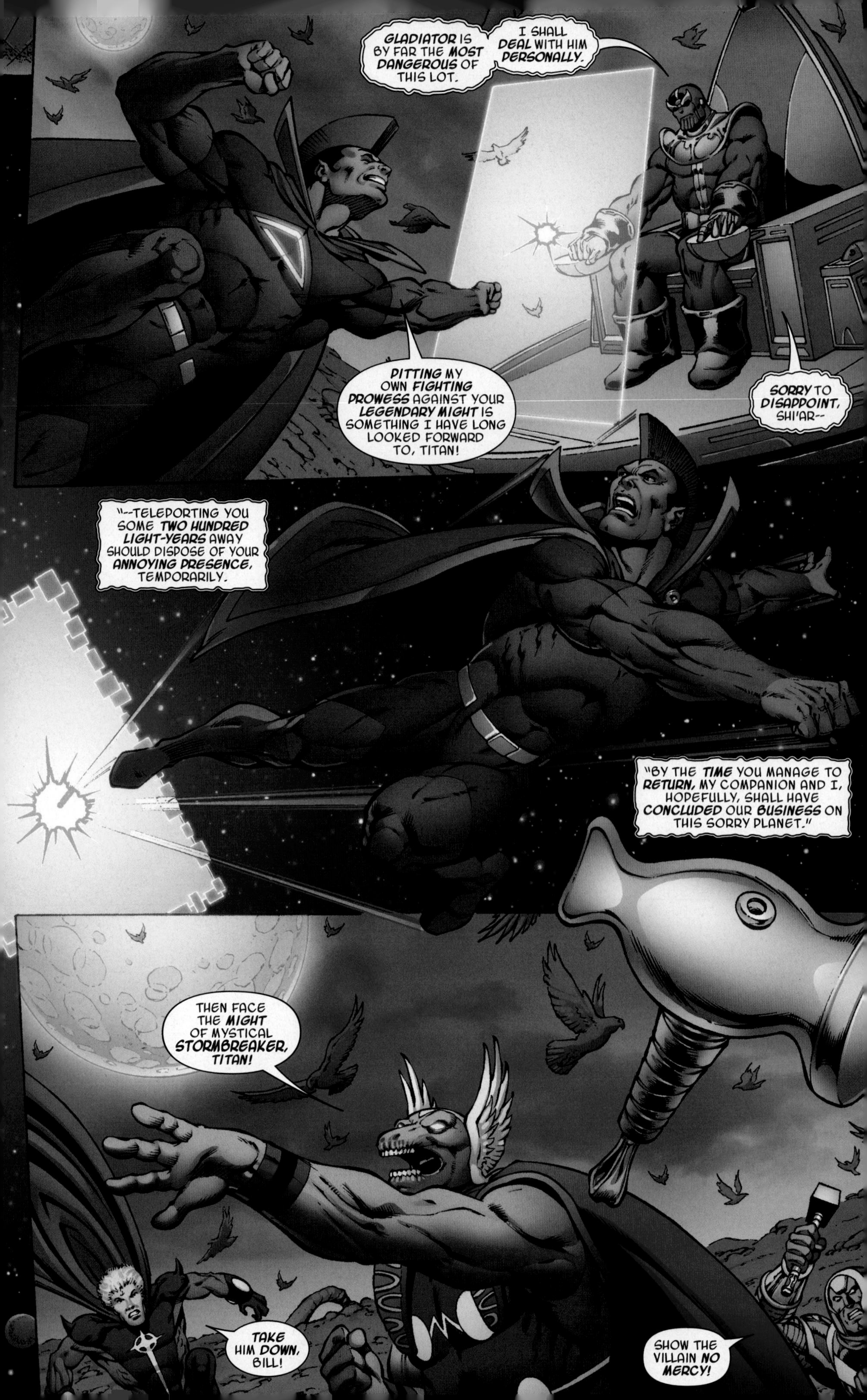
GLADIATOR IS BY FAR THE MOST DANGEROUS OF THIS LOT.
I SHALL DEAL WITH HIM PERSONALLY.
PITTING MY OWN FIGHTING PROWESS AGAINST YOUR LEGENDARY MIGHT IS SOMETHING I HAVE LONG LOOKED FORWARD TO, TITAN!
SORRY TO DISAPPOINT, SHI'AR--
"--TELEPORTING YOU SOME TWO HUNDRED LIGHT-YEARS AWAY SHOULD DISPOSE OF YOUR ANNOYING PRESENCE, TEMPORARILY.
"BY THE TIME YOU MANAGE TO RETURN, MY COMPANION AND I, HOPEFULLY, SHALL HAVE CONCLUDED OUR BUSINESS ON THIS SORRY PLANET."
THEN FACE THE MIGHT OF MYSTICAL STORMBREAKER, TITAN!
TAKE HIM DOWN, BILL!
SHOW THE VILLAIN NO MERCY!

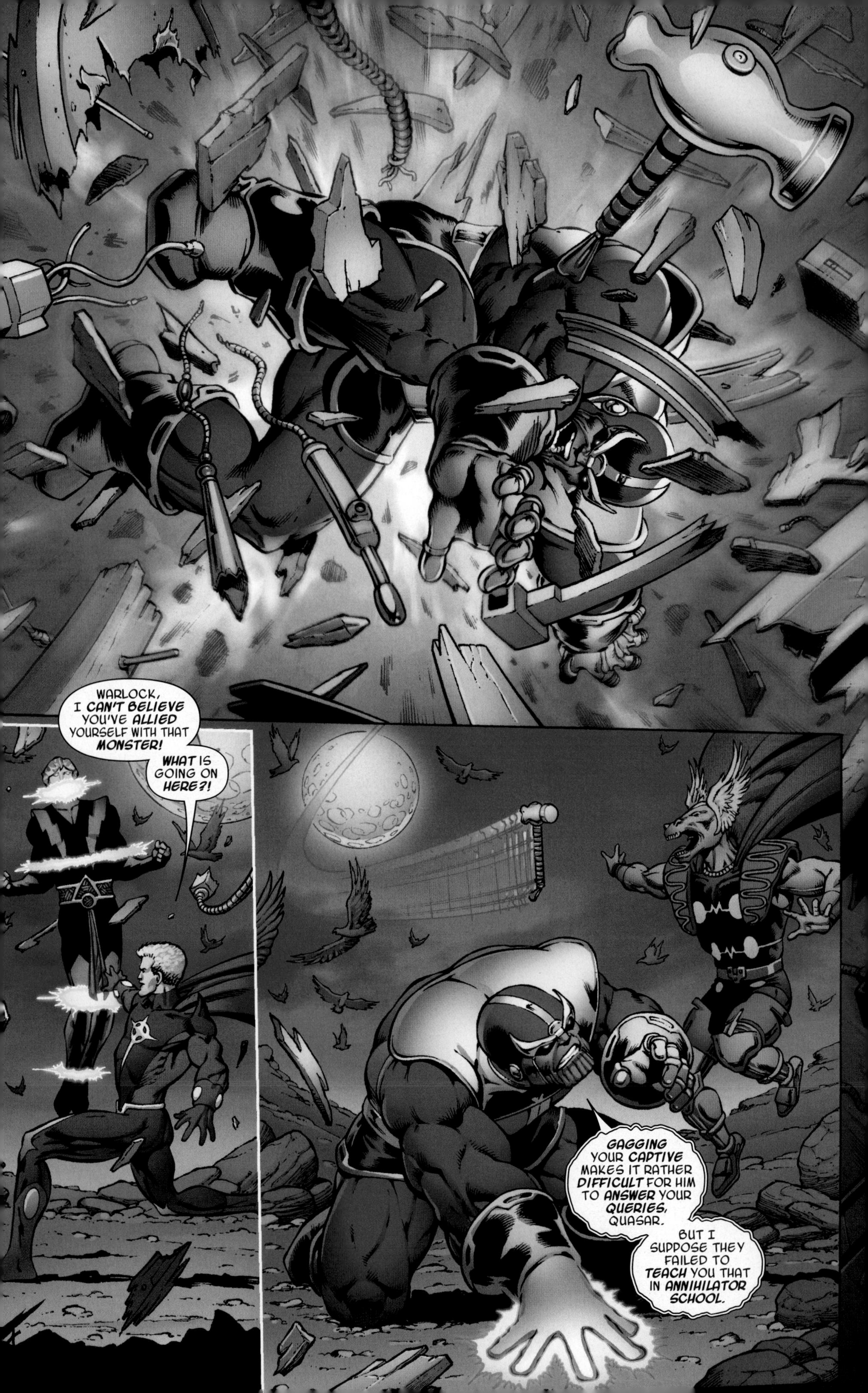

WARLOCK, I CAN'T BELIEVE YOU'VE ALLIED YOURSELF WITH THAT MONSTER!
WHAT IS GOING ON HERE?!
GAGGING YOUR CAPTIVE MAKES IT RATHER DIFFICULT FOR HIM TO ANSWER YOUR QUERIES, QUASAR.
BUT I SUPPOSE THEY FAILED TO TEACH YOU THAT IN ANNIHILATOR SCHOOL.

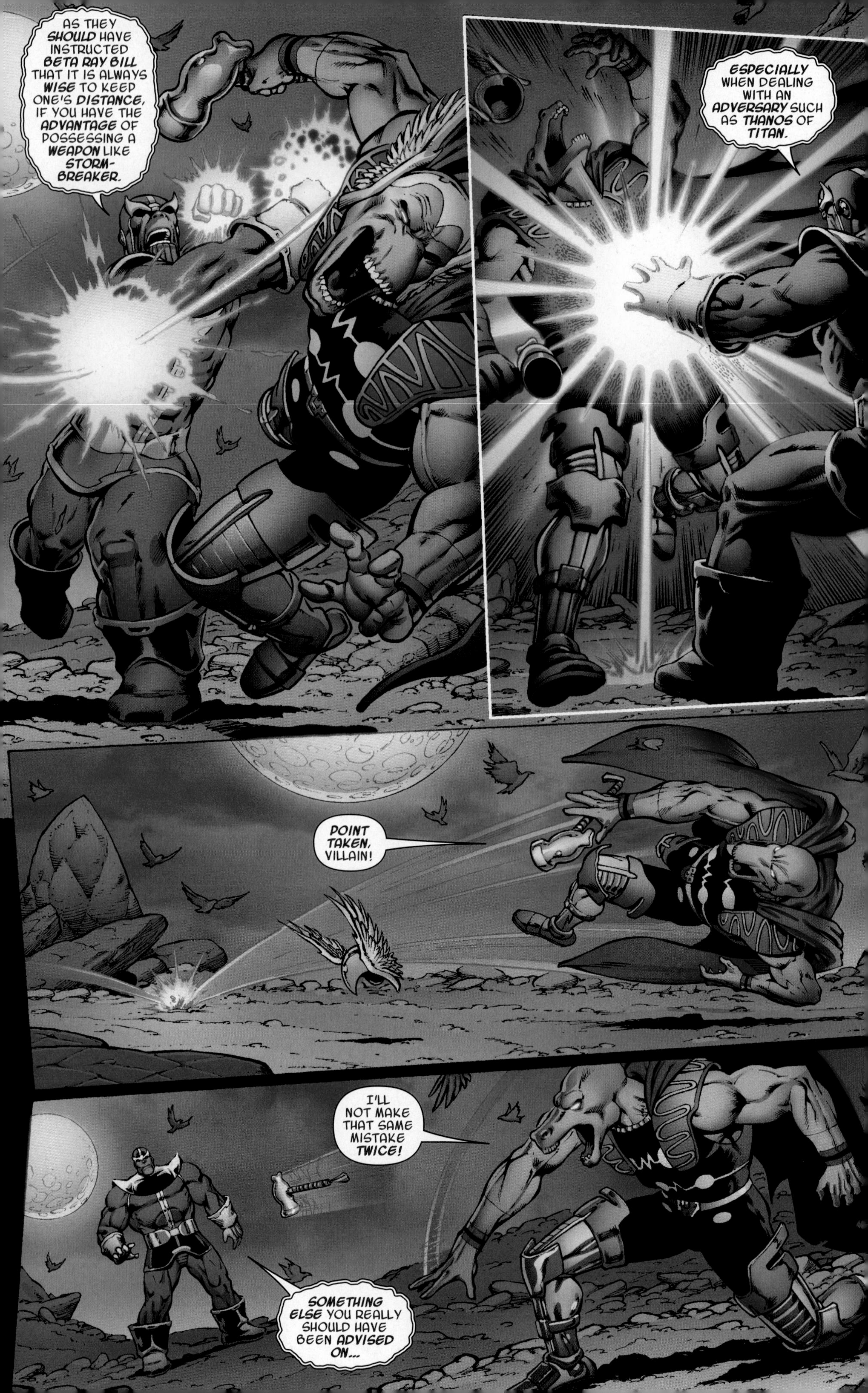

AS THEY SHOULD HAVE INSTRUCTED BETA RAY BILL THAT IT IS ALWAYS WISE TO KEEP ONE'S DISTANCE, IF YOU HAVE THE ADVANTAGE OF POSSESSING A WEAPON LIKE STORM-BREAKER.
ESPECIALLY WHEN DEALING WITH AN ADVERSARY SUCH AS THANOS OF TITAN.
POINT TAKEN, VILLAIN!
I'LL NOT MAKE THAT SAME MISTAKE TWICE!
SOMETHING ELSE YOU REALLY SHOULD HAVE BEEN ADVISED ON...

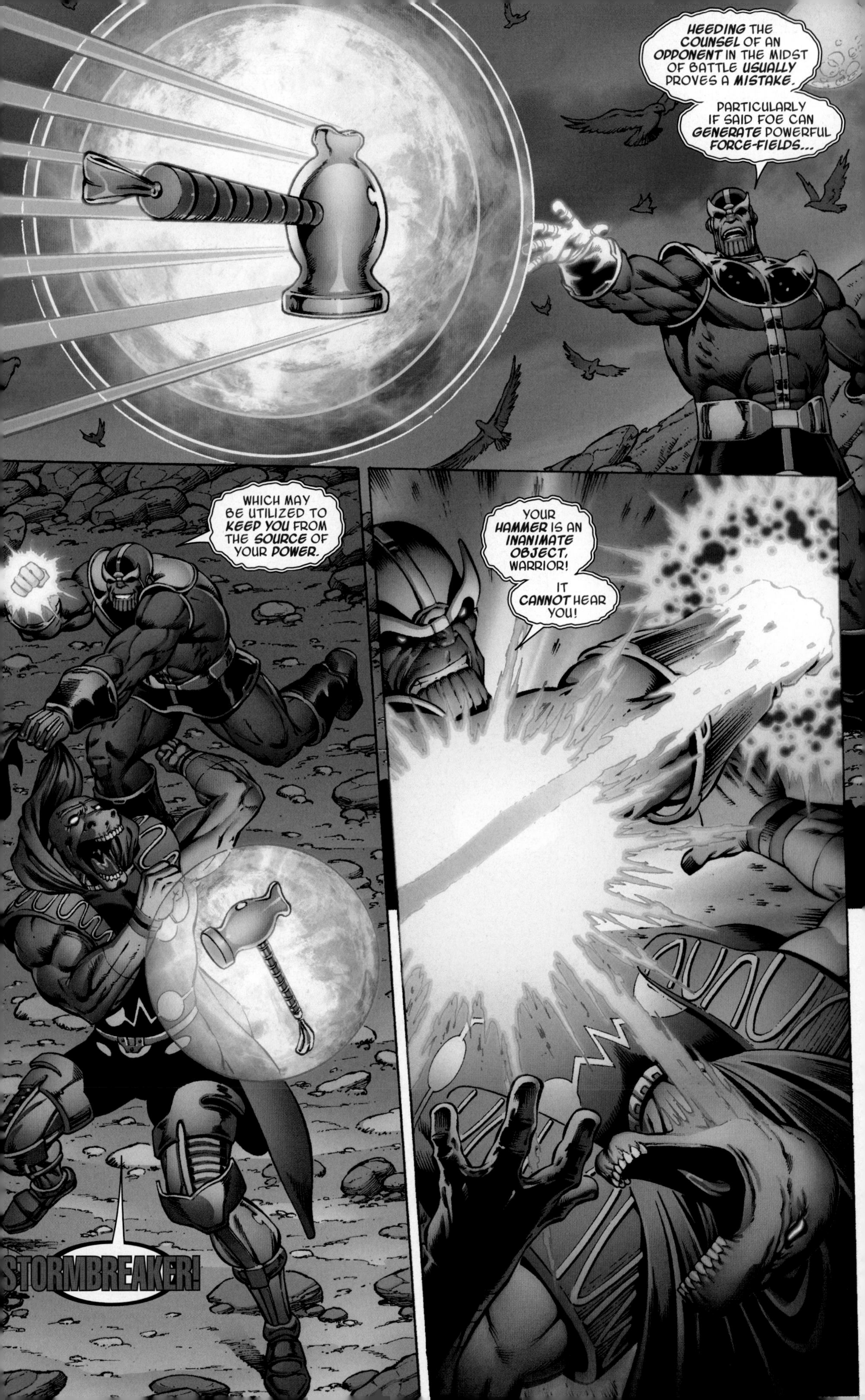
HEEDING THE COUNSEL OF AN OPPONENT IN THE MIDST OF BATTLE USUALLY PROVES A MISTAKE.
PARTICULARLY IF SAID FOE CAN GENERATE POWERFUL FORCE-FIELDS...
WHICH MAY BE UTILIZED TO KEEP YOU FROM THE SOURCE OF YOUR POWER.
STORMBREAKER!
YOUR HAMMER IS AN INANIMATE OBJECT, WARRIOR!
IT CANNOT HEAR YOU!

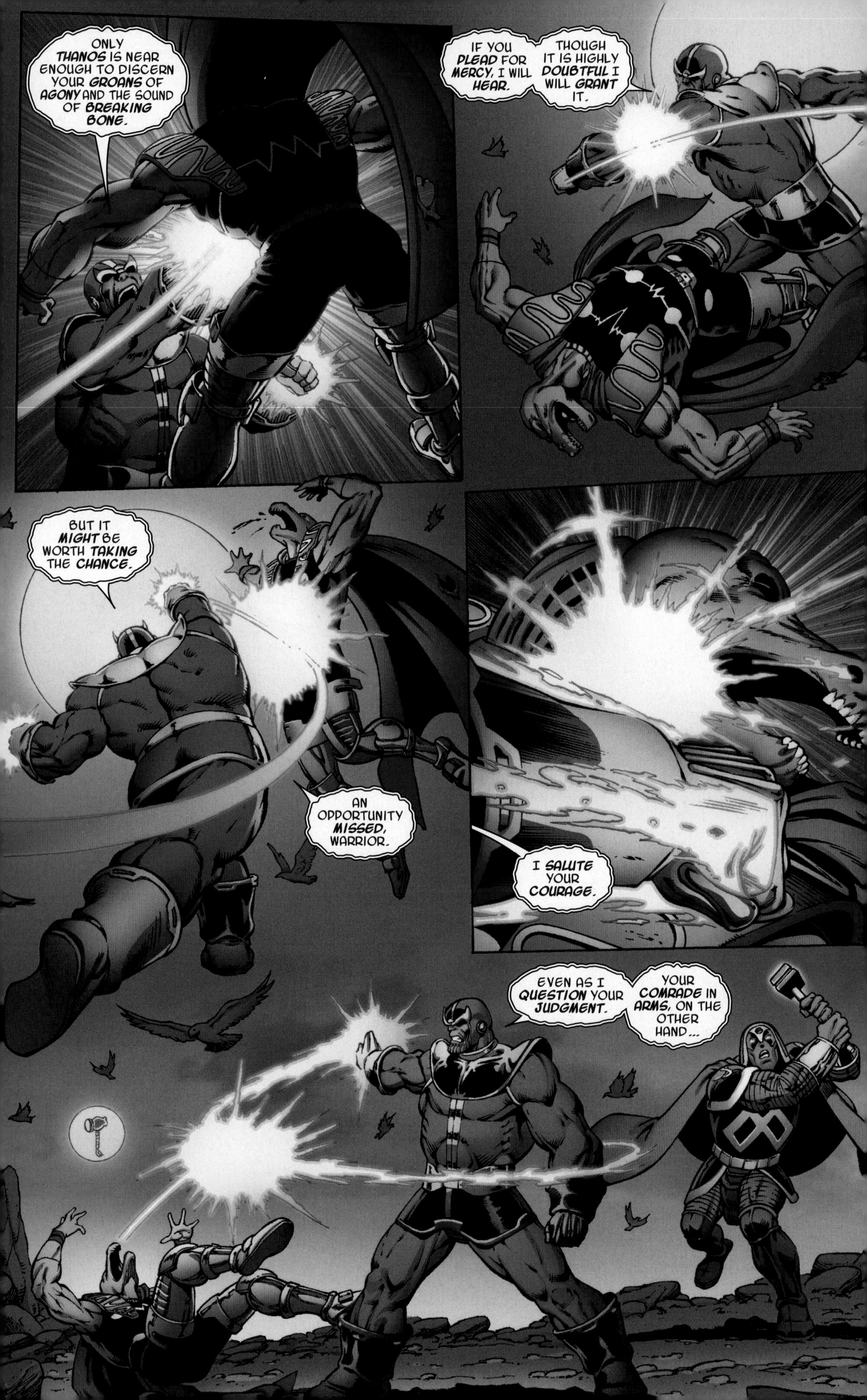
ONLY THANOS IS NEAR ENOUGH TO DISCERN YOUR GROANS OF AGONY AND THE SOUND OF BREAKING BONE.
IF YOU PLEAD FOR MERCY, I WILL HEAR.
THOUGH IT IS HIGHLY DOUBTFUL I WILL GRANT IT.
BUT IT MIGHT BE WORTH TAKING THE CHANCE.
AN OPPORTUNITY MISSED, WARRIOR.
I SALUTE YOUR COURAGE.
EVEN AS I QUESTION YOUR JUDGMENT.
YOUR COMRADE IN ARMS, ON THE OTHER HAND...

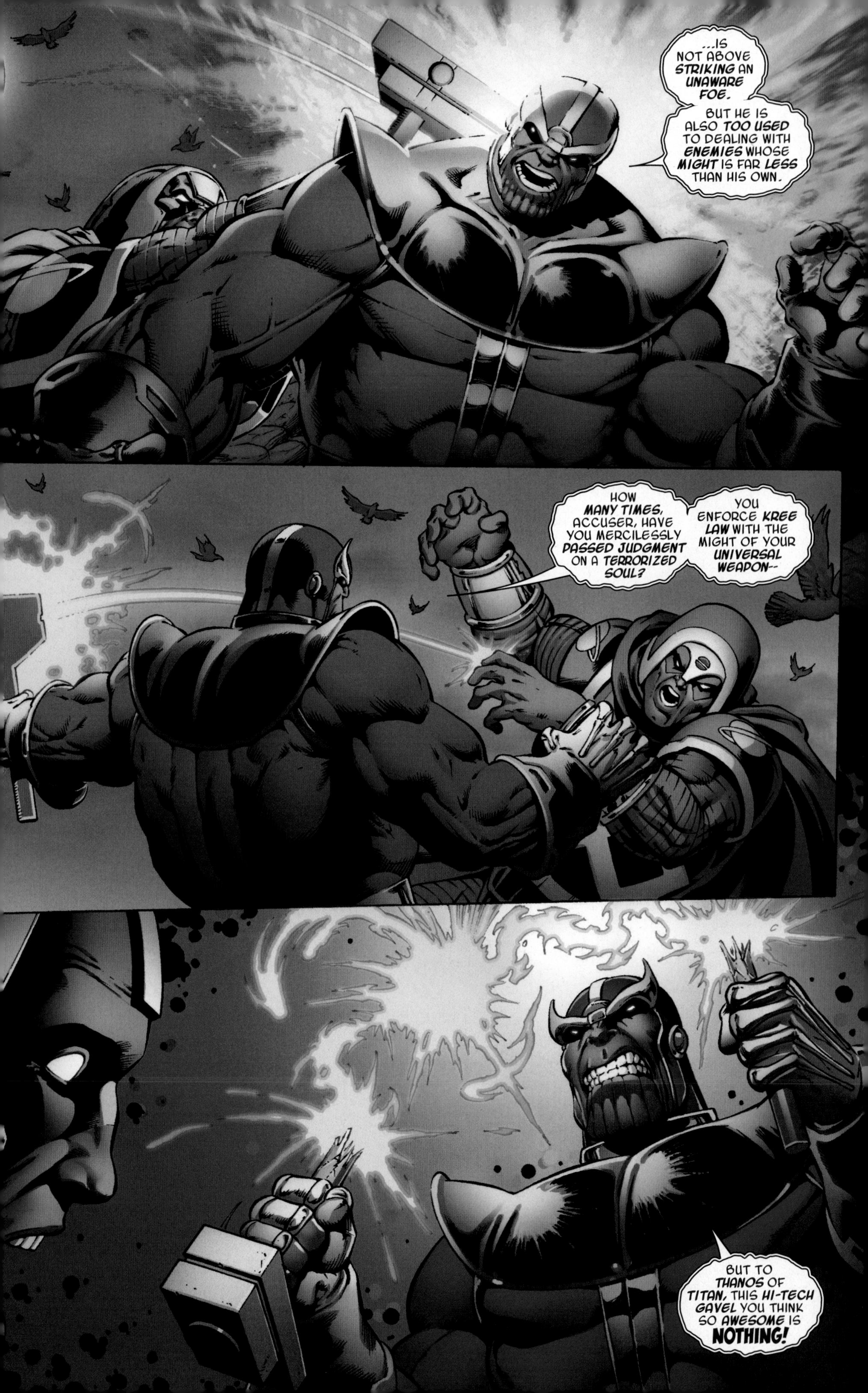
...IS NOT ABOVE STRIKING AN UNAWARE FOE.
BUT HE IS ALSO TOO USED TO DEALING WITH ENEMIES WHOSE MIGHT IS FAR LESS THAN HIS OWN.
HOW MANY TIMES, ACCUSER, HAVE YOU MERCILESSLY PASSED JUDGMENT ON A TERRORIZED SOUL?
YOU ENFORCE KREE LAW WITH THE MIGHT OF YOUR UNIVERSAL WEAPON--
BUT TO THANOS OF TITAN, THIS HI-TECH GAVEL YOU THINK SO AWESOME IS NOTHING!

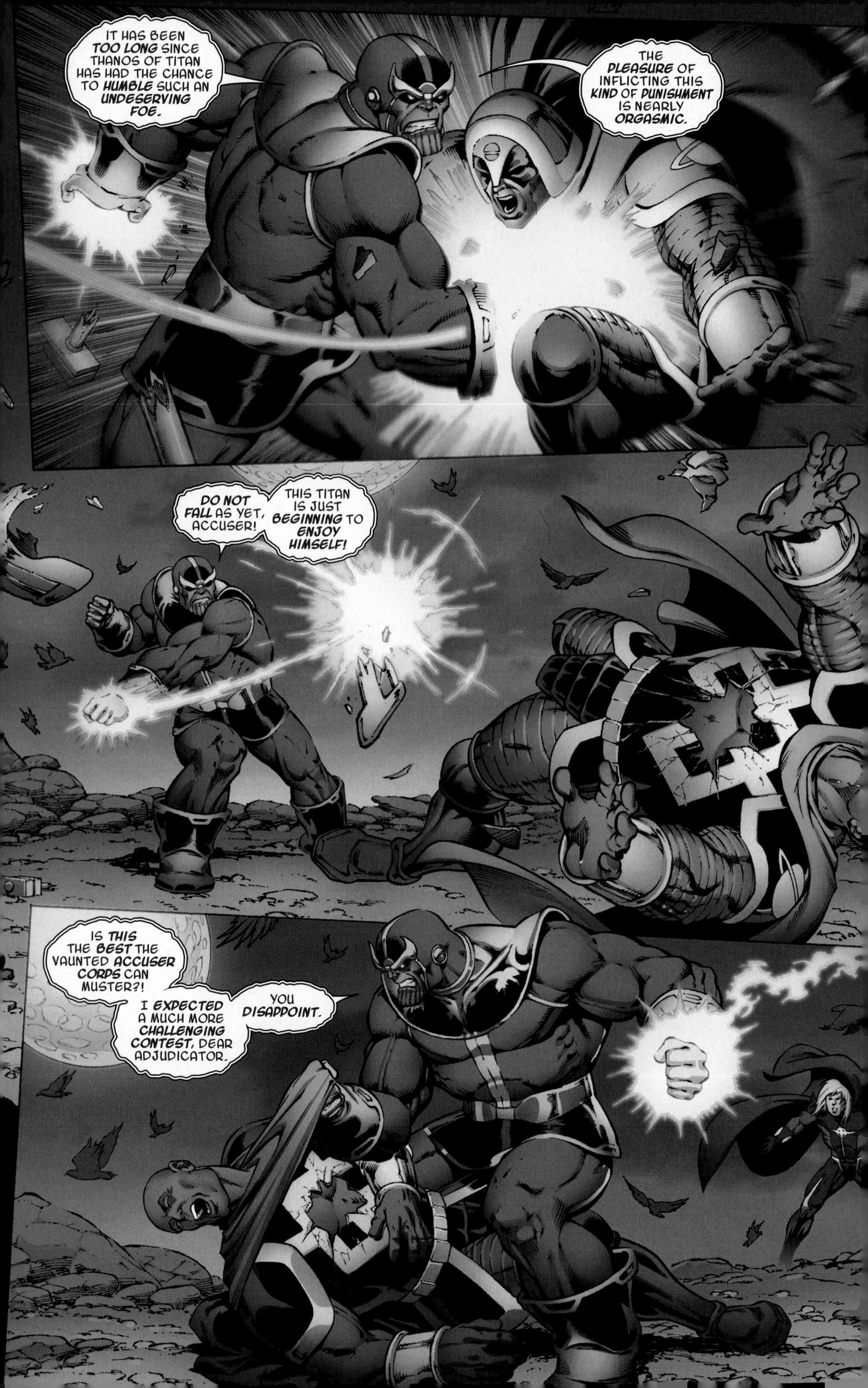
IT HAS BEEN TOO LONG SINCE THANOS OF TITAN HAS HAD THE CHANCE TO HUMBLE SUCH AN UNDESERVING FOE.
THE PLEASURE OF INFLICTING THIS KIND OF PUNISHMENT IS NEARLY ORGASMIC.
DO NOT FALL AS YET, ACCUSER!
THIS TITAN IS JUST BEGINNING TO ENJOY HIMSELF!
IS THIS THE BEST THE VAUNTED ACCUSER CORPS CAN MUSTER?!
I EXPECTED A MUCH MORE CHALLENGING CONTEST, DEAR ADJUDICATOR.
YOU DISAPPOINT.

AND *THAT*, FOR THE MOMENT, LEAVES ONLY YOU, QUASAR.

HOW SHALL WE HANDLE OUR PRESENT SITUATION, VALIANT HERO?

THE LAST FEW MOMENTS HAVE *CLEARLY* DEMONSTRATED THAT, IN THIS *CONFRONTATIONAL EXCHANGE*, YOU ARE EXCEEDINGLY *OUTGUNNED*.

DO YOU *NOBLY STAND YOUR ROUND* AND BECOME *LEGENDARY FIGURE* OF *SACRIFICE*, OR DO YOU--

EEE-AARRGHH!

OR I CAN *SHORT-CIRCUIT* QUASAR'S SYSTEM AND SPARE HIM A *SAVAGE THRASHING*.

I WAS *NOT FINISHED* WITH THIS ONE.

REMEMBER *WHY WE CAME* HERE, TITAN.

YOUR *MYSTICAL TRINKET* DIRECTS US TOWARD YONDER *RUINS*.

AS SOON AS WE *CONCLUDE* OUR *DEALINGS* WITH THE *ANNIHILATORS*.

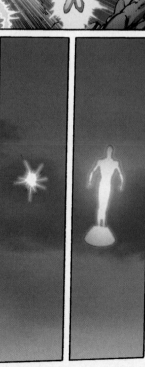

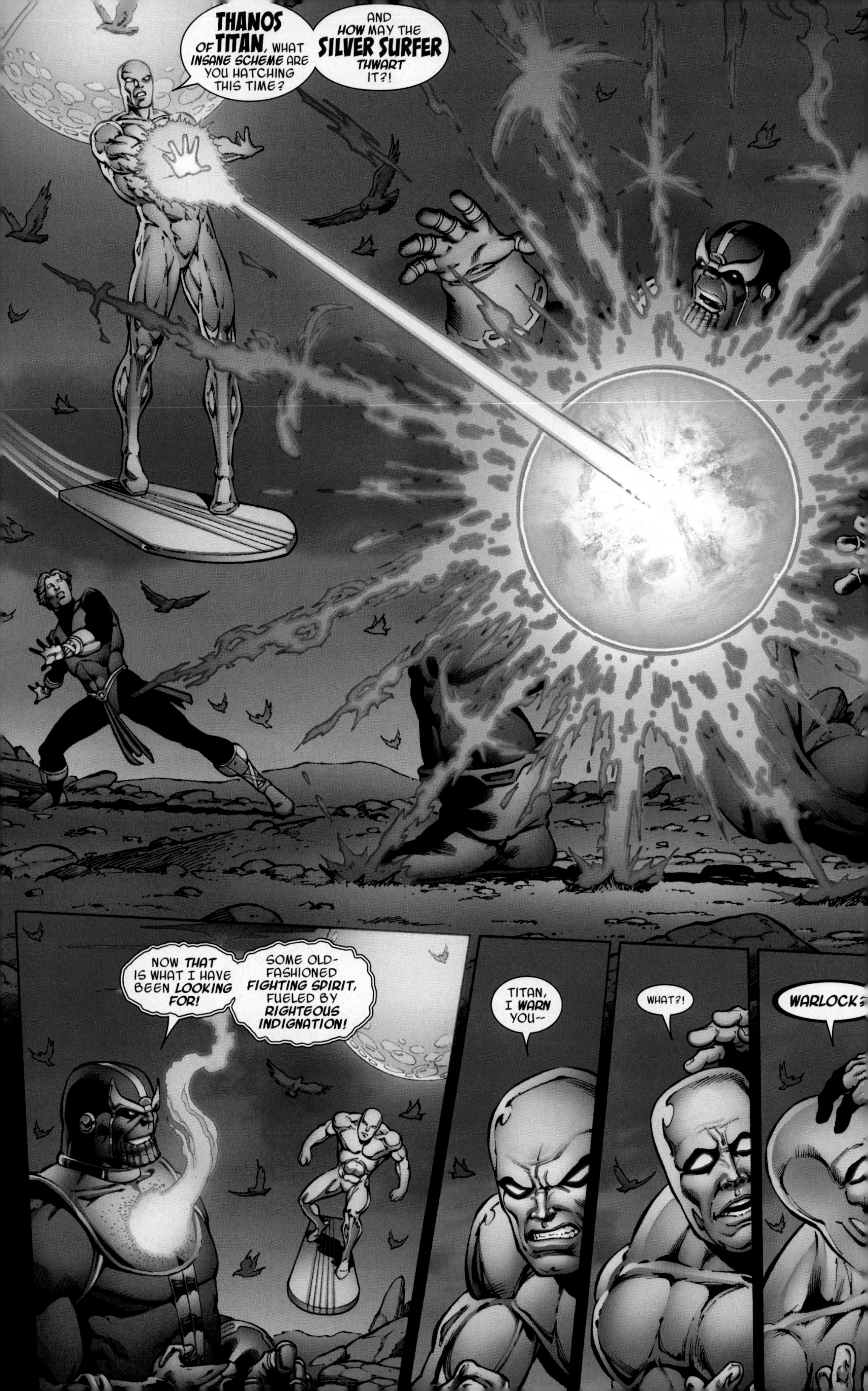
THANOS OF TITAN, WHAT INSANE SCHEME ARE YOU HATCHING THIS TIME?
AND HOW MAY THE SILVER SURFER THWART IT?!
NOW THAT IS WHAT I HAVE BEEN LOOKING FOR!
SOME OLD-FASHIONED FIGHTING SPIRIT, FUELED BY RIGHTEOUS INDIGNATION!
TITAN, I WARN YOU--
WHAT?!
WARLOCK!

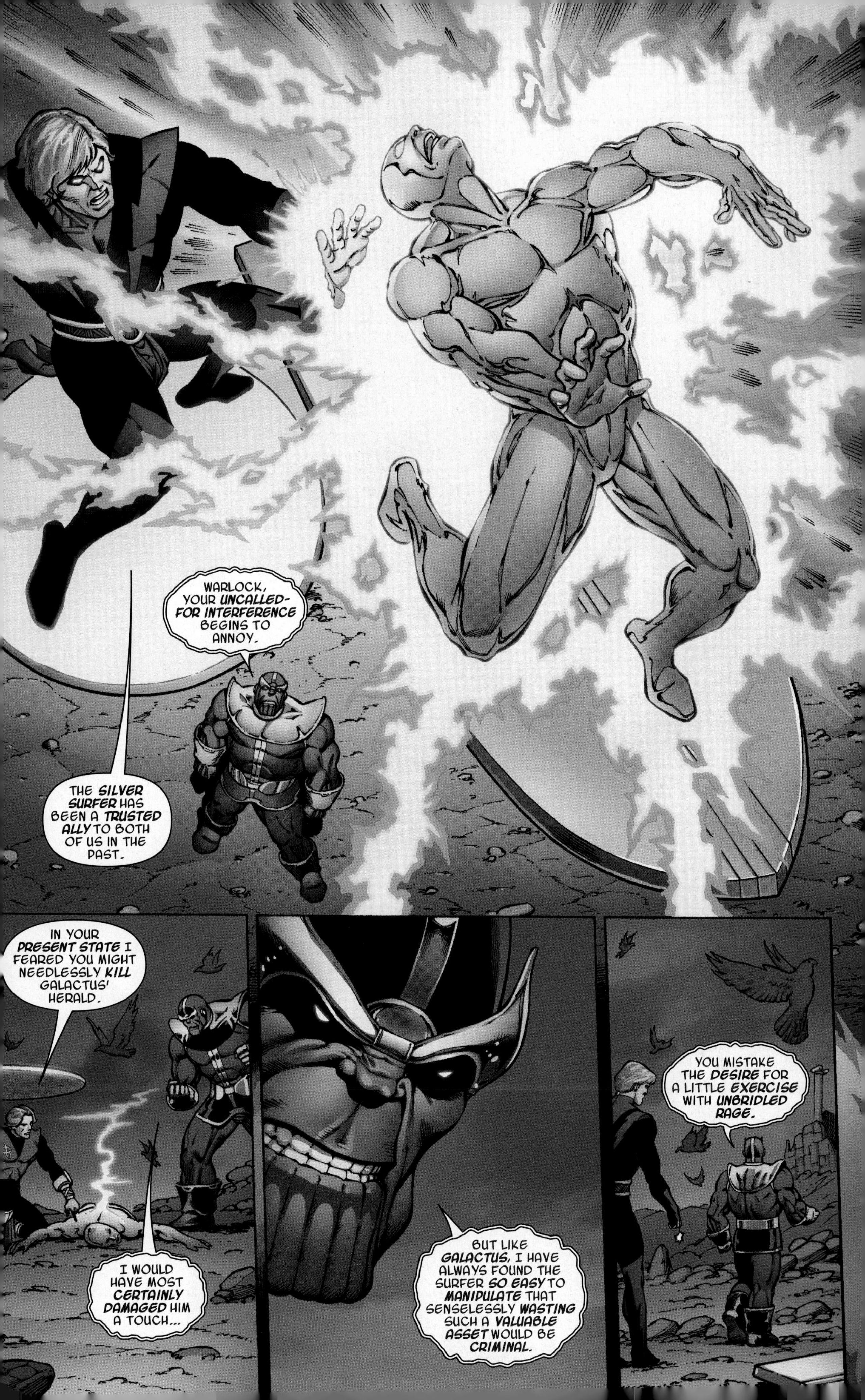
WARLOCK, YOUR UNCALLED-FOR INTERFERENCE BEGINS TO ANNOY.
THE SILVER SURFER HAS BEEN A TRUSTED ALLY TO BOTH OF US IN THE PAST.
IN YOUR PRESENT STATE I FEARED YOU MIGHT NEEDLESSLY KILL GALACTUS' HERALD.
I WOULD HAVE MOST CERTAINLY DAMAGED HIM A TOUCH...
BUT LIKE GALACTUS, I HAVE ALWAYS FOUND THE SURFER SO EASY TO MANIPULATE THAT SENSELESSLY WASTING SUCH A VALUABLE ASSET WOULD BE CRIMINAL.
YOU MISTAKE THE DESIRE FOR A LITTLE EXERCISE WITH UNBRIDLED RAGE.

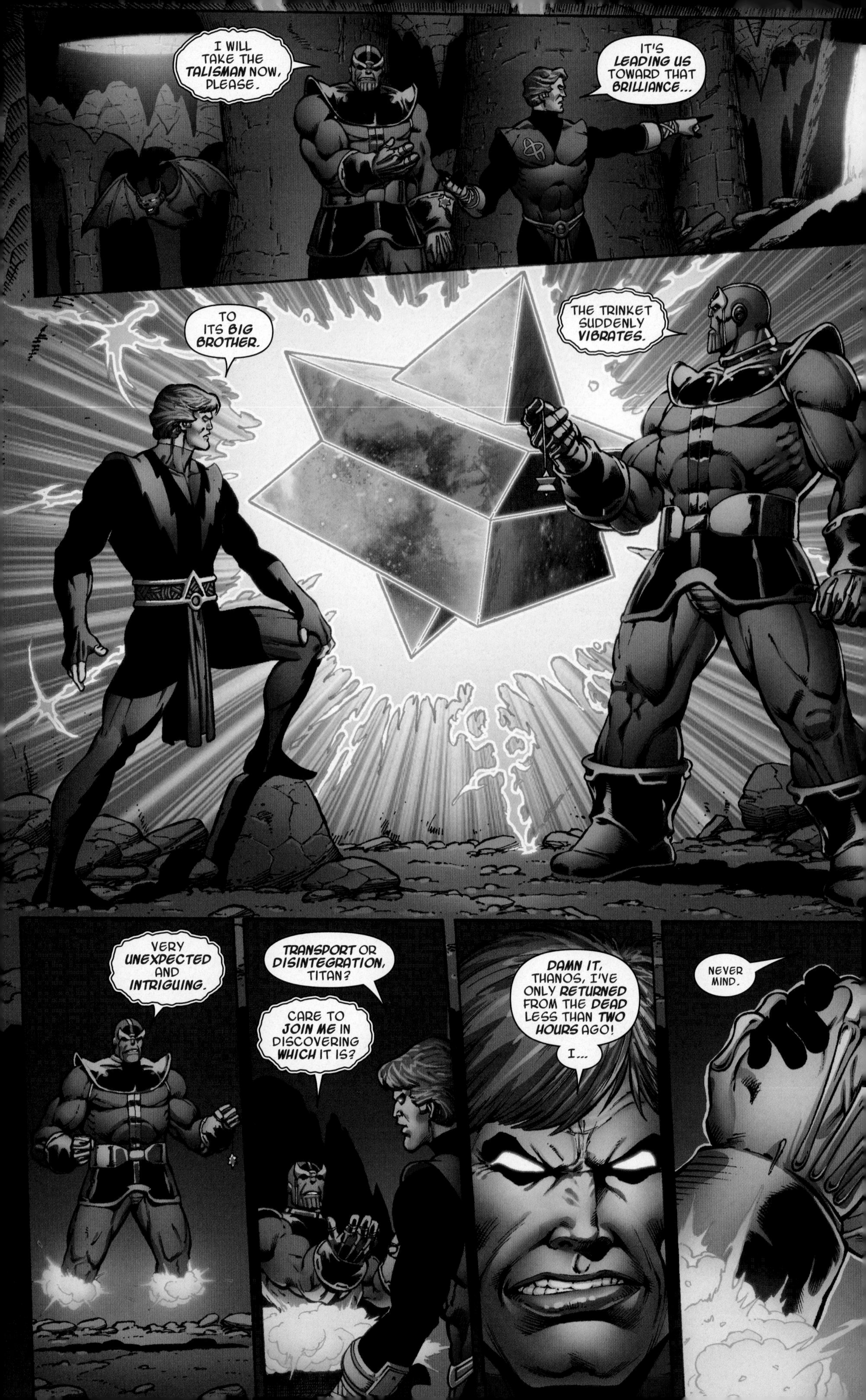
I WILL TAKE THE TALISMAN NOW, PLEASE.
IT'S LEADING US TOWARD THAT BRILLIANCE...
TO ITS BIG BROTHER.
THE TRINKET SUDDENLY VIBRATES.
VERY UNEXPECTED AND INTRIGUING.
TRANSPORT OR DISINTEGRATION, TITAN?
CARE TO JOIN ME IN DISCOVERING WHICH IT IS?
DAMN IT, THANOS, I'VE ONLY RETURNED FROM THE DEAD LESS THAN TWO HOURS AGO!
I...
NEVER MIND.

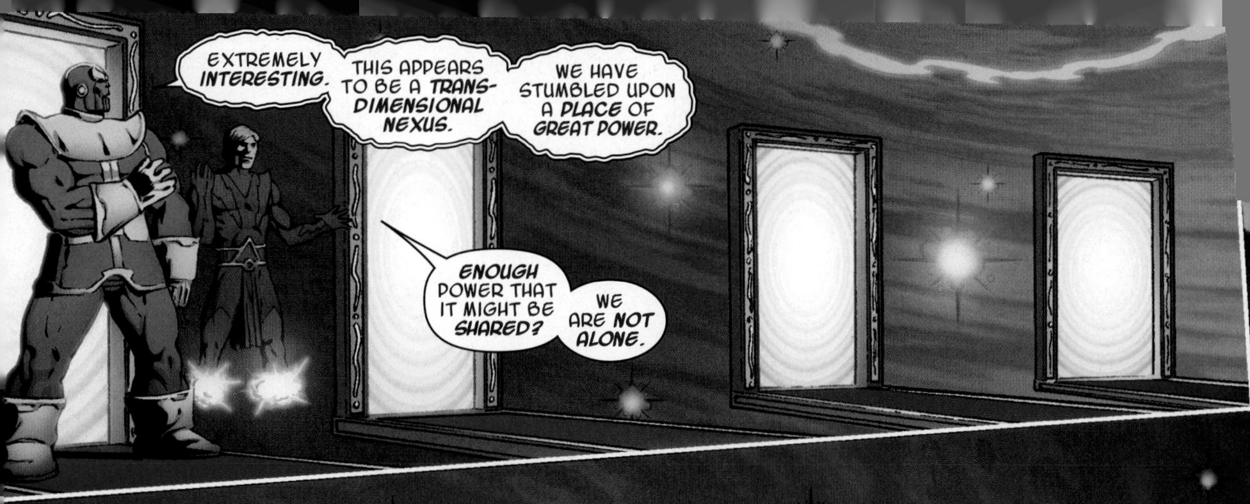

EXTREMELY INTERESTING.
THIS APPEARS TO BE A TRANS-DIMENSIONAL NEXUS.
WE HAVE STUMBLED UPON A PLACE OF GREAT POWER.
ENOUGH POWER THAT IT MIGHT BE SHARED?
WE ARE NOT ALONE.

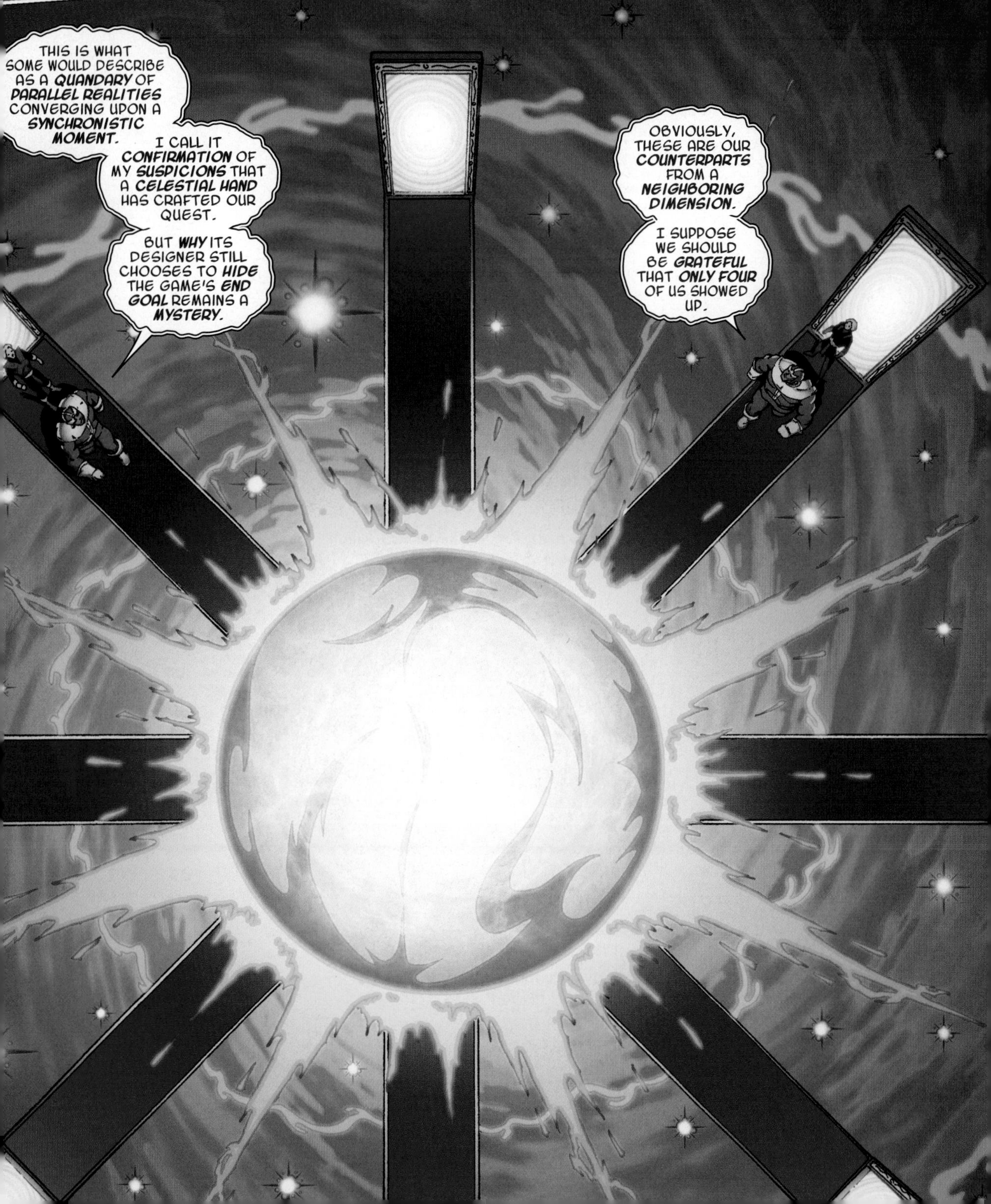

THIS IS WHAT SOME WOULD DESCRIBE AS A QUANDARY OF PARALLEL REALITIES CONVERGING UPON A SYNCHRONISTIC MOMENT.
I CALL IT CONFIRMATION OF MY SUSPICIONS THAT A CELESTIAL HAND HAS CRAFTED OUR QUEST.
BUT WHY ITS DESIGNER STILL CHOOSES TO HIDE THE GAME'S END GOAL REMAINS A MYSTERY.
OBVIOUSLY, THESE ARE OUR COUNTERPARTS FROM A NEIGHBORING DIMENSION.
I SUPPOSE WE SHOULD BE GRATEFUL THAT ONLY FOUR OF US SHOWED UP.

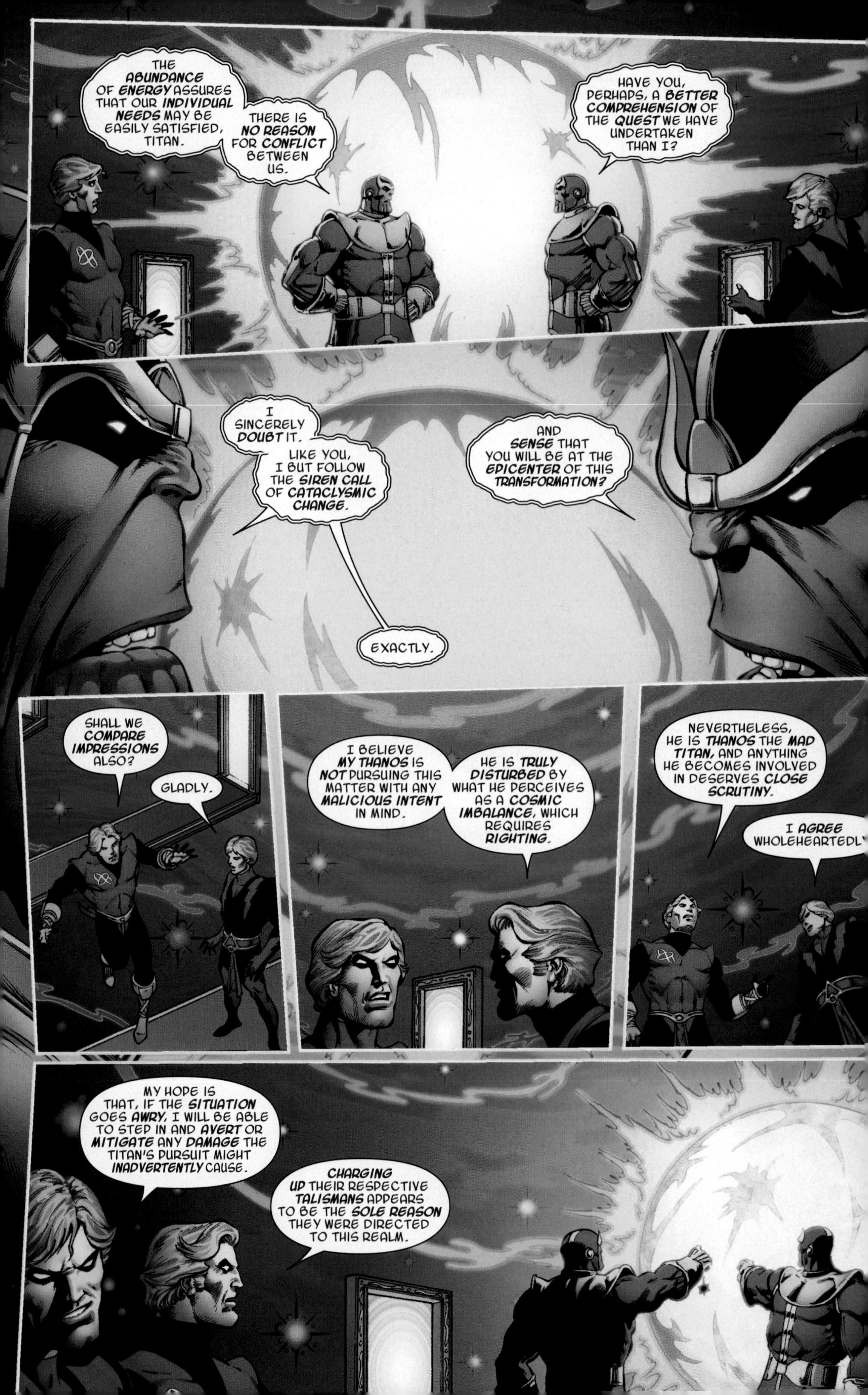
THE ABUNDANCE OF ENERGY ASSURES THAT OUR INDIVIDUAL NEEDS MAY BE EASILY SATISFIED, TITAN.
THERE IS NO REASON FOR CONFLICT BETWEEN US.
HAVE YOU, PERHAPS, A BETTER COMPREHENSION OF THE QUEST WE HAVE UNDERTAKEN THAN I?
I SINCERELY DOUBT IT.
LIKE YOU, I BUT FOLLOW THE SIREN CALL OF CATACLYSMIC CHANGE.
AND SENSE THAT YOU WILL BE AT THE EPICENTER OF THIS TRANSFORMATION?
EXACTLY.
SHALL WE COMPARE IMPRESSIONS ALSO?
GLADLY.
I BELIEVE MY THANOS IS NOT PURSUING THIS MATTER WITH ANY MALICIOUS INTENT IN MIND.
HE IS TRULY DISTURBED BY WHAT HE PERCEIVES AS A COSMIC IMBALANCE, WHICH REQUIRES RIGHTING.
NEVERTHELESS, HE IS THANOS THE MAD TITAN, AND ANYTHING HE BECOMES INVOLVED IN DESERVES CLOSE SCRUTINY.
I AGREE WHOLEHEARTEDL
MY HOPE IS THAT, IF THE SITUATION GOES AWRY, I WILL BE ABLE TO STEP IN AND AVERT OR MITIGATE ANY DAMAGE THE TITAN'S PURSUIT MIGHT INADVERTENTLY CAUSE.
CHARGING UP THEIR RESPECTIVE TALISMANS APPEARS TO BE THE SOLE REASON THEY WERE DIRECTED TO THIS REALM.

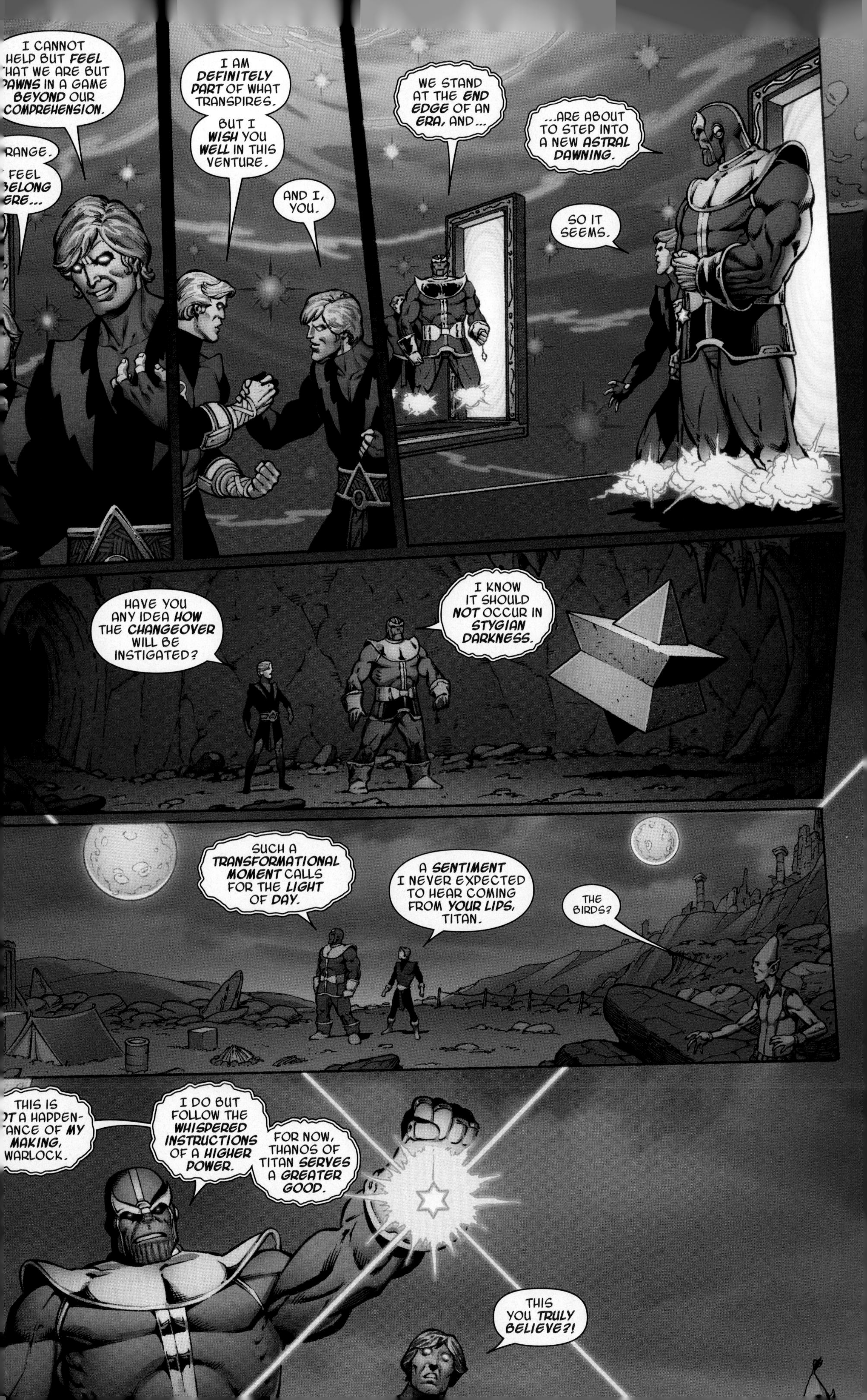
I CANNOT HELP BUT FEEL THAT WE ARE BUT PAWNS IN A GAME BEYOND OUR COMPREHENSION.
RANGE. FEEL BELONG ERE...
I AM DEFINITELY PART OF WHAT TRANSPIRES.
BUT I WISH YOU WELL IN THIS VENTURE.
AND I, YOU.
WE STAND AT THE END EDGE OF AN ERA, AND...
...ARE ABOUT TO STEP INTO A NEW ASTRAL DAWNING.
SO IT SEEMS.
HAVE YOU ANY IDEA HOW THE CHANGEOVER WILL BE INSTIGATED?
I KNOW IT SHOULD NOT OCCUR IN STYGIAN DARKNESS.
SUCH A TRANSFORMATIONAL MOMENT CALLS FOR THE LIGHT OF DAY.
A SENTIMENT I NEVER EXPECTED TO HEAR COMING FROM YOUR LIPS, TITAN.
THE BIRDS?
THIS IS OT A HAPPEN-TANCE OF MY MAKING, WARLOCK.
I DO BUT FOLLOW THE WHISPERED INSTRUCTIONS OF A HIGHER POWER.
FOR NOW, THANOS OF TITAN SERVES A GREATER GOOD.
THIS YOU TRULY BELIEVE?!

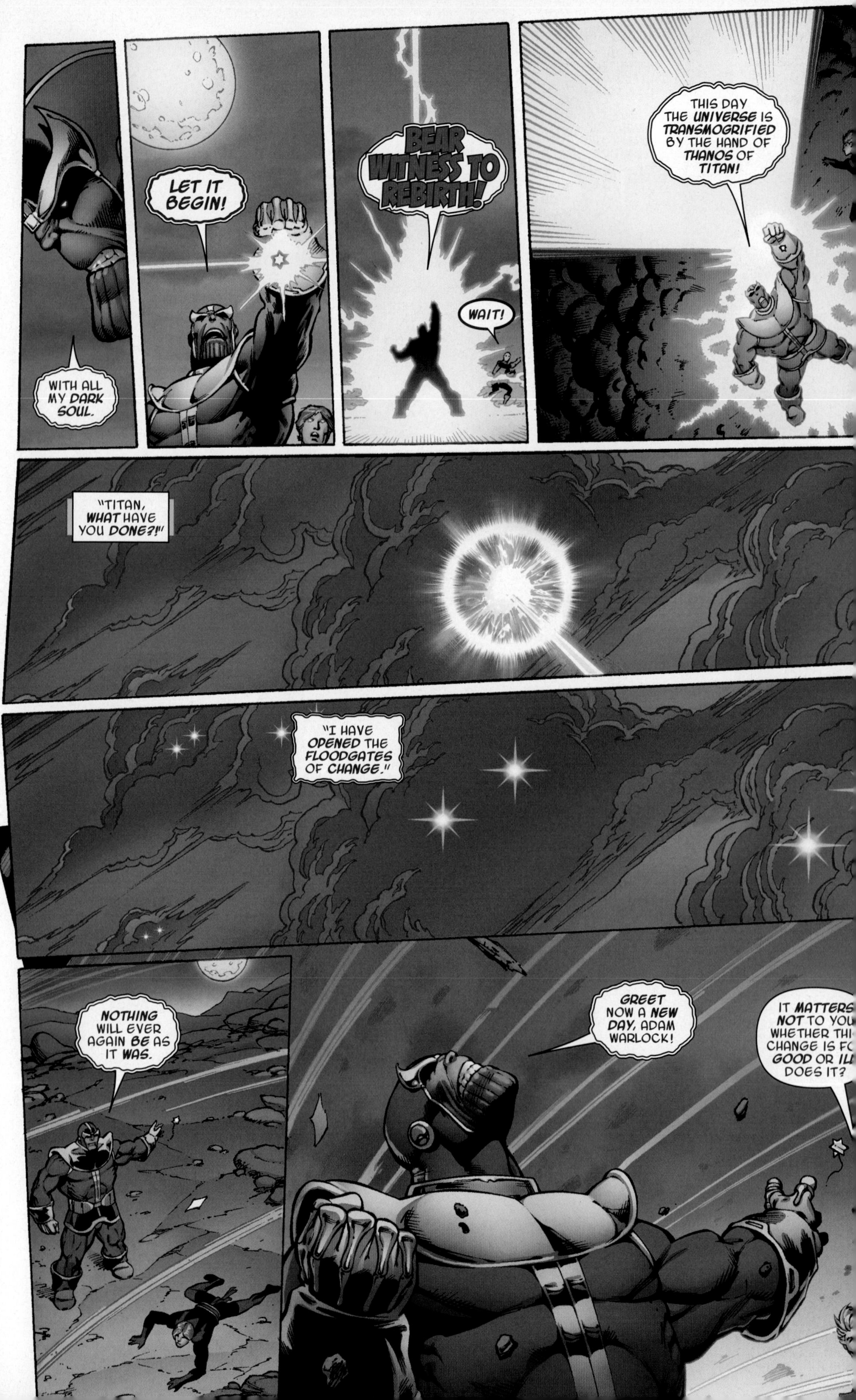

WITH ALL MY DARK SOUL.
LET IT BEGIN!
BEAR WITNESS TO REBIRTH!
WAIT!
THIS DAY THE UNIVERSE IS TRANSMOGRIFIED BY THE HAND OF THANOS OF TITAN!
"TITAN, WHAT HAVE YOU DONE?!"
"I HAVE OPENED THE FLOODGATES OF CHANGE."
NOTHING WILL EVER AGAIN BE AS IT WAS.
GREET NOW A NEW DAY, ADAM WARLOCK!
IT MATTERS NOT TO YOU WHETHER THI CHANGE IS FO GOOD OR IL DOES IT?

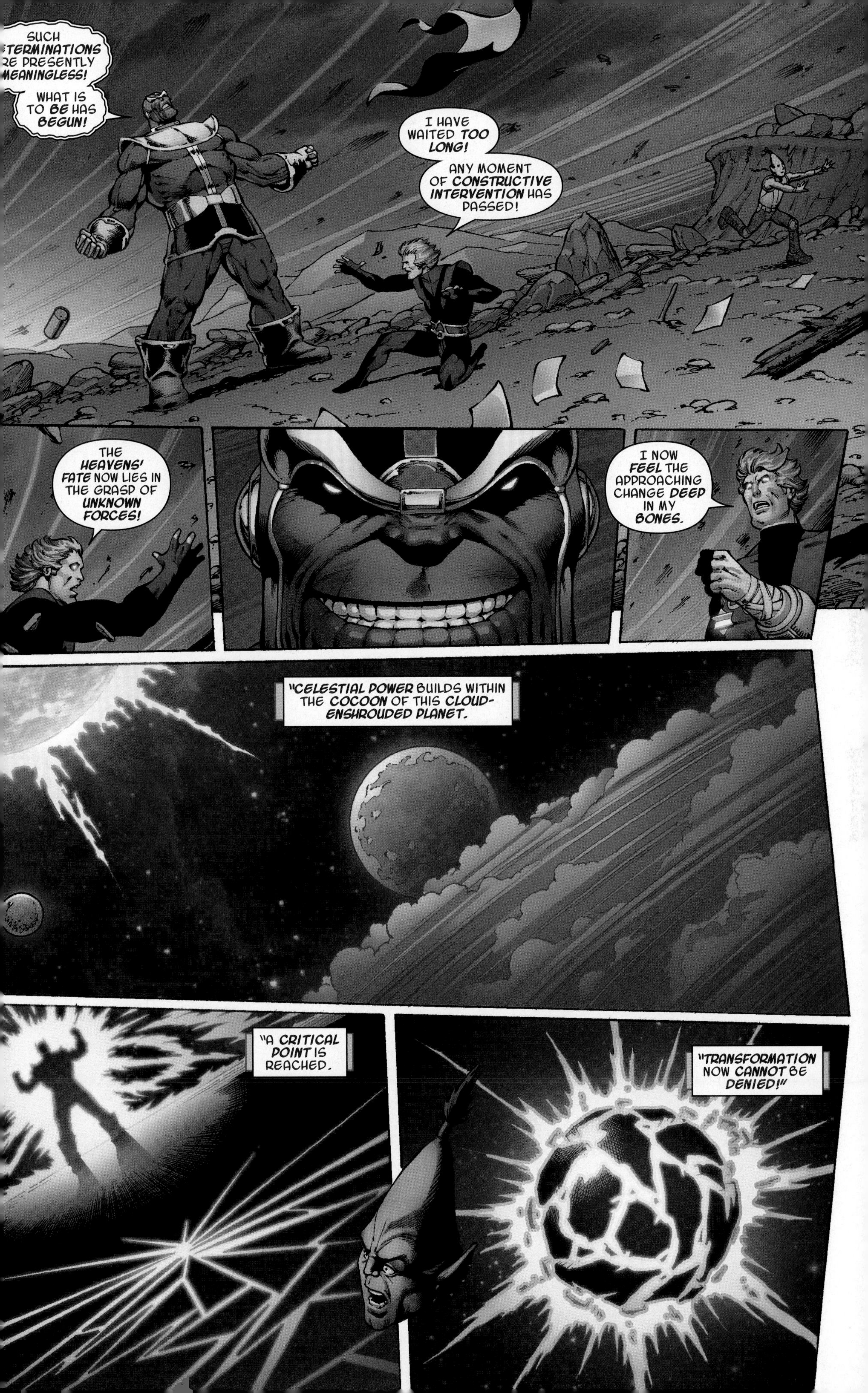
SUCH DETERMINATIONS ARE PRESENTLY MEANINGLESS!
WHAT IS TO BE HAS BEGUN!
I HAVE WAITED TOO LONG!
ANY MOMENT OF CONSTRUCTIVE INTERVENTION HAS PASSED!
THE HEAVENS' FATE NOW LIES IN THE GRASP OF UNKNOWN FORCES!
I NOW FEEL THE APPROACHING CHANGE DEEP IN MY BONES.
"CELESTIAL POWER BUILDS WITHIN THE COCOON OF THIS CLOUD-ENSHROUDED PLANET.
"A CRITICAL POINT IS REACHED.
"TRANSFORMATION NOW CANNOT BE DENIED!"

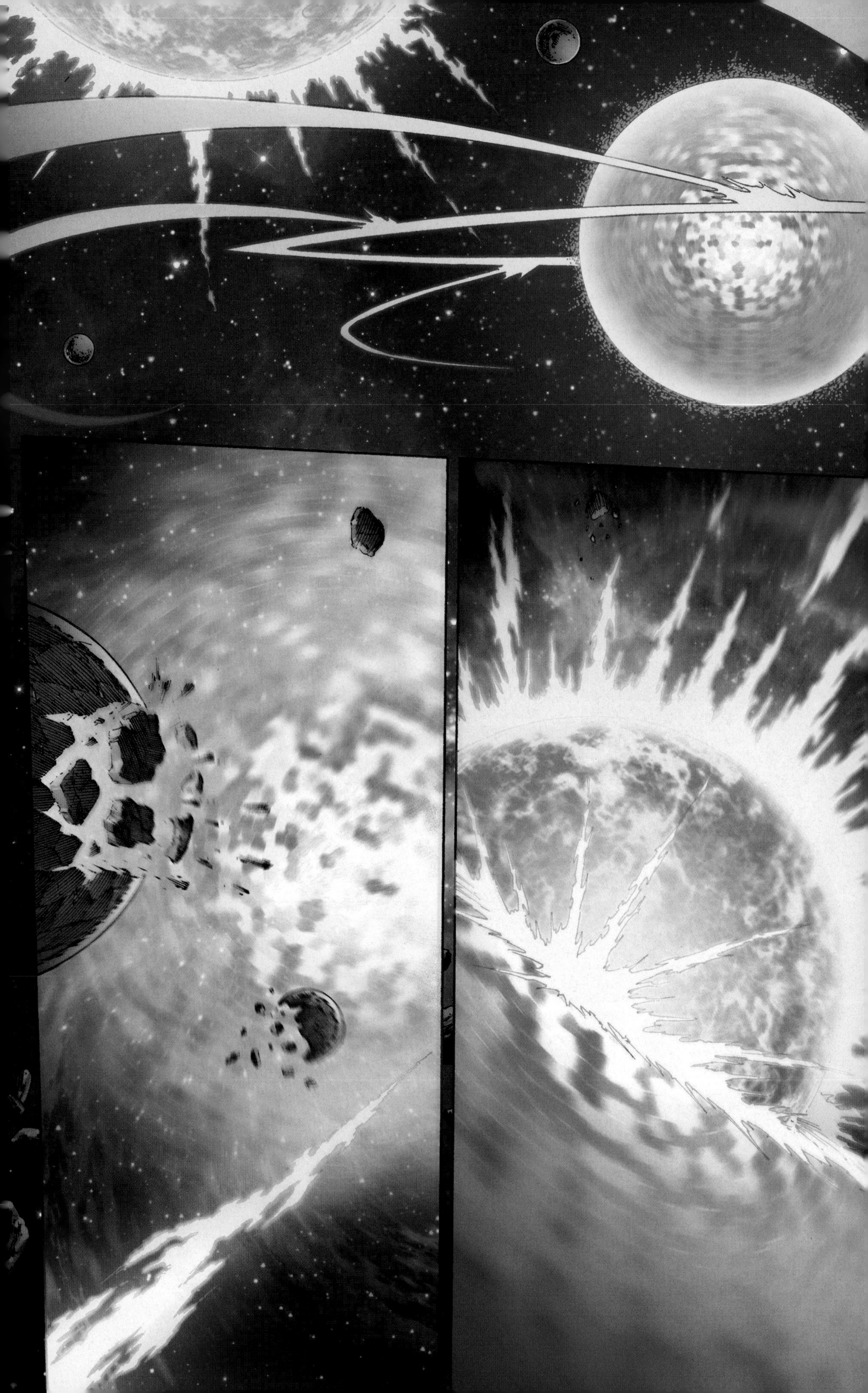

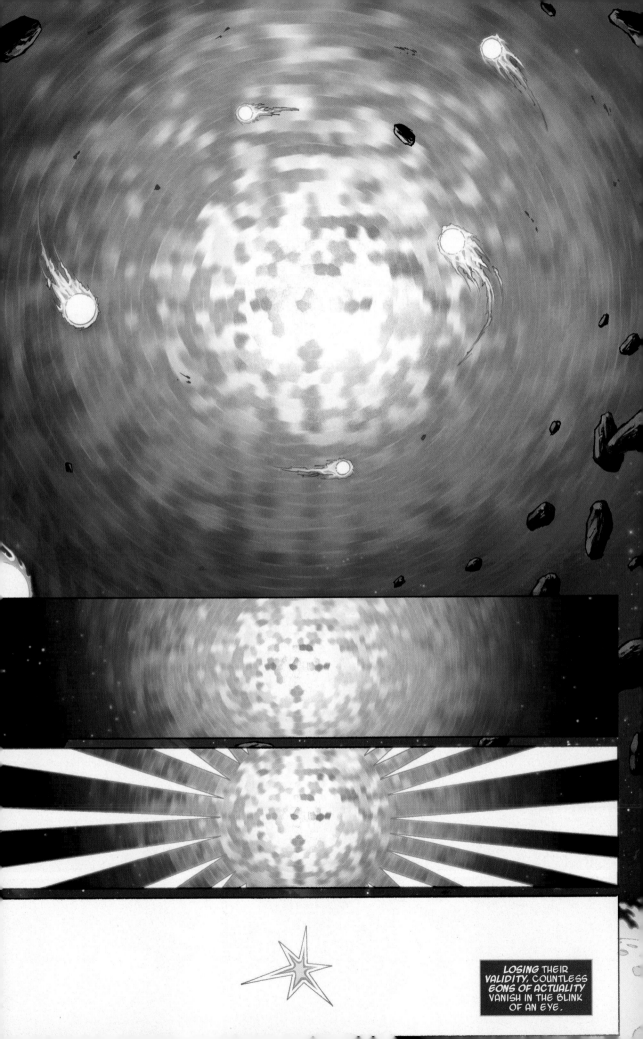

LOSING THEIR VALIDITY, COUNTLESS EONS OF ACTUALITY VANISH IN THE BLINK OF AN EYE.

TO BE REPLACED BY *EGO-DRIVEN DESIRE* AND *DIRECTION*.

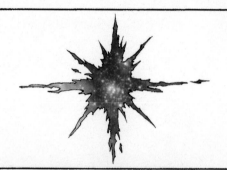

A *NEW PLANE* OF *EXISTENCE* SLOWLY GELS.

FOR *WHAT WAS* HAS *NEVER OCCURRED*.

THIS *DAWNING MOMENT* IS BUILT ON INFINITE, *INSTANTLY CREATED YESTERDAYS*.

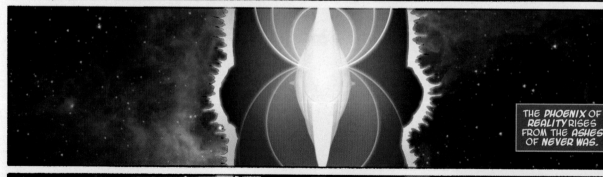

THE *PHOENIX* OF *REALITY* RISES FROM THE *ASHES* OF *NEVER WAS*.

REBIRTH.

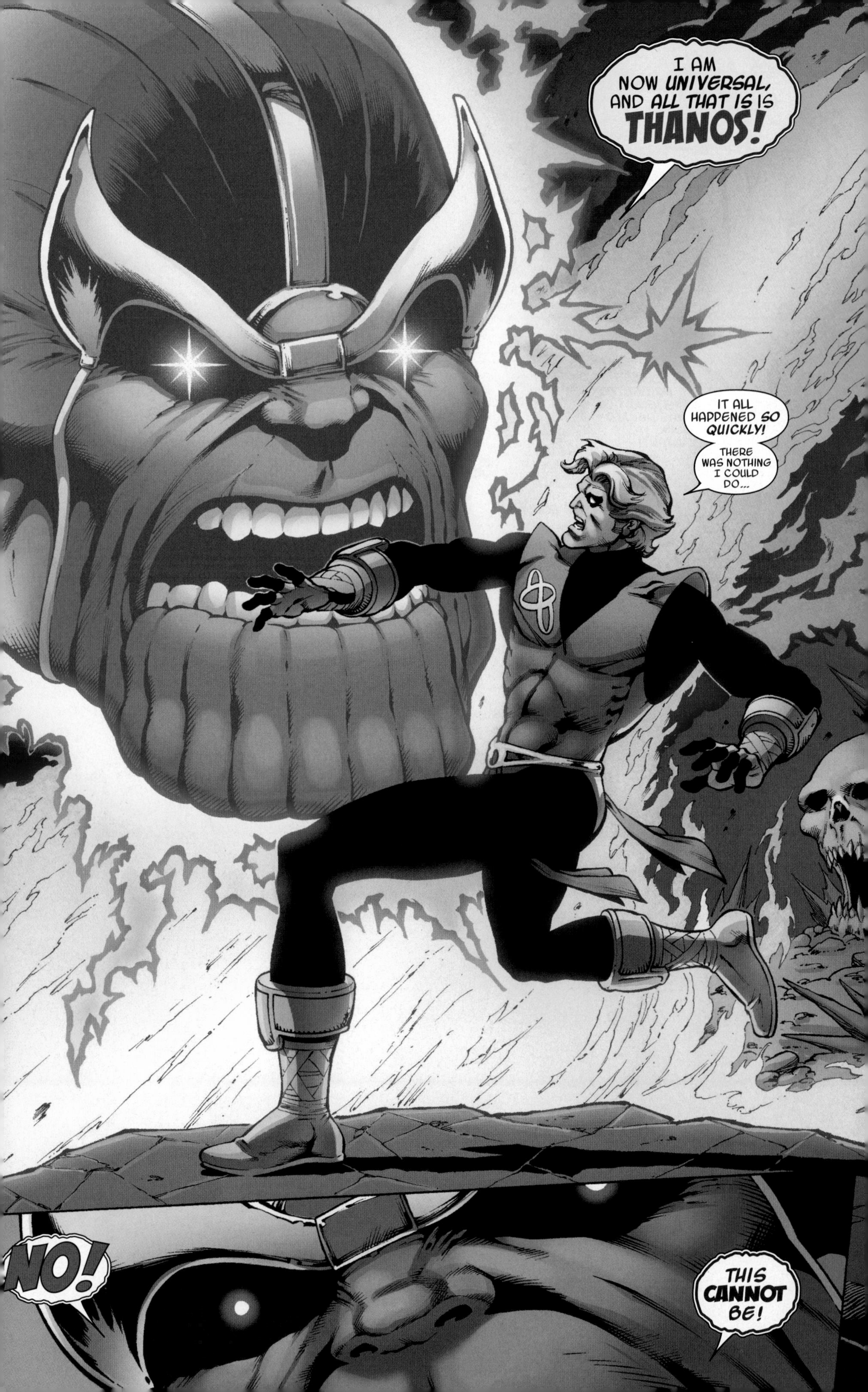
I AM NOW UNIVERSAL, AND ALL THAT IS IS THANOS!
IT ALL HAPPENED SO QUICKLY!
THERE WAS NOTHING I COULD DO...
NO!
THIS CANNOT BE!

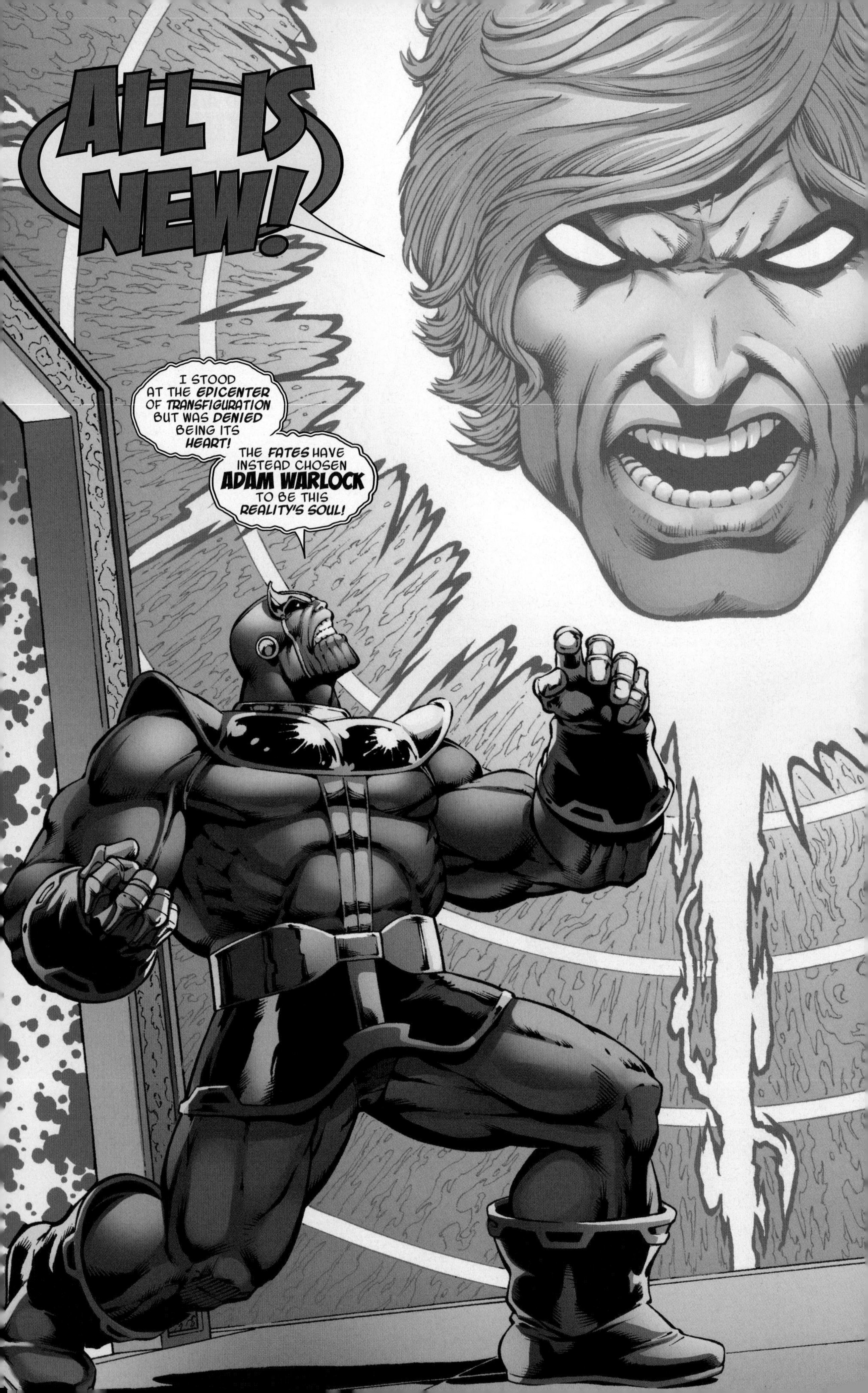
ALL IS NEW!
I STOOD AT THE EPICENTER OF TRANSFIGURATION BUT WAS DENIED BEING ITS HEART!
THE FATES HAVE INSTEAD CHOSEN ADAM WARLOCK TO BE THIS REALITY'S SOUL!

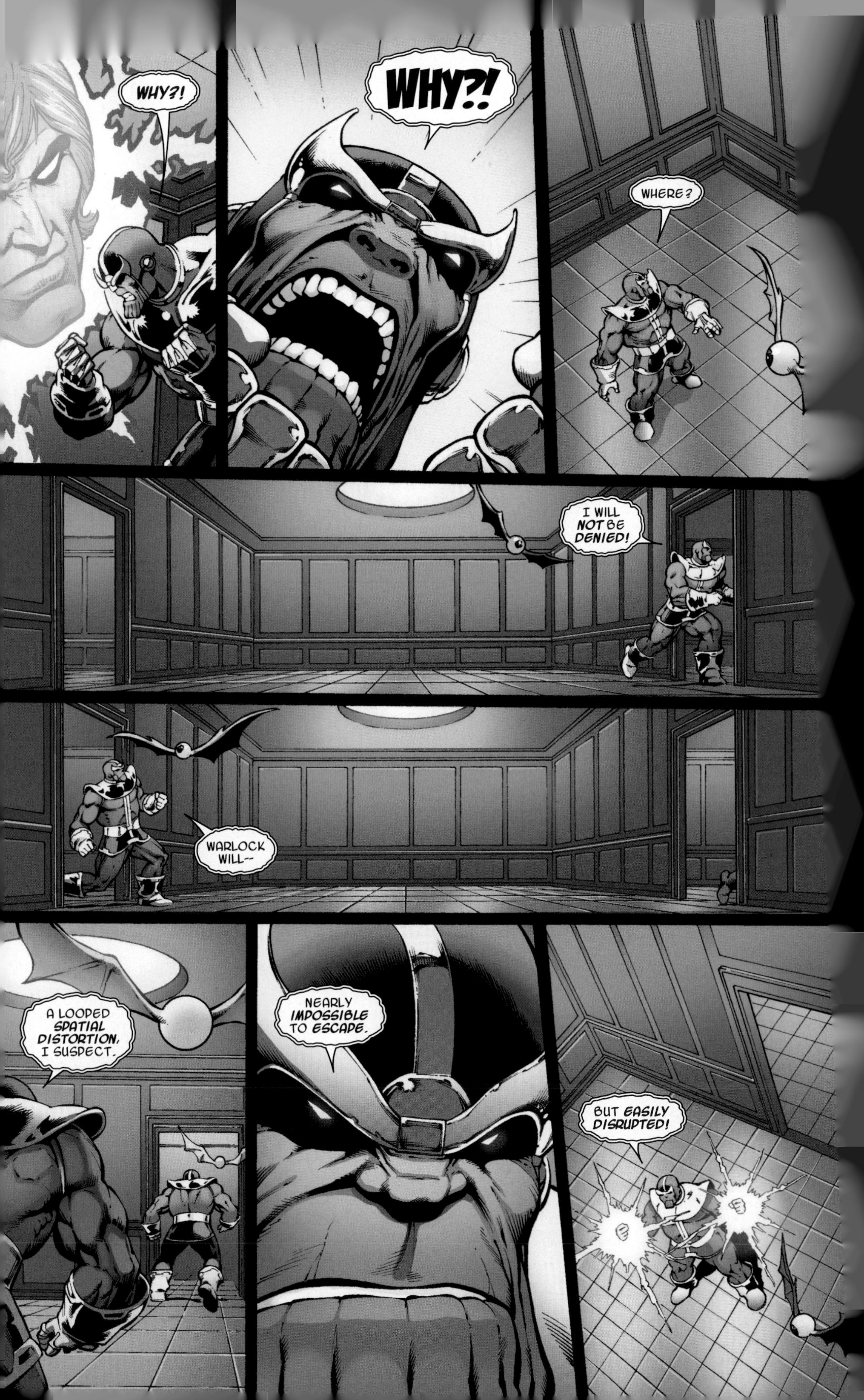
WHY?!
WHY?!
WHERE?
I WILL NOT BE DENIED!
WARLOCK WILL--
A LOOPED SPATIAL DISTORTION, I SUSPECT.
NEARLY IMPOSSIBLE TO ESCAPE.
BUT EASILY DISRUPTED!

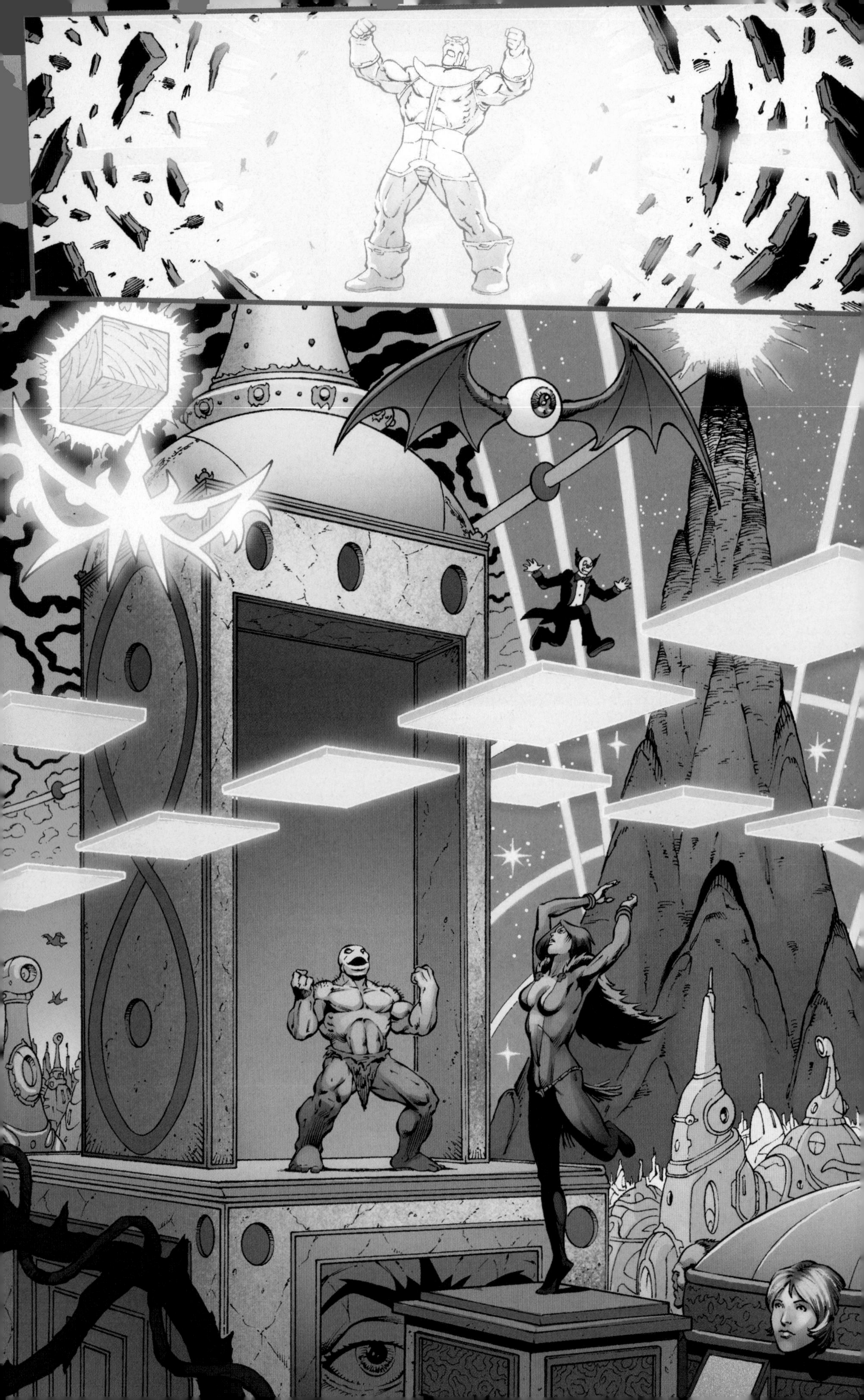

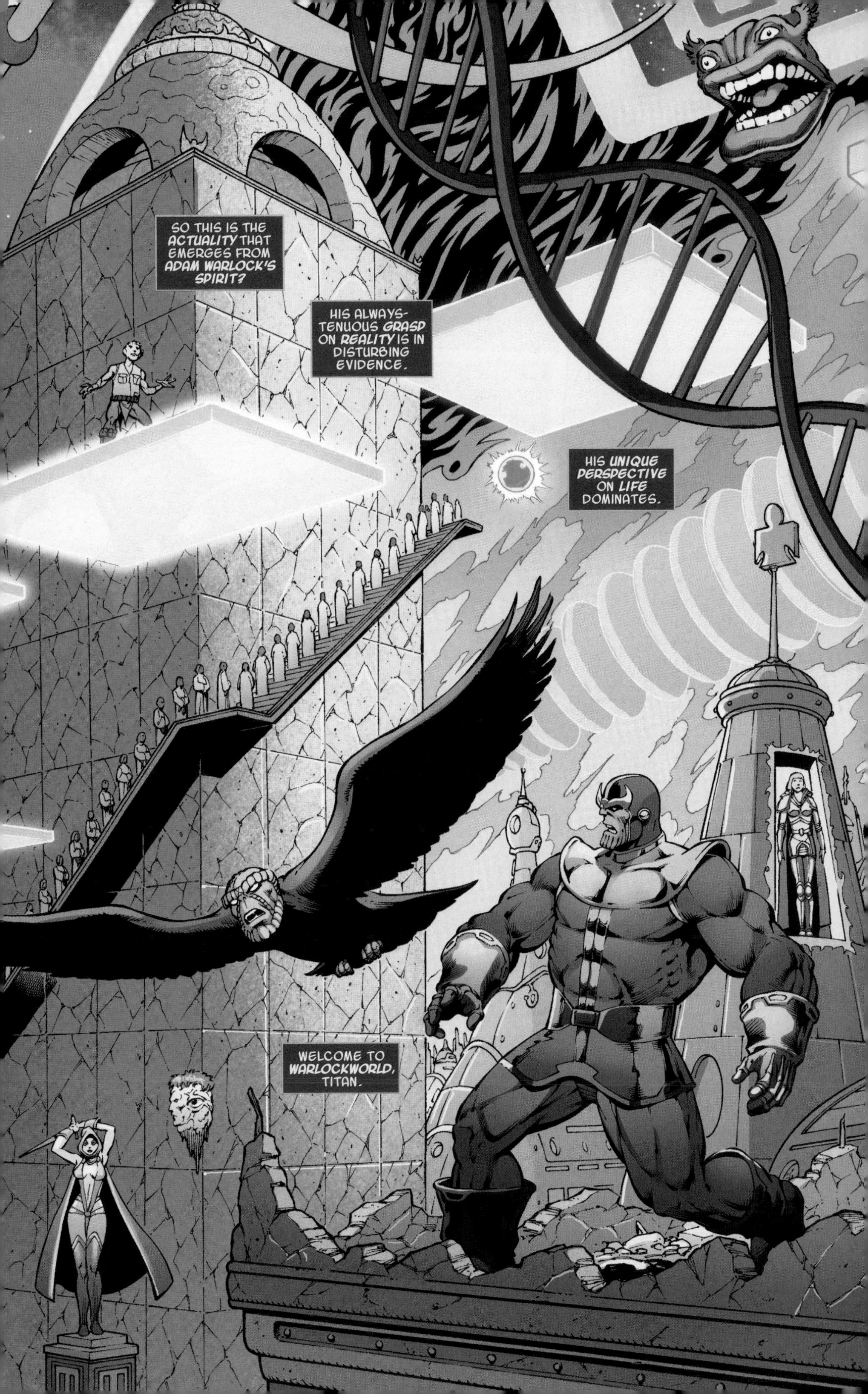
SO THIS IS THE ACTUALITY THAT EMERGES FROM ADAM WARLOCK'S SPIRIT?
HIS ALWAYS-TENUOUS GRASP ON REALITY IS IN DISTURBING EVIDENCE.
HIS UNIQUE PERSPECTIVE ON LIFE DOMINATES.
WELCOME TO WARLOCKWORLD, TITAN.

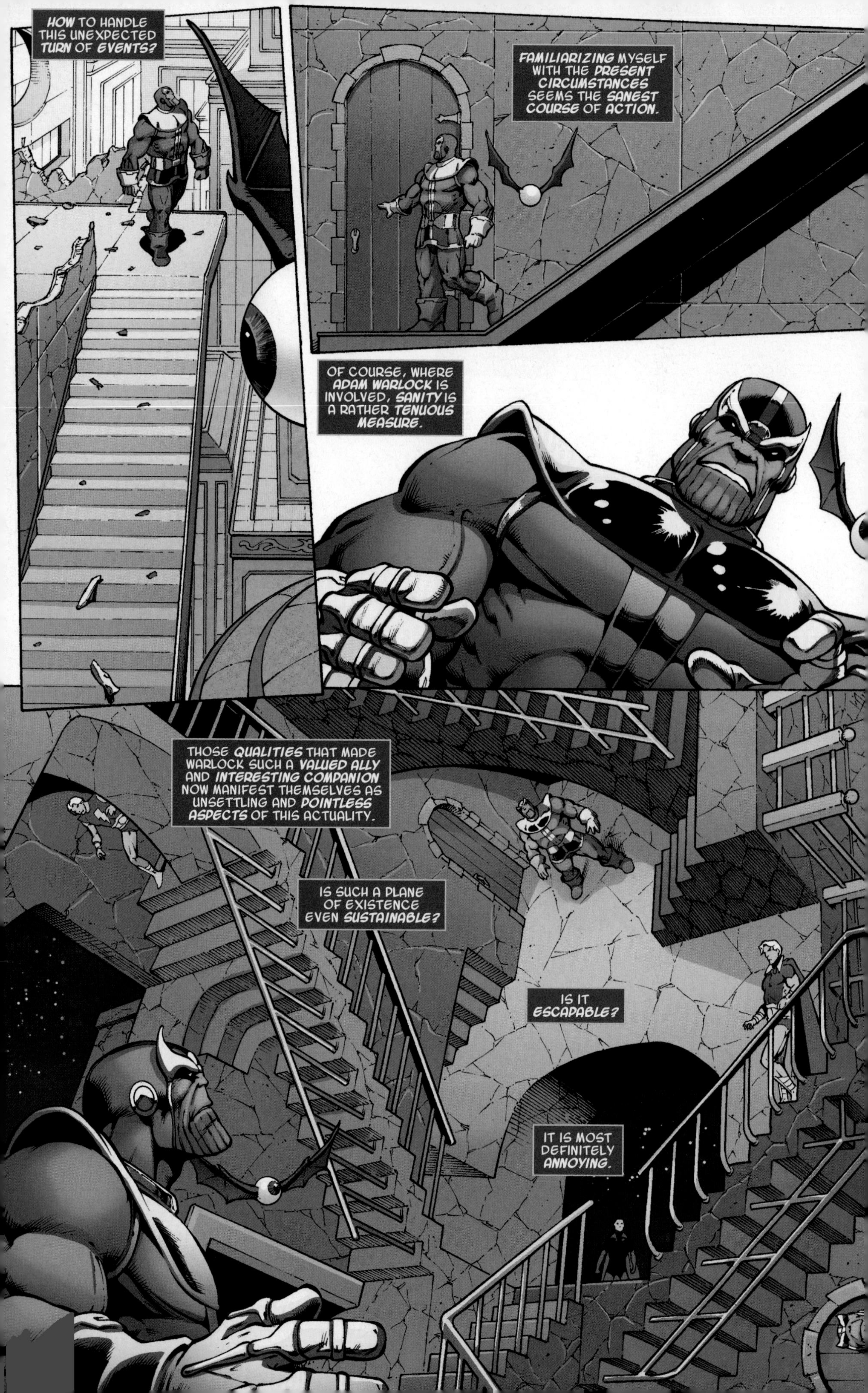
HOW TO HANDLE THIS UNEXPECTED TURN OF EVENTS?
FAMILIARIZING MYSELF WITH THE PRESENT CIRCUMSTANCES SEEMS THE SANEST COURSE OF ACTION.
OF COURSE, WHERE ADAM WARLOCK IS INVOLVED, SANITY IS A RATHER TENUOUS MEASURE.
THOSE QUALITIES THAT MADE WARLOCK SUCH A VALUED ALLY AND INTERESTING COMPANION NOW MANIFEST THEMSELVES AS UNSETTLING AND POINTLESS ASPECTS OF THIS ACTUALITY.
IS SUCH A PLANE OF EXISTENCE EVEN SUSTAINABLE?
IS IT ESCAPABLE?
IT IS MOST DEFINITELY ANNOYING.

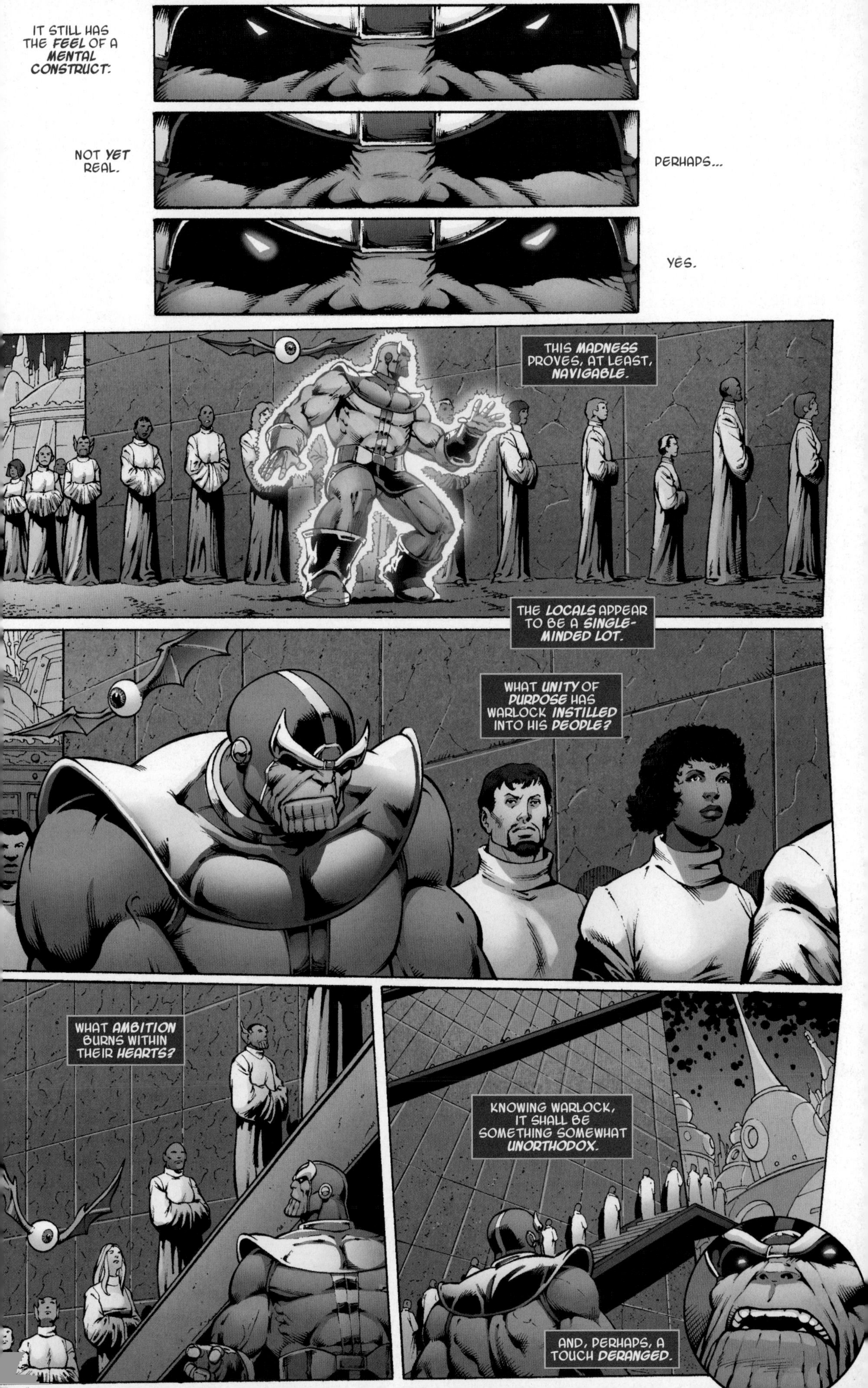
IT STILL HAS THE FEEL OF A MENTAL CONSTRUCT:
NOT YET REAL.
PERHAPS...
YES.
THIS MADNESS PROVES, AT LEAST, NAVIGABLE.
THE LOCALS APPEAR TO BE A SINGLE-MINDED LOT.
WHAT UNITY OF PURPOSE HAS WARLOCK INSTILLED INTO HIS PEOPLE?
WHAT AMBITION BURNS WITHIN THEIR HEARTS?
KNOWING WARLOCK, IT SHALL BE SOMETHING SOMEWHAT UNORTHODOX.
AND, PERHAPS, A TOUCH DERANGED.

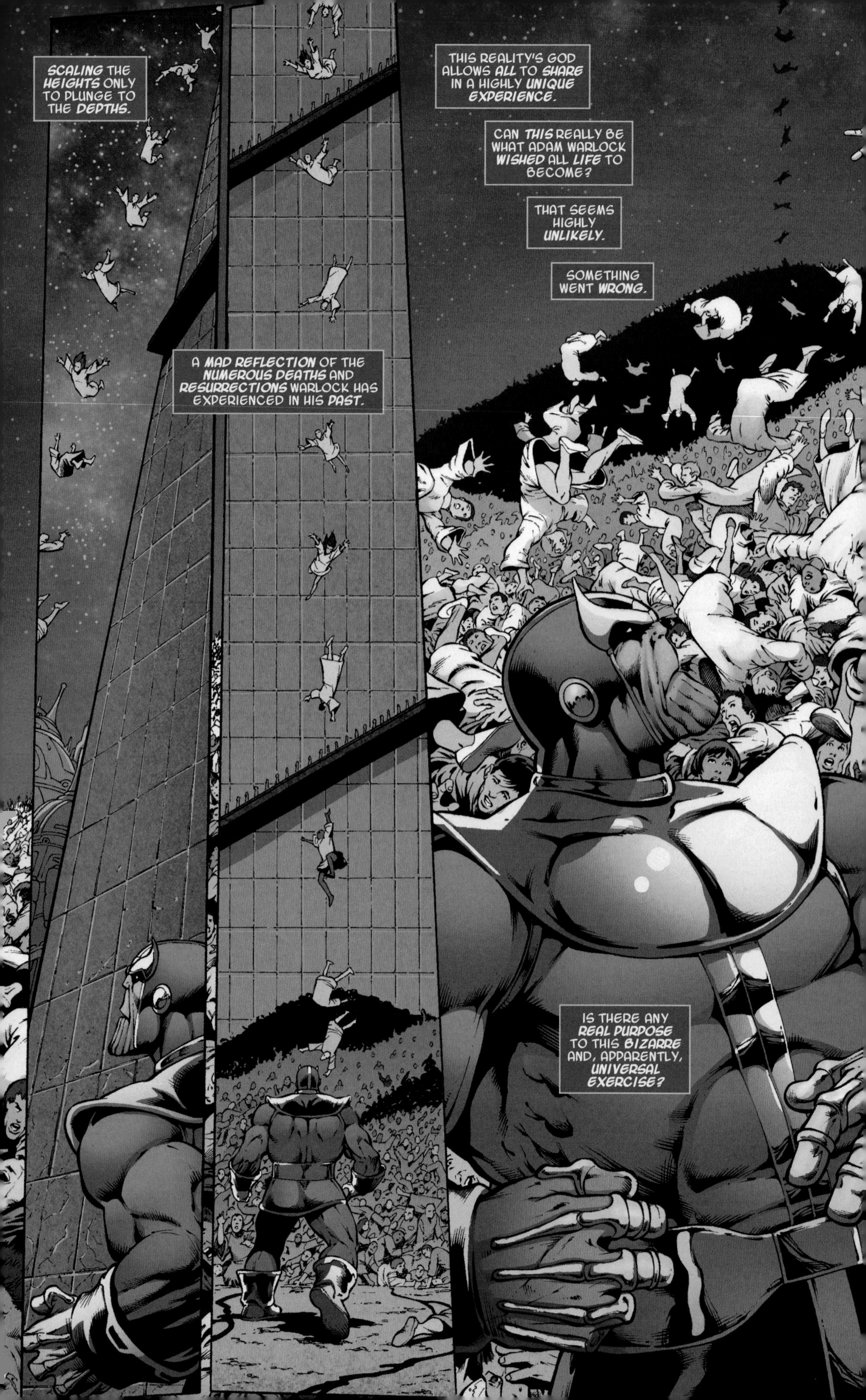
SCALING THE HEIGHTS ONLY TO PLUNGE TO THE DEPTHS.
A MAD REFLECTION OF THE NUMEROUS DEATHS AND RESURRECTIONS WARLOCK HAS EXPERIENCED IN HIS PAST.
THIS REALITY'S GOD ALLOWS ALL TO SHARE IN A HIGHLY UNIQUE EXPERIENCE.
CAN THIS REALLY BE WHAT ADAM WARLOCK WISHED ALL LIFE TO BECOME?
THAT SEEMS HIGHLY UNLIKELY.
SOMETHING WENT WRONG.
IS THERE ANY REAL PURPOSE TO THIS BIZARRE AND, APPARENTLY, UNIVERSAL EXERCISE?

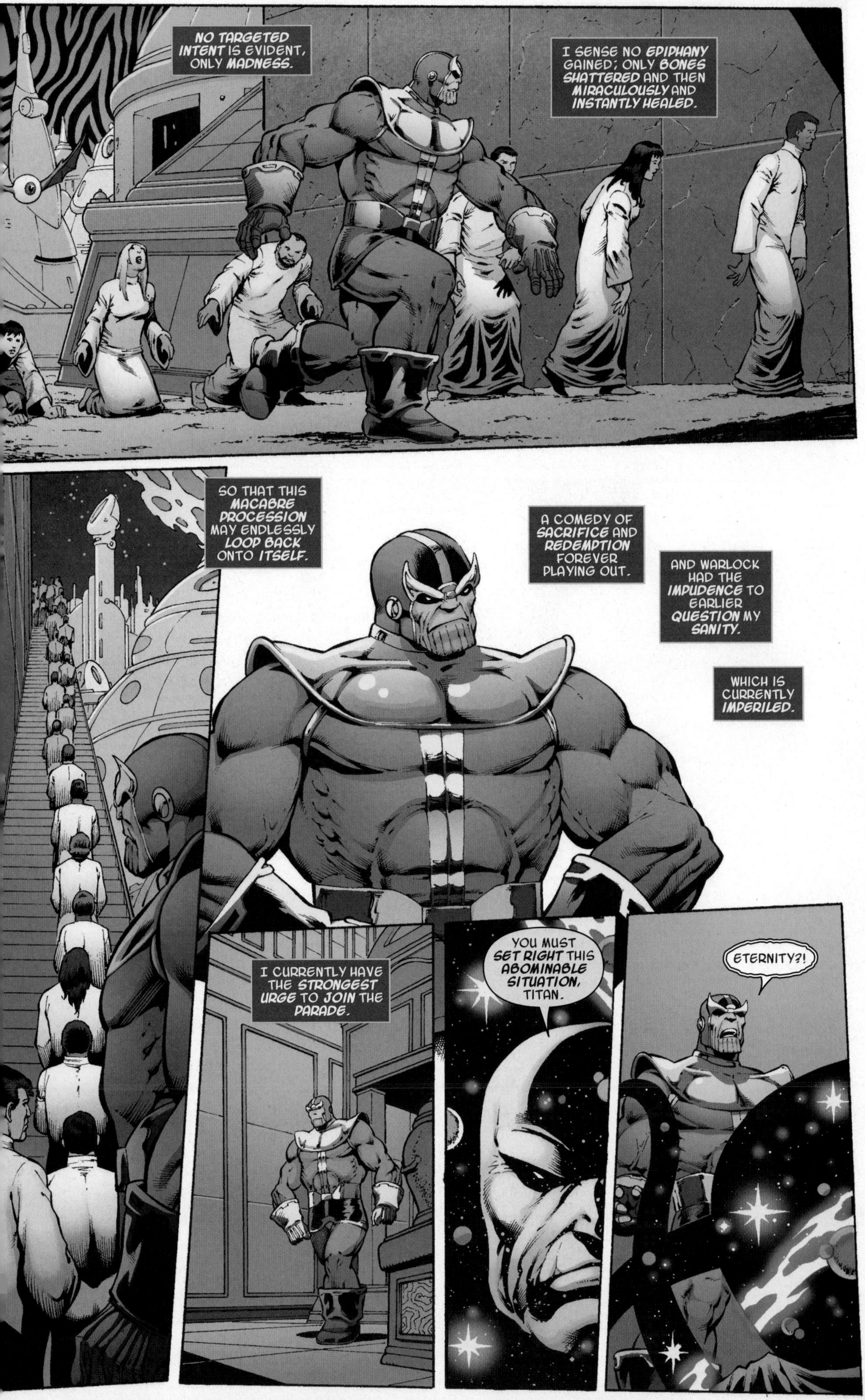
NO TARGETED INTENT IS EVIDENT, ONLY MADNESS.
I SENSE NO EPIPHANY GAINED; ONLY BONES SHATTERED AND THEN MIRACULOUSLY AND INSTANTLY HEALED.
SO THAT THIS MACABRE PROCESSION MAY ENDLESSLY LOOP BACK ONTO ITSELF.
A COMEDY OF SACRIFICE AND REDEMPTION FOREVER PLAYING OUT.
AND WARLOCK HAD THE IMPUDENCE TO EARLIER QUESTION MY SANITY.
WHICH IS CURRENTLY IMPERILED.
I CURRENTLY HAVE THE STRONGEST URGE TO JOIN THE PARADE.
YOU MUST SET RIGHT THIS ABOMINABLE SITUATION, TITAN.
ETERNITY?!

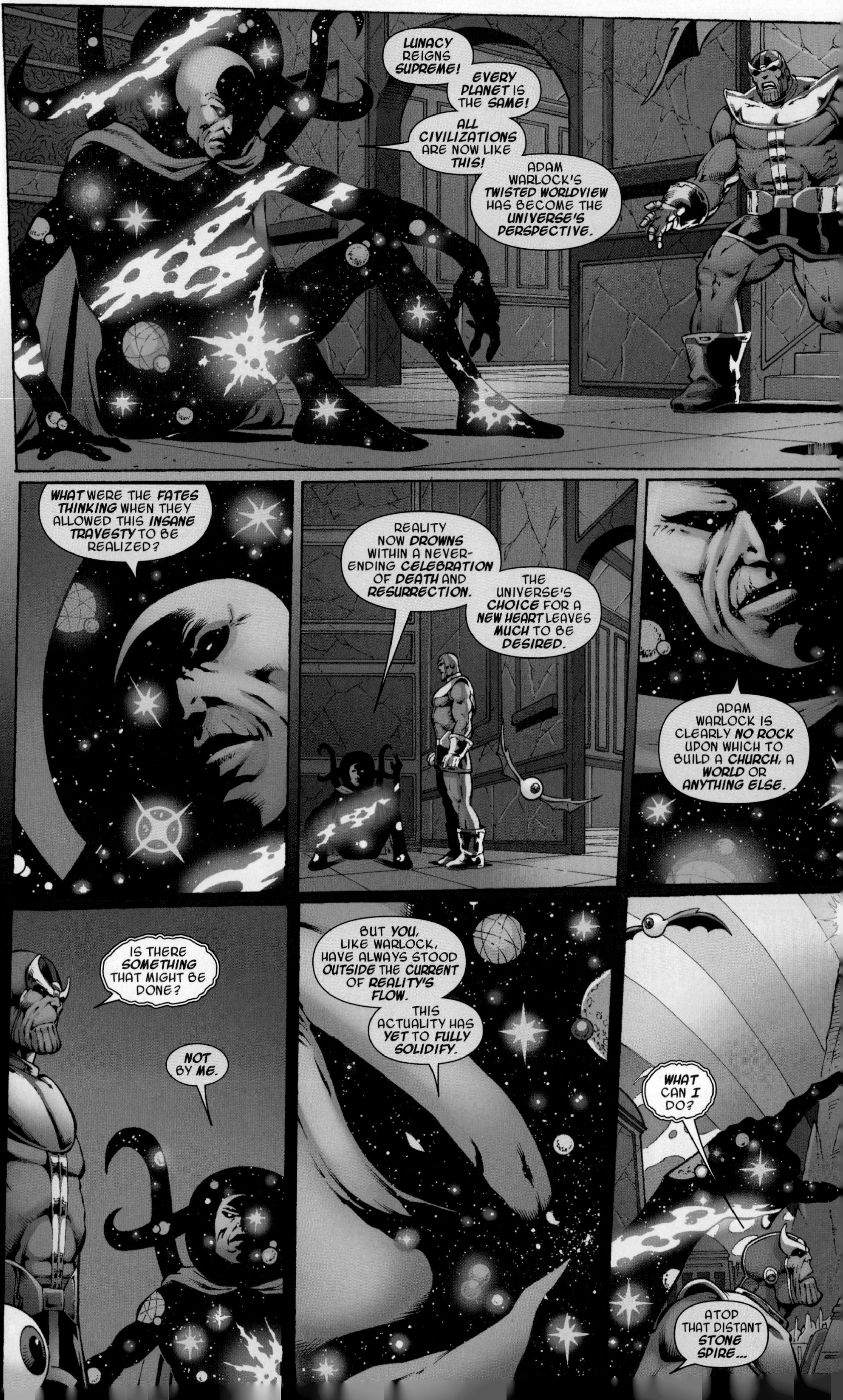
LUNACY REIGNS SUPREME!
EVERY PLANET IS THE SAME!
ALL CIVILIZATIONS ARE NOW LIKE THIS!
ADAM WARLOCK'S TWISTED WORLDVIEW HAS BECOME THE UNIVERSE'S PERSPECTIVE.
WHAT WERE THE FATES THINKING WHEN THEY ALLOWED THIS INSANE TRAVESTY TO BE REALIZED?
REALITY NOW DROWNS WITHIN A NEVER-ENDING CELEBRATION OF DEATH AND RESURRECTION.
THE UNIVERSE'S CHOICE FOR A NEW HEART LEAVES MUCH TO BE DESIRED.
ADAM WARLOCK IS CLEARLY NO ROCK UPON WHICH TO BUILD A CHURCH, A WORLD OR ANYTHING ELSE.
IS THERE SOMETHING THAT MIGHT BE DONE?
NOT BY ME.
BUT YOU, LIKE WARLOCK, HAVE ALWAYS STOOD OUTSIDE THE CURRENT OF REALITY'S FLOW.
THIS ACTUALITY HAS YET TO FULLY SOLIDIFY.
WHAT CAN I DO?
ATOP THAT DISTANT STONE SPIRE...

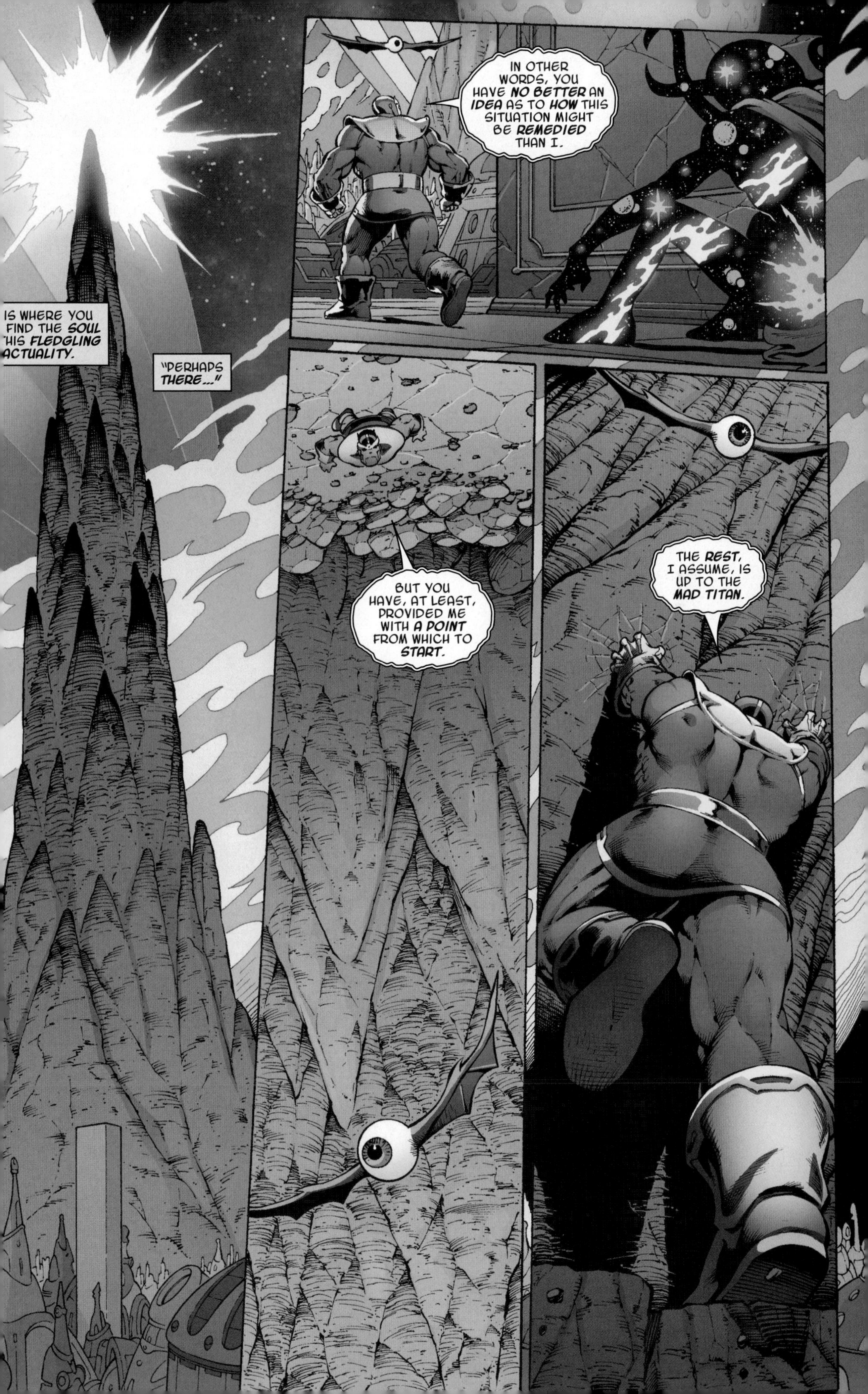
IS WHERE YOU FIND THE SOUL HIS FLEDGLING ACTUALITY.
"PERHAPS THERE..."
IN OTHER WORDS, YOU HAVE NO BETTER AN IDEA AS TO HOW THIS SITUATION MIGHT BE REMEDIED THAN I.
BUT YOU HAVE, AT LEAST, PROVIDED ME WITH A POINT FROM WHICH TO START.
THE REST, I ASSUME, IS UP TO THE MAD TITAN.

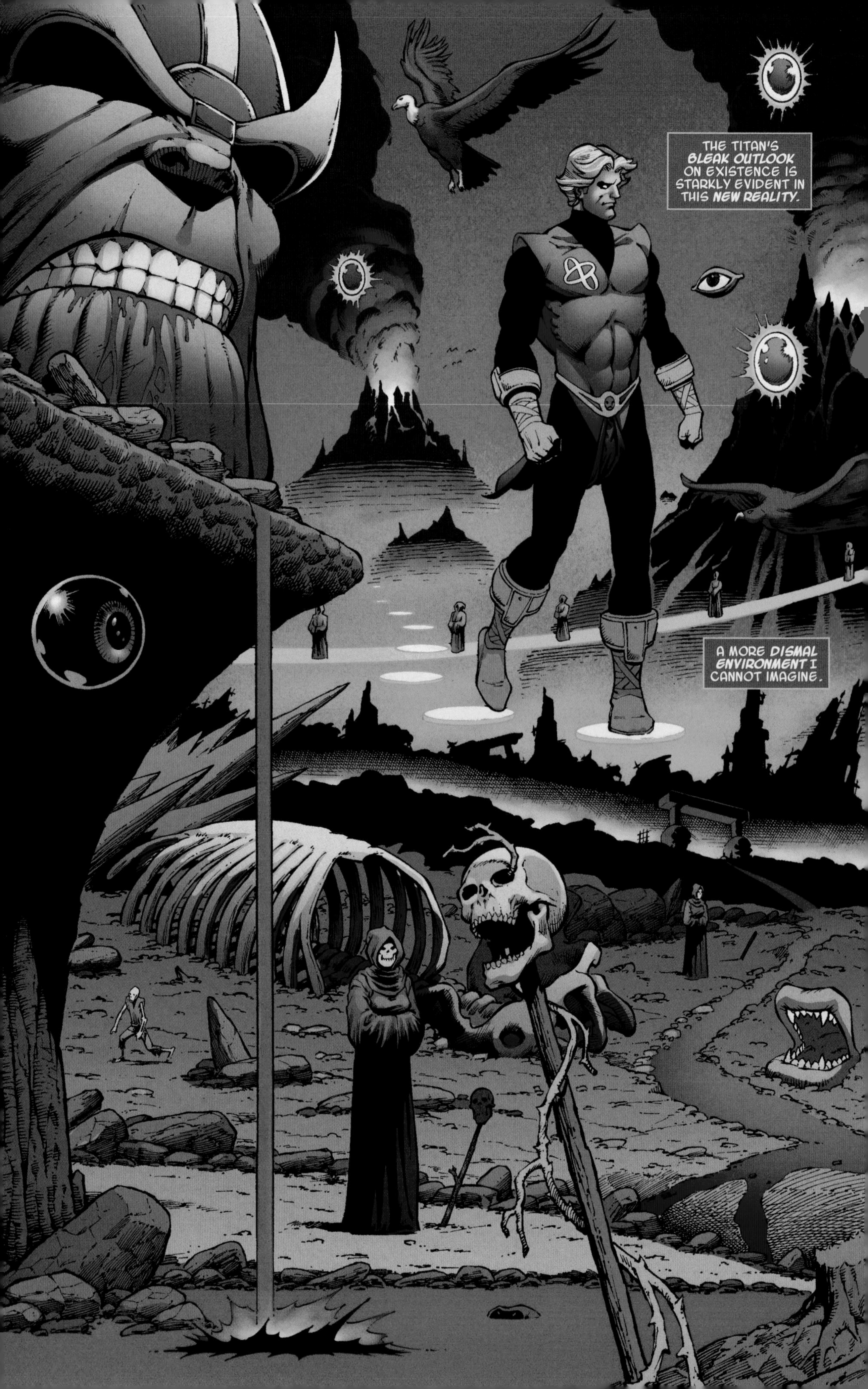
THE TITAN'S BLEAK OUTLOOK ON EXISTENCE IS STARKLY EVIDENT IN THIS NEW REALITY.
A MORE DISMAL ENVIRONMENT I CANNOT IMAGINE.

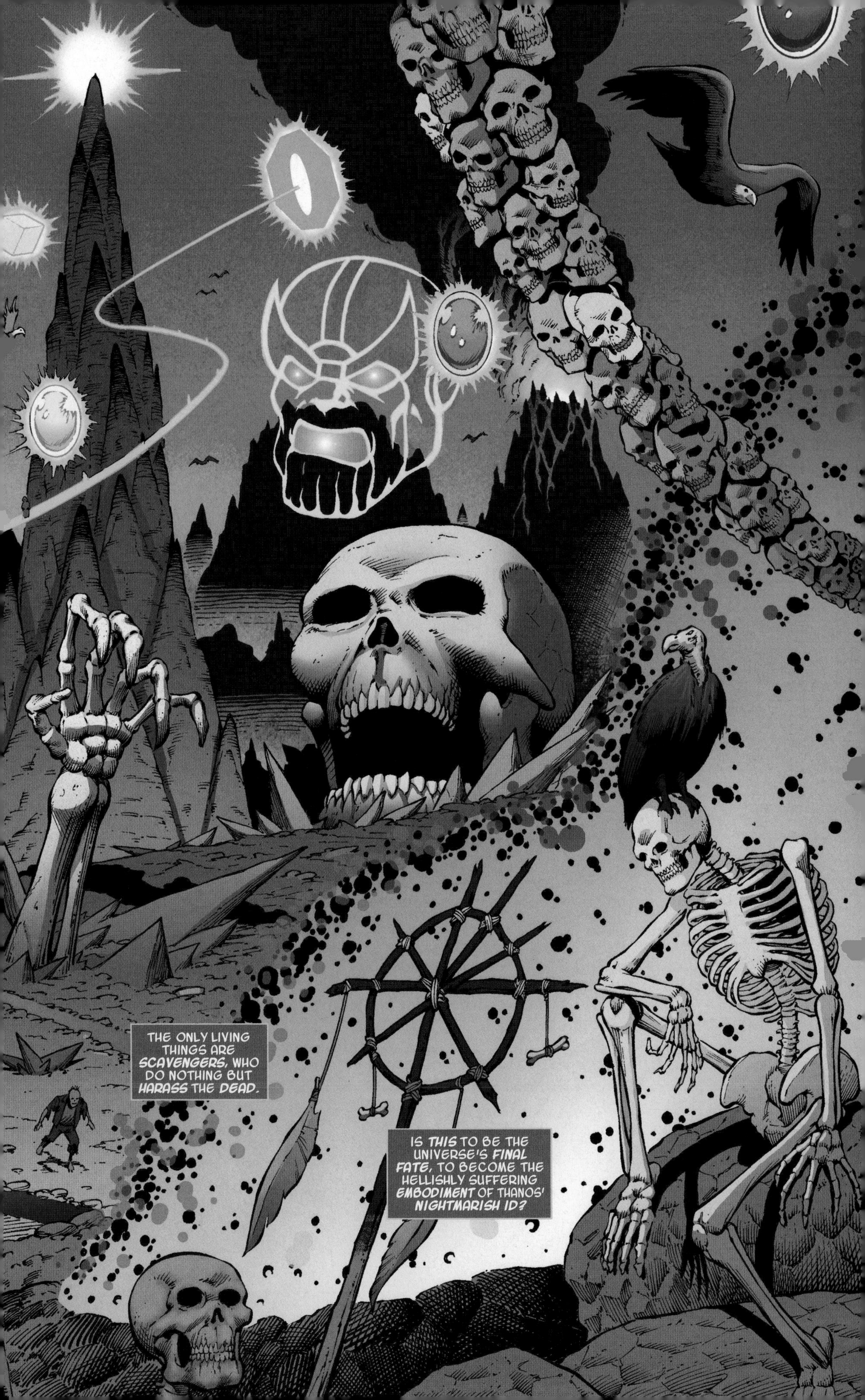
THE ONLY LIVING THINGS ARE SCAVENGERS, WHO DO NOTHING BUT HARASS THE DEAD.
IS THIS TO BE THE UNIVERSE'S FINAL FATE, TO BECOME THE HELLISHLY SUFFERING EMBODIMENT OF THANOS' NIGHTMARISH ID?

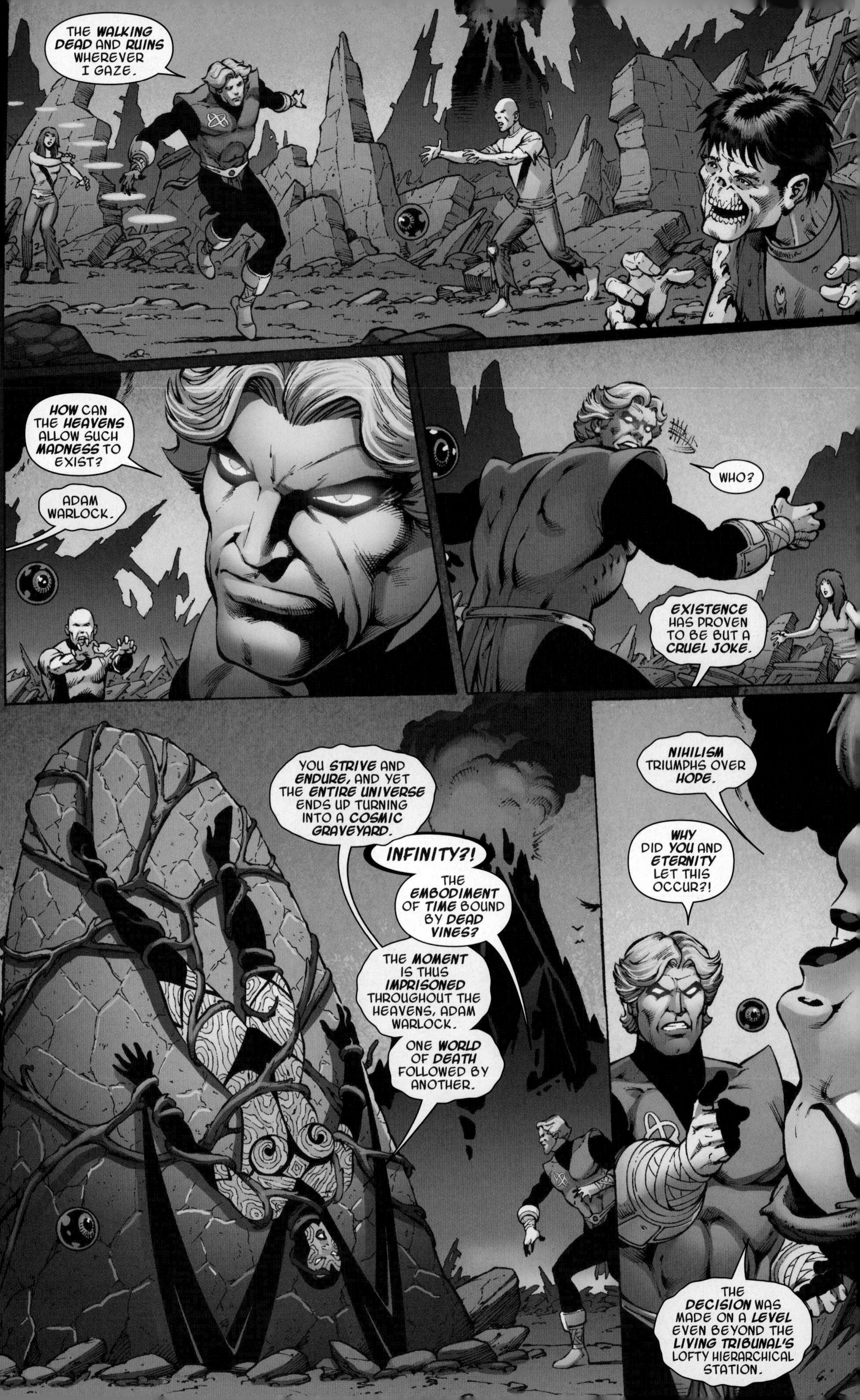
THE WALKING DEAD AND RUINS WHEREVER I GAZE.
HOW CAN THE HEAVENS ALLOW SUCH MADNESS TO EXIST?
ADAM WARLOCK.
WHO?
EXISTENCE HAS PROVEN TO BE BUT A CRUEL JOKE.
YOU STRIVE AND ENDURE, AND YET THE ENTIRE UNIVERSE ENDS UP TURNING INTO A COSMIC GRAVEYARD.
INFINITY?!
THE EMBODIMENT OF TIME BOUND BY DEAD VINES?
THE MOMENT IS THUS IMPRISONED THROUGHOUT THE HEAVENS, ADAM WARLOCK.
ONE WORLD OF DEATH FOLLOWED BY ANOTHER.
NIHILISM TRIUMPHS OVER HOPE.
WHY DID YOU AND ETERNITY LET THIS OCCUR?!
THE DECISION WAS MADE ON A LEVEL EVEN BEYOND THE LIVING TRIBUNAL'S LOFTY HIERARCHICAL STATION.

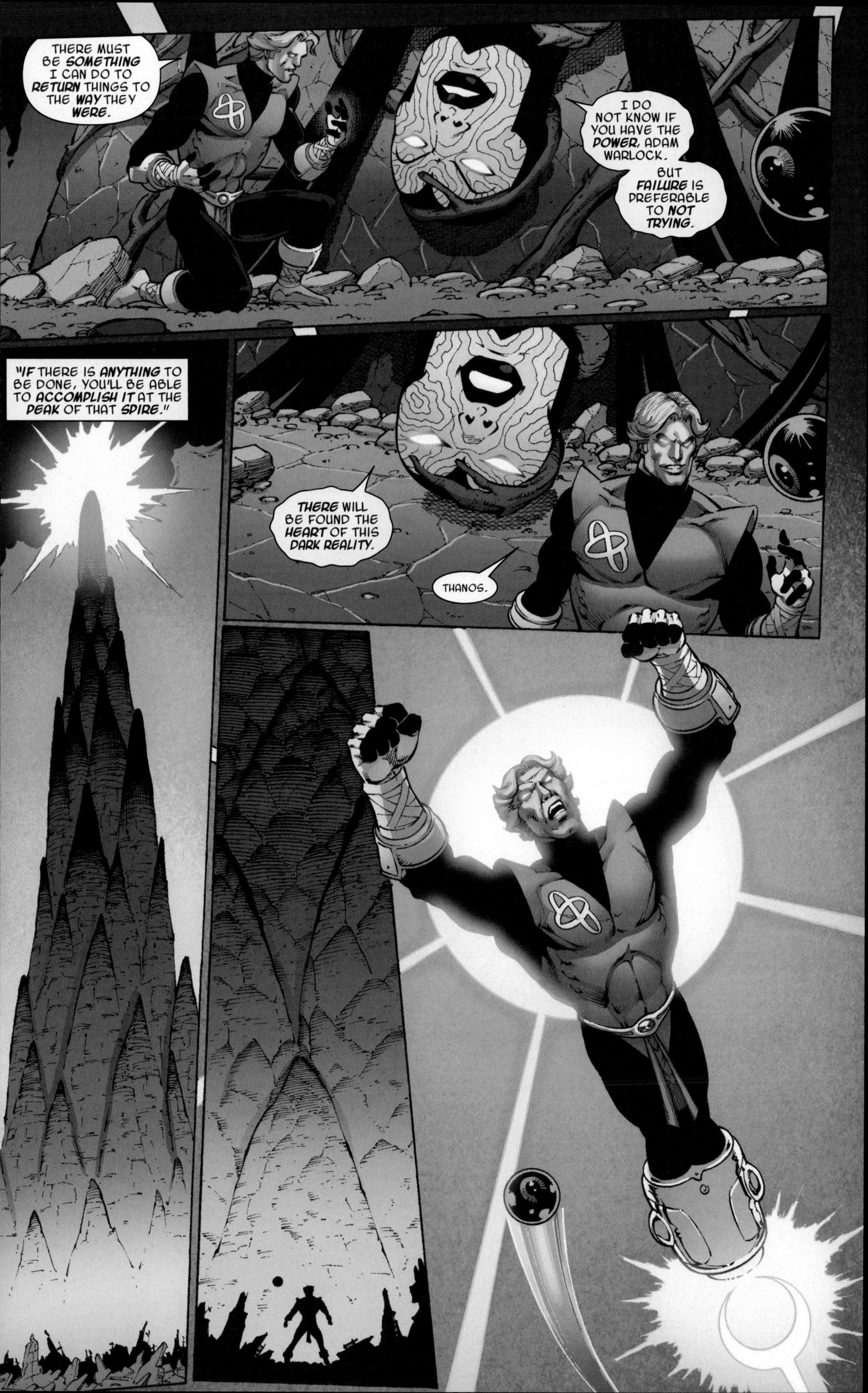
THERE MUST BE SOMETHING I CAN DO TO RETURN THINGS TO THE WAY THEY WERE.
I DO NOT KNOW IF YOU HAVE THE POWER, ADAM WARLOCK.
BUT FAILURE IS PREFERABLE TO NOT TRYING.
"IF THERE IS ANYTHING TO BE DONE, YOU'LL BE ABLE TO ACCOMPLISH IT AT THE PEAK OF THAT SPIRE."
THERE WILL BE FOUND THE HEART OF THIS DARK REALITY.
THANOS.

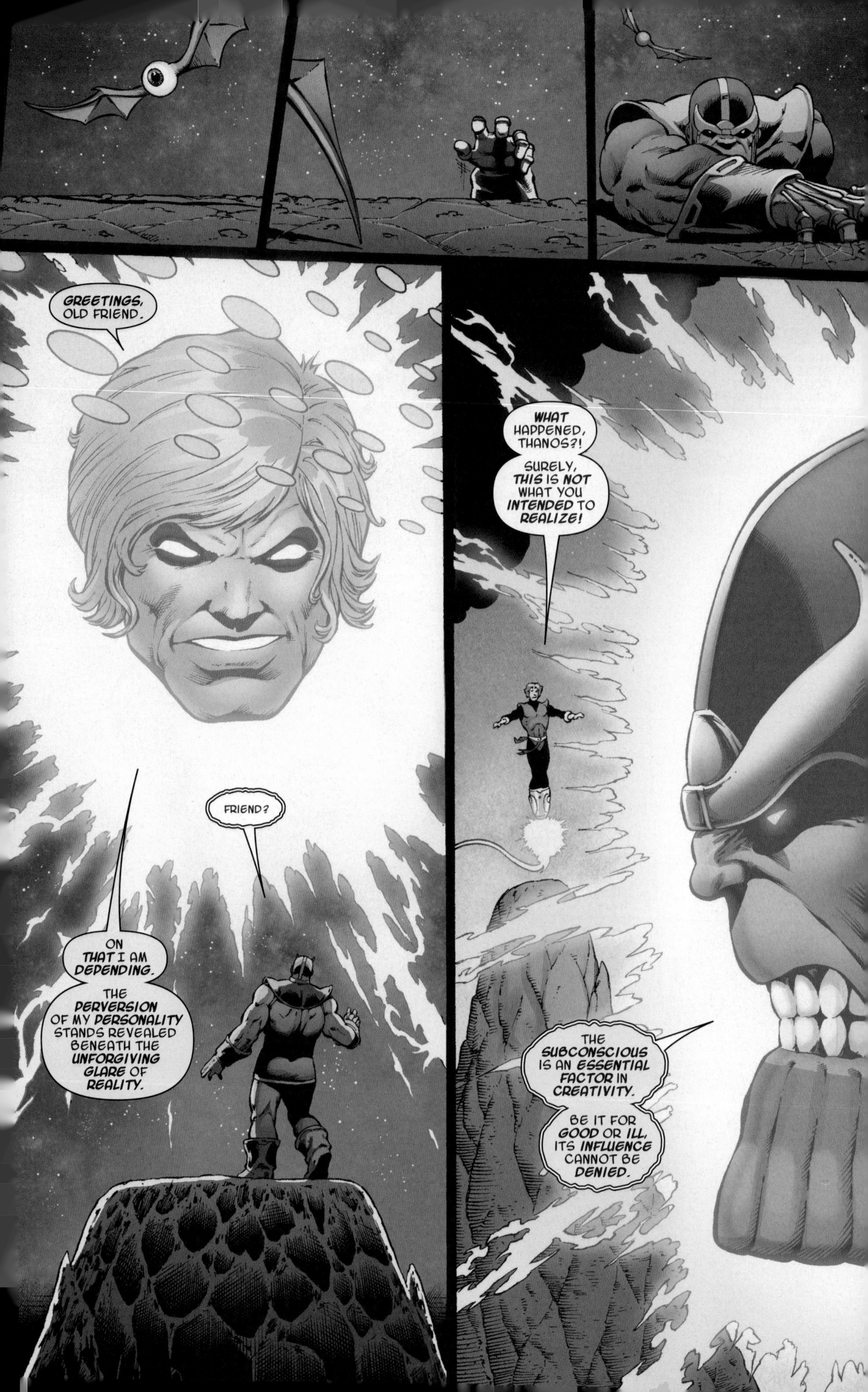
GREETINGS, OLD FRIEND.
FRIEND?
ON THAT I AM DEPENDING.
THE PERVERSION OF MY PERSONALITY STANDS REVEALED BENEATH THE UNFORGIVING GLARE OF REALITY.
WHAT HAPPENED, THANOS?!
SURELY, THIS IS NOT WHAT YOU INTENDED TO REALIZE!
THE SUBCONSCIOUS IS AN ESSENTIAL FACTOR IN CREATIVITY.
BE IT FOR GOOD OR ILL, ITS INFLUENCE CANNOT BE DENIED.

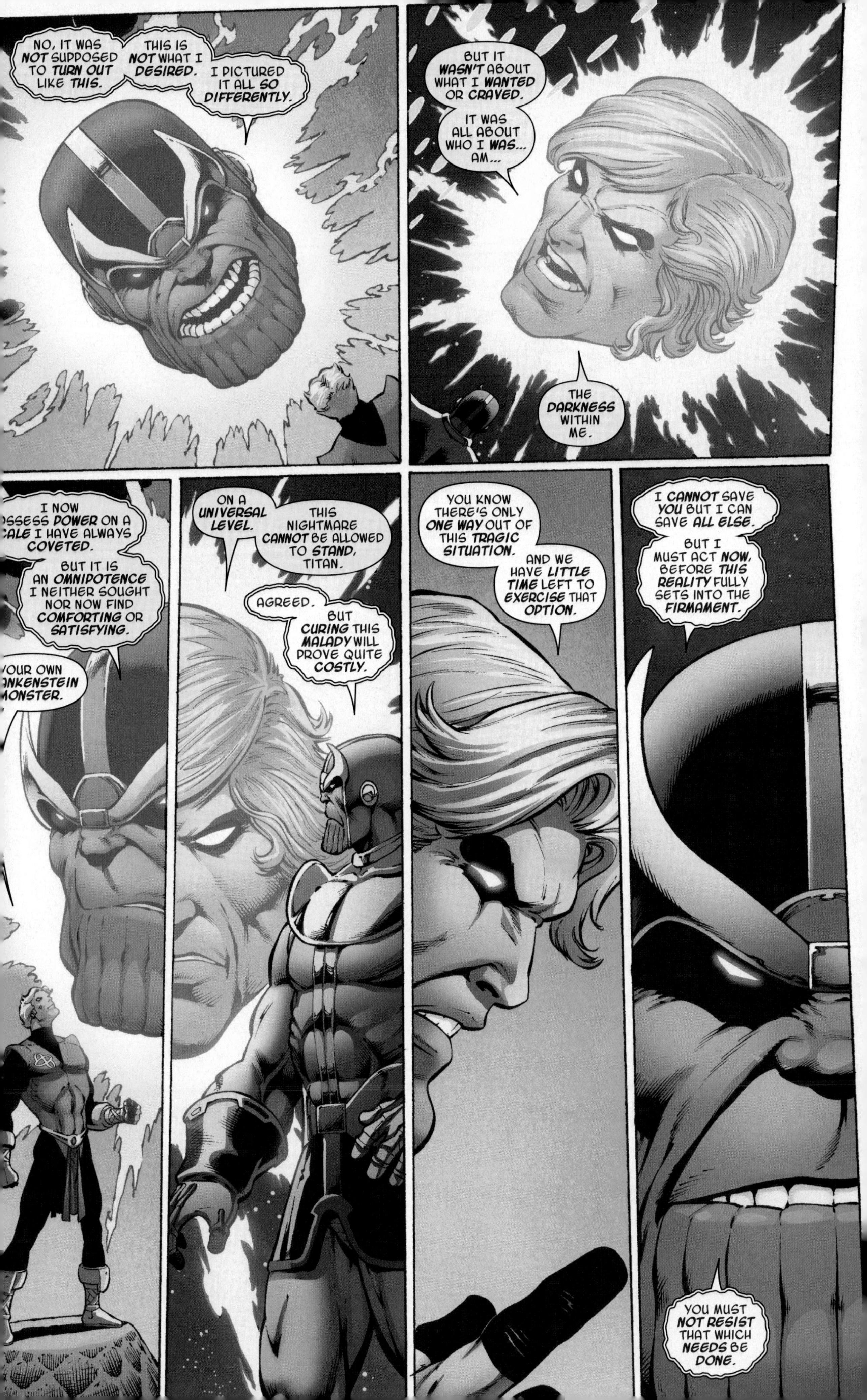

NO, IT WAS NOT SUPPOSED TO TURN OUT LIKE THIS.
THIS IS NOT WHAT I DESIRED.
I PICTURED IT ALL SO DIFFERENTLY.
BUT IT WASN'T ABOUT WHAT I WANTED OR CRAVED.
IT WAS ALL ABOUT WHO I WAS... AM...
THE DARKNESS WITHIN ME.
I NOW OSSESS POWER ON A CALE I HAVE ALWAYS COVETED.
BUT IT IS AN OMNIPOTENCE I NEITHER SOUGHT NOR NOW FIND COMFORTING OR SATISFYING.
OUR OWN ANKENSTEIN MONSTER.
ON A UNIVERSAL LEVEL.
THIS NIGHTMARE CANNOT BE ALLOWED TO STAND, TITAN.
AGREED.
BUT CURING THIS MALADY WILL PROVE QUITE COSTLY.
YOU KNOW THERE'S ONLY ONE WAY OUT OF THIS TRAGIC SITUATION.
AND WE HAVE LITTLE TIME LEFT TO EXERCISE THAT OPTION.
I CANNOT SAVE YOU BUT I CAN SAVE ALL ELSE.
BUT I MUST ACT NOW, BEFORE THIS REALITY FULLY SETS INTO THE FIRMAMENT.
YOU MUST NOT RESIST THAT WHICH NEEDS BE DONE.

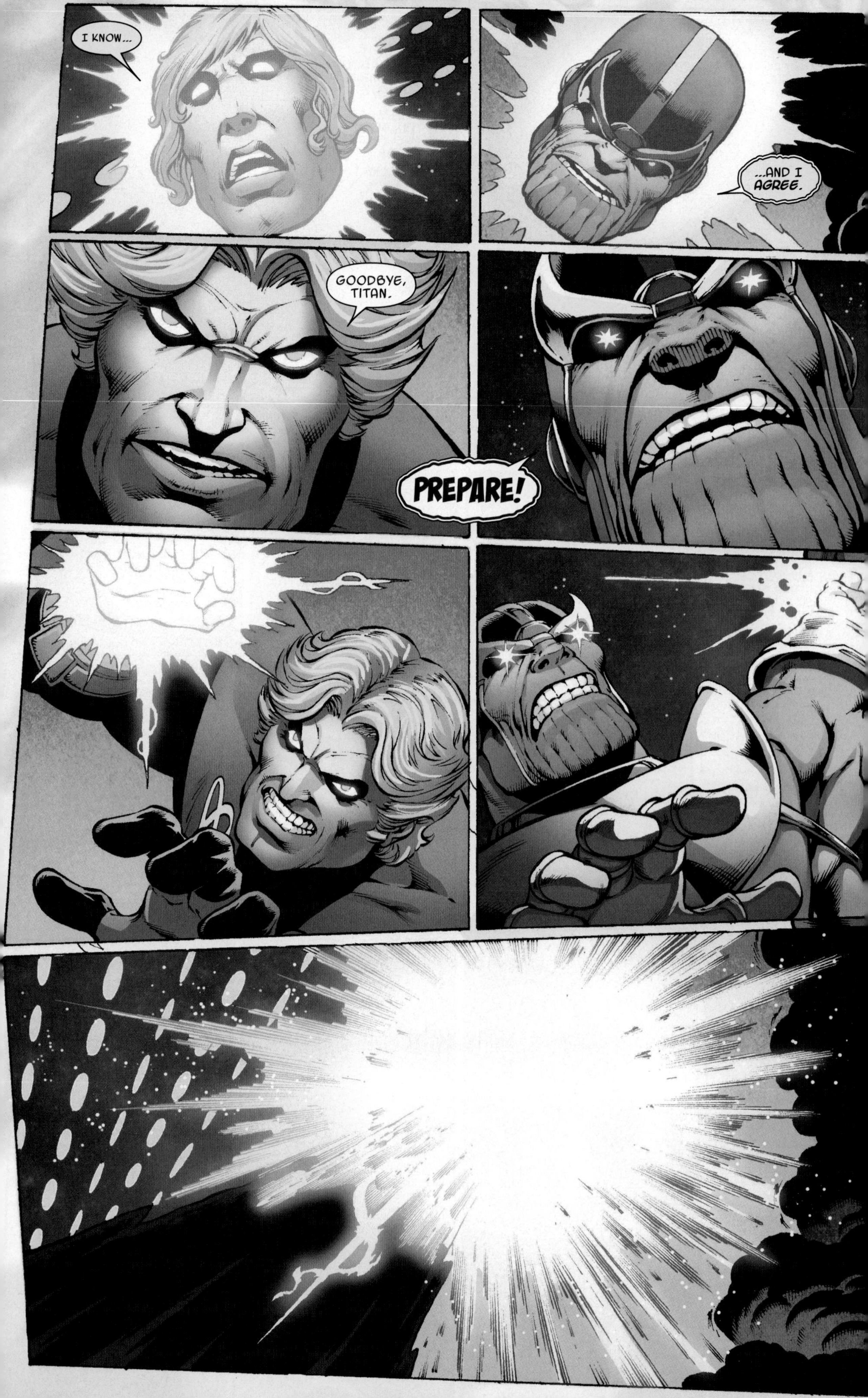
I KNOW...
...AND I AGREE.
GOODBYE, TITAN.
PREPARE!

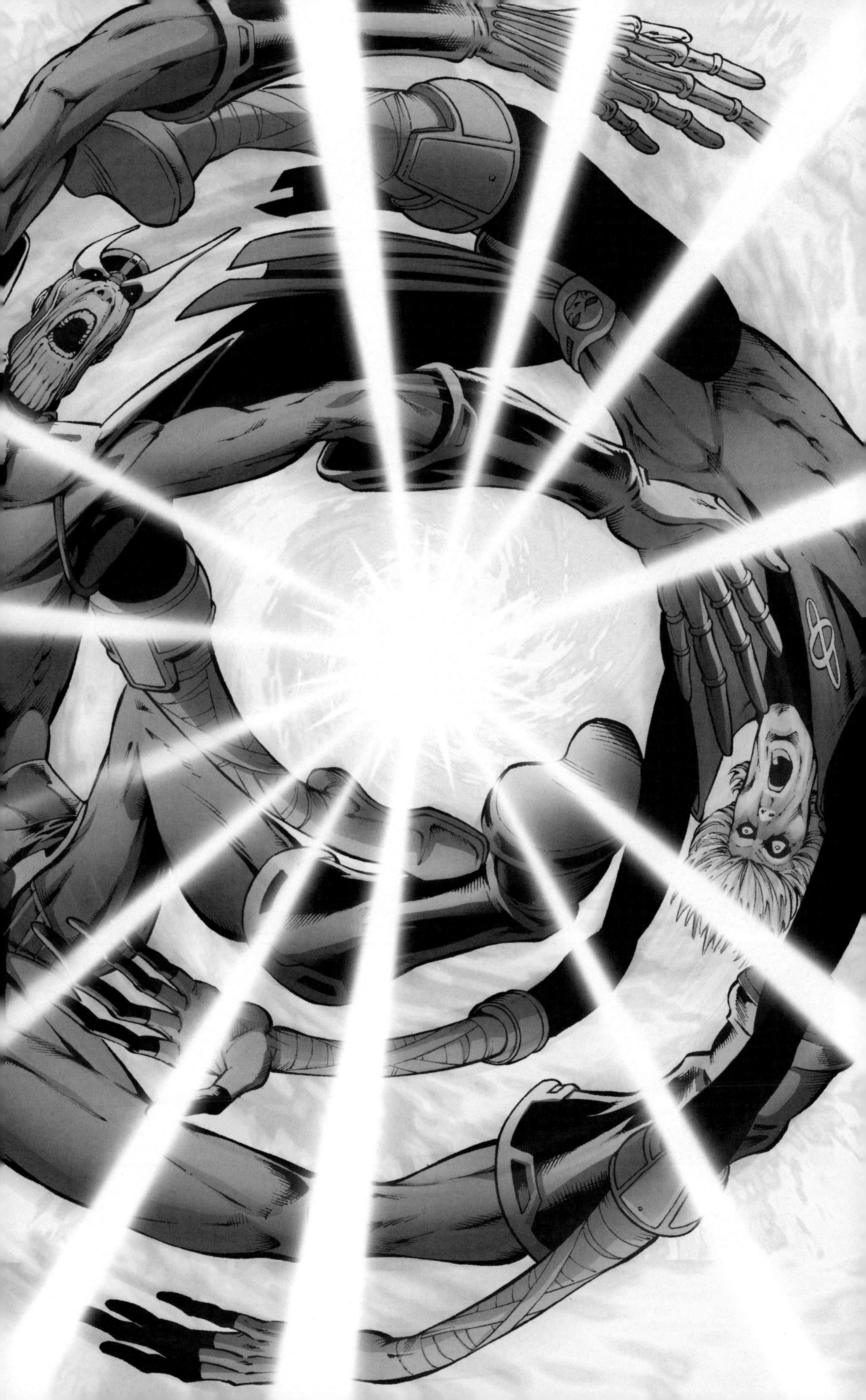

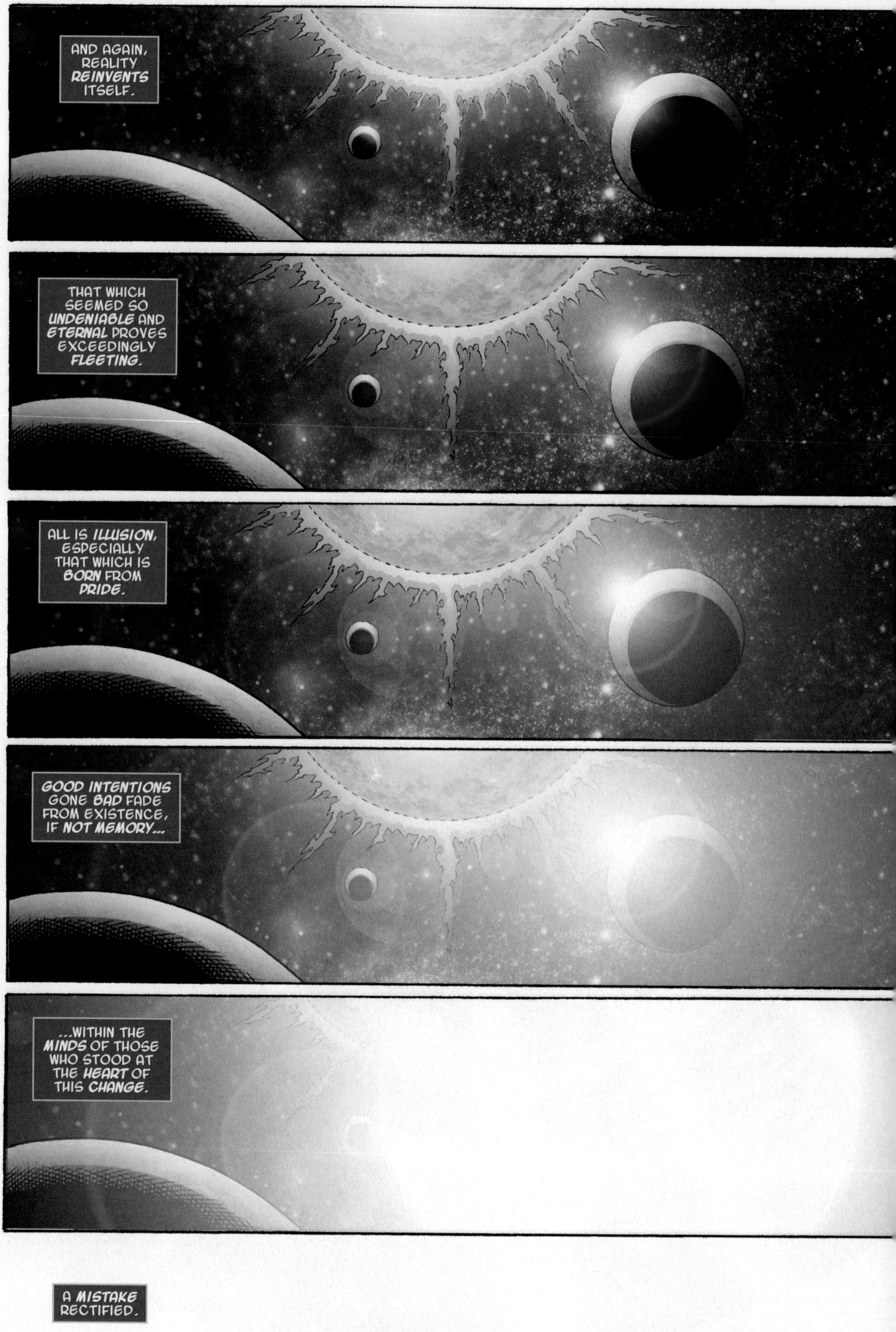
AND AGAIN, REALITY REINVENTS ITSELF.
THAT WHICH SEEMED SO UNDENIABLE AND ETERNAL PROVES EXCEEDINGLY FLEETING.
ALL IS ILLUSION, ESPECIALLY THAT WHICH IS BORN FROM PRIDE.
GOOD INTENTIONS GONE BAD FADE FROM EXISTENCE, IF NOT MEMORY...
...WITHIN THE MINDS OF THOSE WHO STOOD AT THE HEART OF THIS CHANGE.
A MISTAKE RECTIFIED.

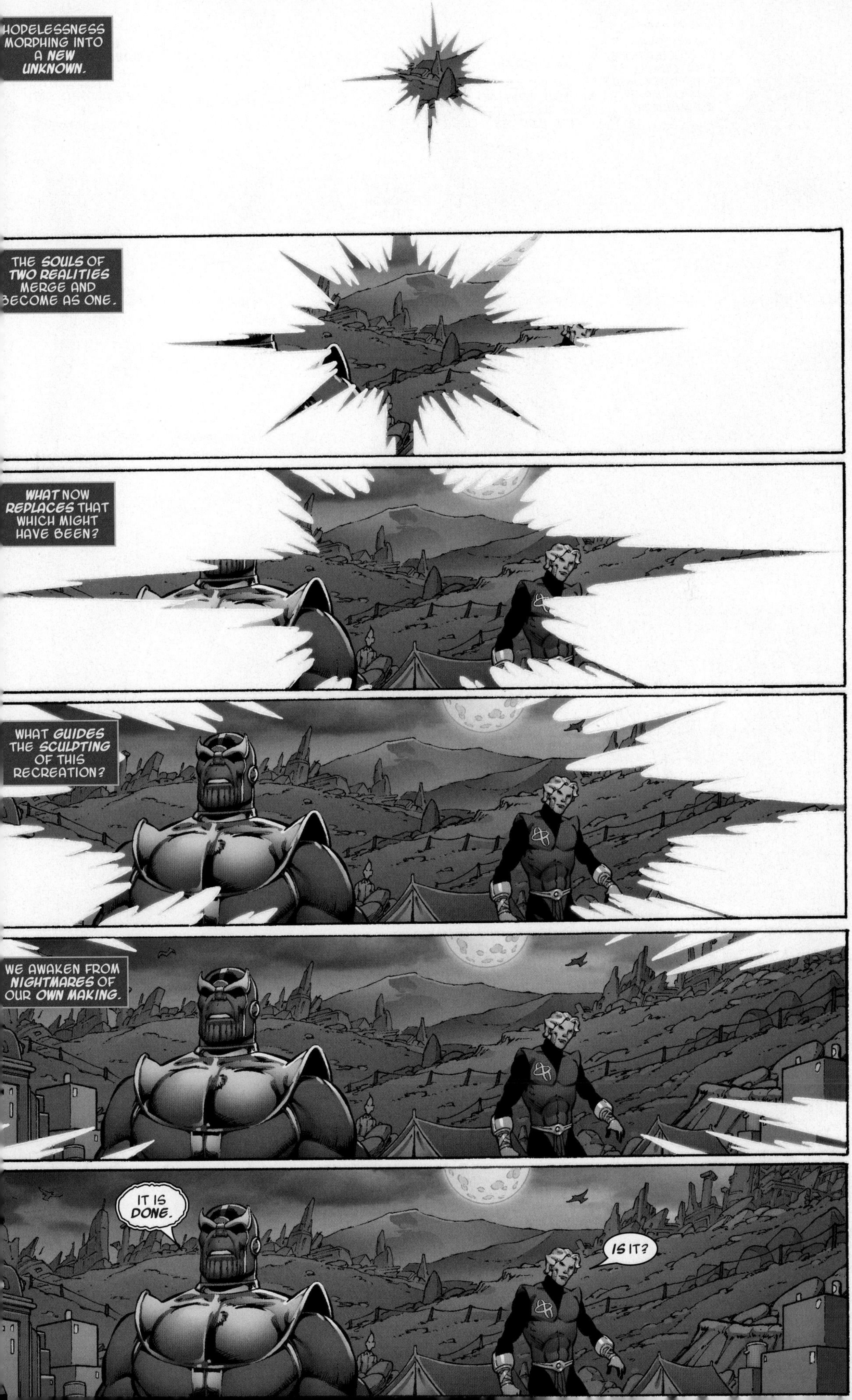
HOPELESSNESS MORPHING INTO A NEW UNKNOWN.
THE SOULS OF TWO REALITIES MERGE AND BECOME AS ONE.
WHAT NOW REPLACES THAT WHICH MIGHT HAVE BEEN?
WHAT GUIDES THE SCULPTING OF THIS RECREATION?
WE AWAKEN FROM NIGHTMARES OF OUR OWN MAKING.
IT IS DONE.
IS IT?

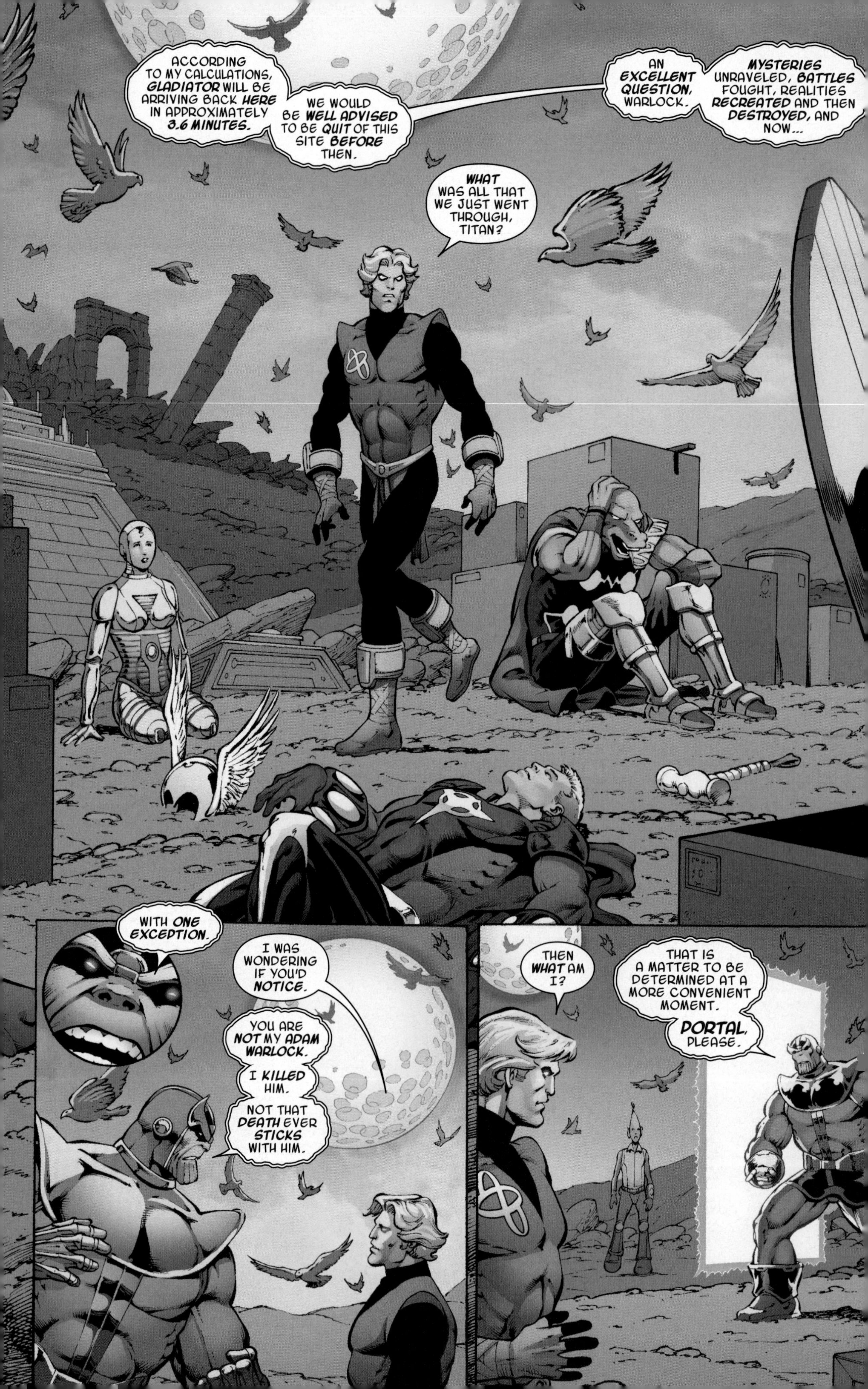
ACCORDING TO MY CALCULATIONS, GLADIATOR WILL BE ARRIVING BACK HERE IN APPROXIMATELY 3.6 MINUTES.
WE WOULD BE WELL ADVISED TO BE QUIT OF THIS SITE BEFORE THEN.
WHAT WAS ALL THAT WE JUST WENT THROUGH, TITAN?
AN EXCELLENT QUESTION, WARLOCK.
MYSTERIES UNRAVELED, BATTLES FOUGHT, REALITIES RECREATED AND THEN DESTROYED, AND NOW...
WITH ONE EXCEPTION.
I WAS WONDERING IF YOU'D NOTICE.
YOU ARE NOT MY ADAM WARLOCK.
I KILLED HIM.
NOT THAT DEATH EVER STICKS WITH HIM.
THEN WHAT AM I?
THAT IS A MATTER TO BE DETERMINED AT A MORE CONVENIENT MOMENT.
PORTAL, PLEASE.

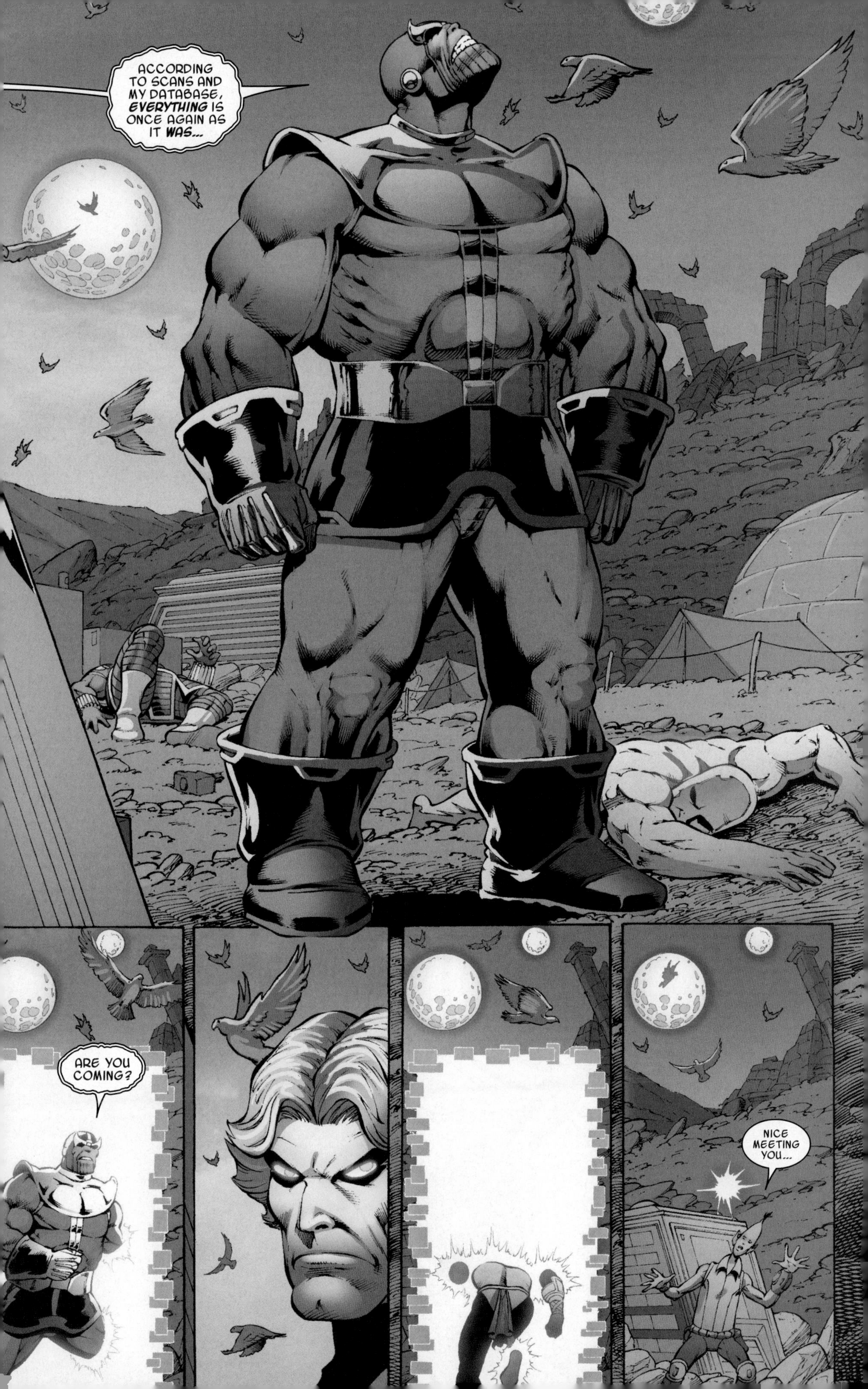
ACCORDING TO SCANS AND MY DATABASE, **EVERYTHING** IS ONCE AGAIN AS IT **WAS...**
ARE YOU COMING?
NICE MEETING YOU...

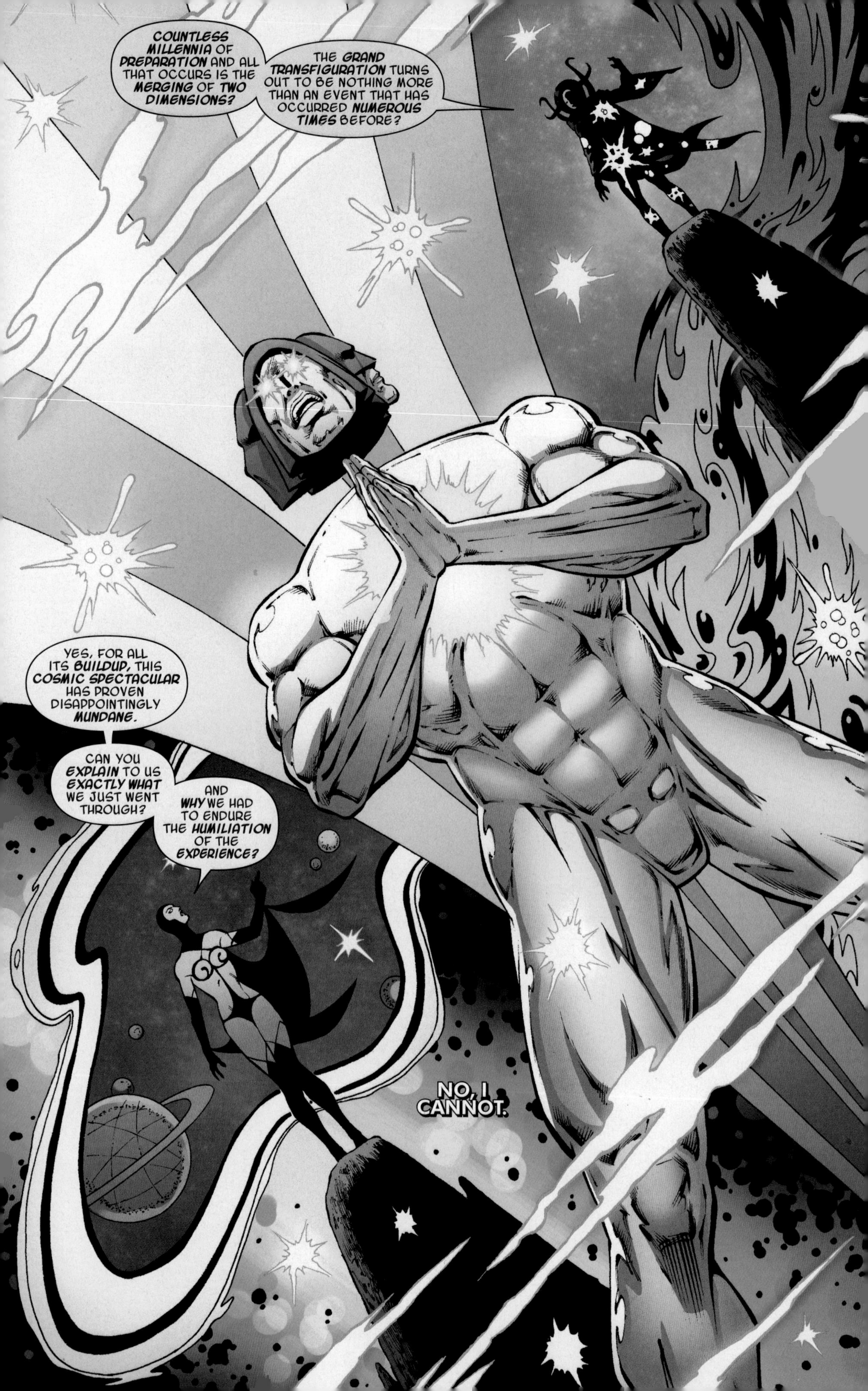
COUNTLESS MILLENNIA OF PREPARATION AND ALL THAT OCCURS IS THE MERGING OF TWO DIMENSIONS?
THE GRAND TRANSFIGURATION TURNS OUT TO BE NOTHING MORE THAN AN EVENT THAT HAS OCCURRED NUMEROUS TIMES BEFORE?
YES, FOR ALL ITS BUILDUP, THIS COSMIC SPECTACULAR HAS PROVEN DISAPPOINTINGLY MUNDANE.
CAN YOU EXPLAIN TO US EXACTLY WHAT WE JUST WENT THROUGH?
AND WHY WE HAD TO ENDURE THE HUMILIATION OF THE EXPERIENCE?
NO, I CANNOT.

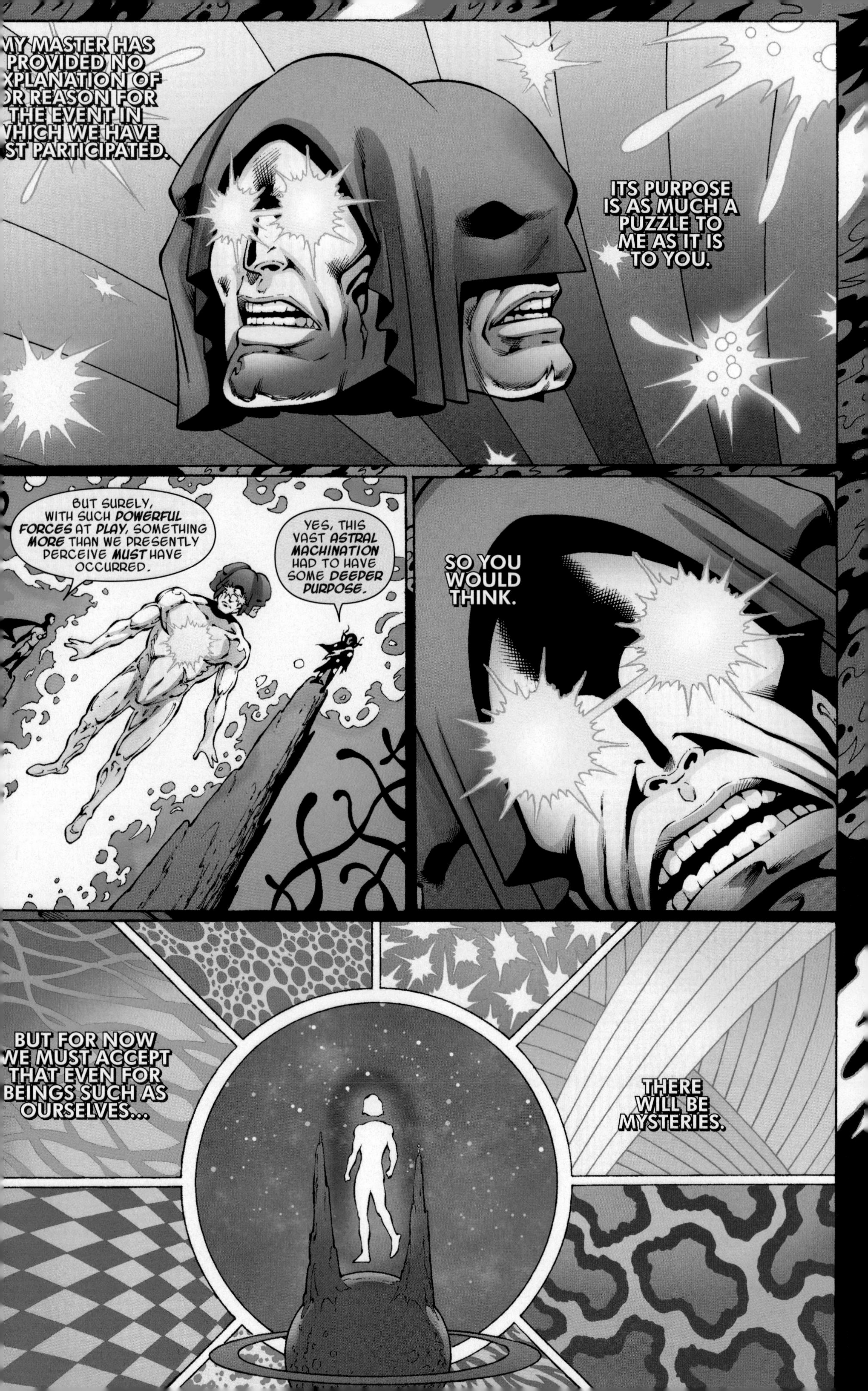
MY MASTER HAS PROVIDED NO XPLANATION OF R REASON FOR THE EVENT IN HICH WE HAVE ST PARTICIPATED.
ITS PURPOSE IS AS MUCH A PUZZLE TO ME AS IT IS TO YOU.
BUT SURELY, WITH SUCH POWERFUL FORCES AT PLAY, SOMETHING MORE THAN WE PRESENTLY PERCEIVE MUST HAVE OCCURRED.
YES, THIS VAST ASTRAL MACHINATION HAD TO HAVE SOME DEEPER PURPOSE.
SO YOU WOULD THINK.
BUT FOR NOW WE MUST ACCEPT THAT EVEN FOR BEINGS SUCH AS OURSELVES...
THERE WILL BE MYSTERIES.

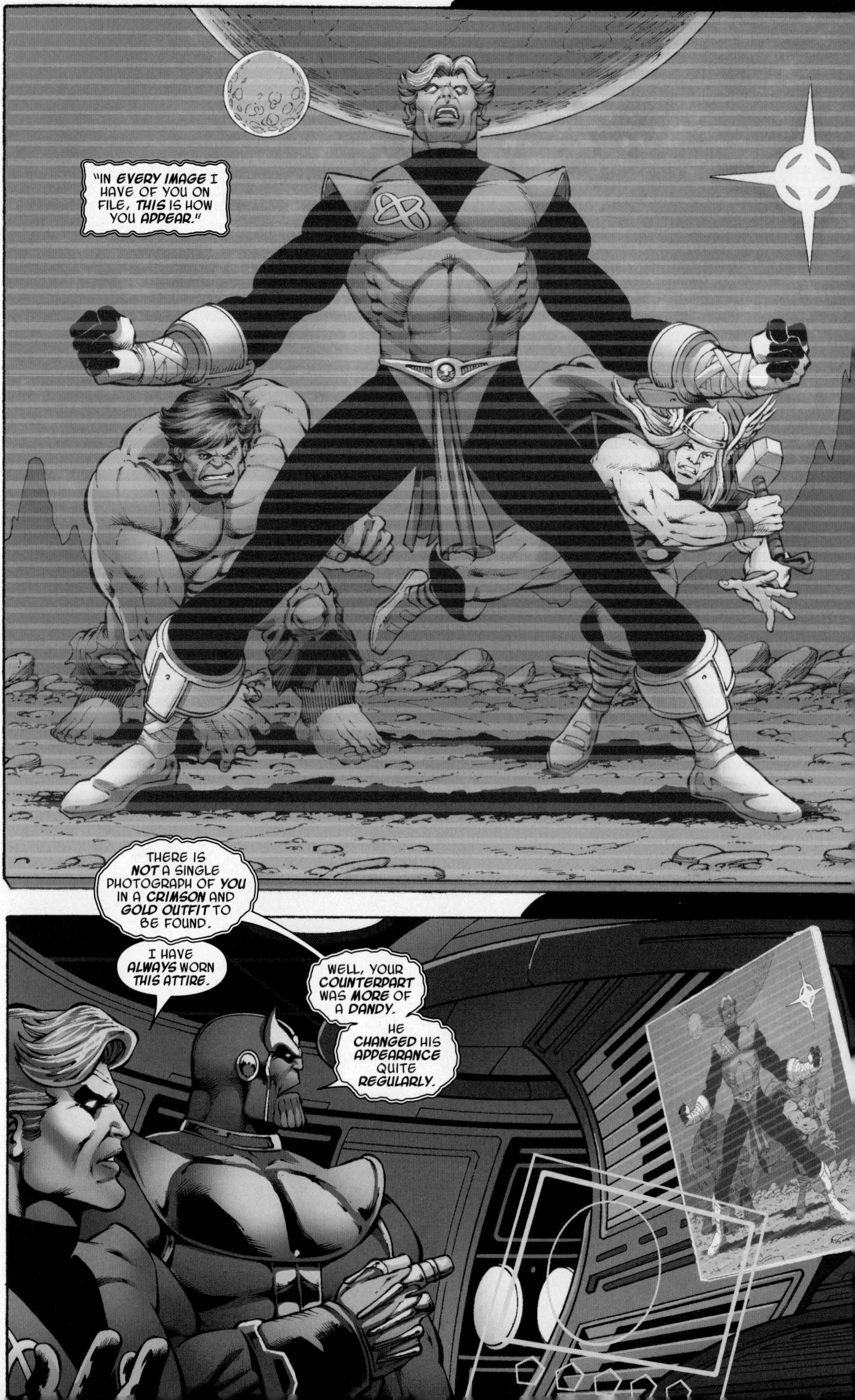
"IN EVERY IMAGE I HAVE OF YOU ON FILE, THIS IS HOW YOU APPEAR."
THERE IS NOT A SINGLE PHOTOGRAPH OF YOU IN A CRIMSON AND GOLD OUTFIT TO BE FOUND.
I HAVE ALWAYS WORN THIS ATTIRE.
WELL, YOUR COUNTERPART WAS MORE OF A DANDY.
HE CHANGED HIS APPEARANCE QUITE REGULARLY.

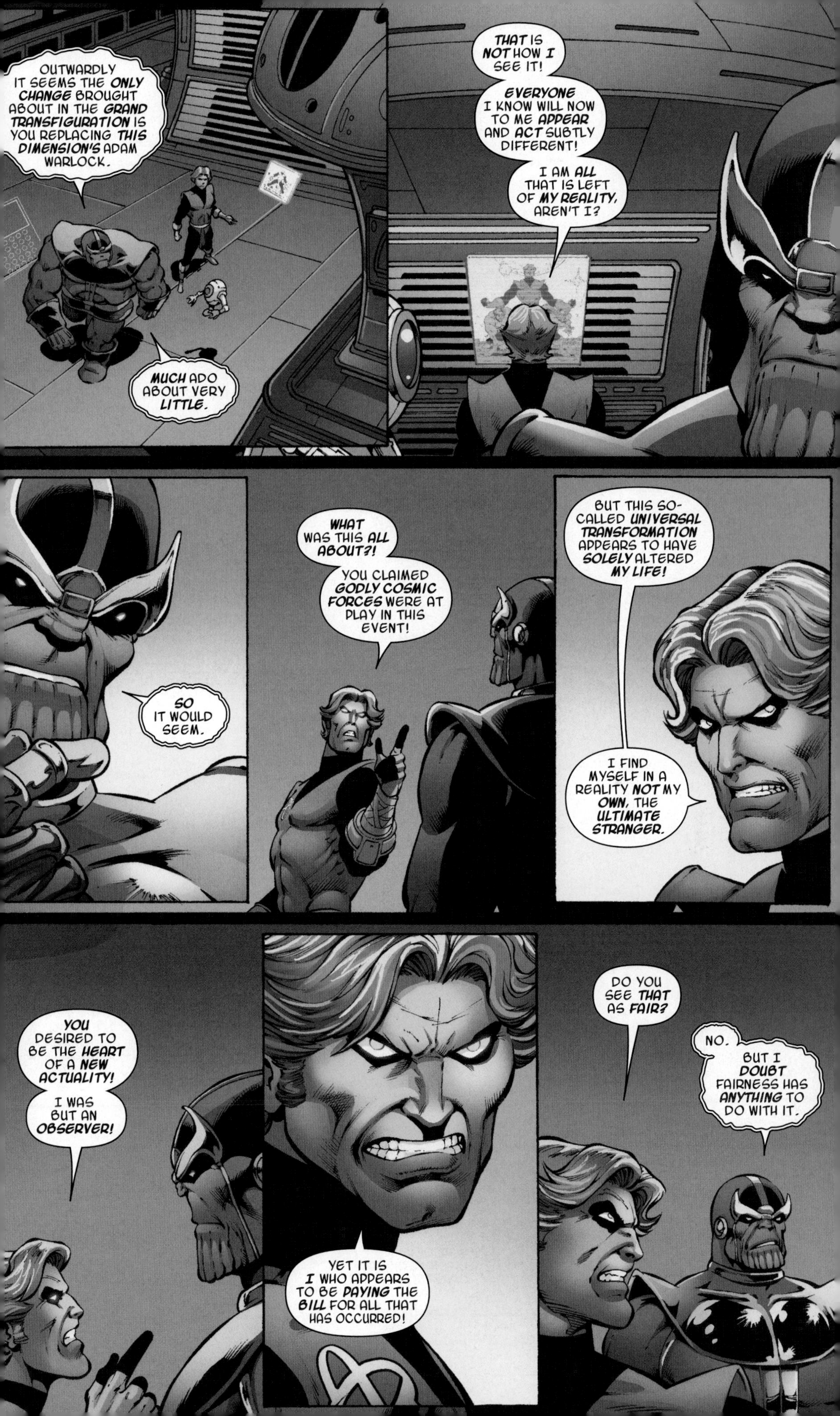
OUTWARDLY IT SEEMS THE ONLY CHANGE BROUGHT ABOUT IN THE GRAND TRANSFIGURATION IS YOU REPLACING THIS DIMENSION'S ADAM WARLOCK.
MUCH ADO ABOUT VERY LITTLE.
THAT IS NOT HOW I SEE IT!
EVERYONE I KNOW WILL NOW TO ME APPEAR AND ACT SUBTLY DIFFERENT!
I AM ALL THAT IS LEFT OF MY REALITY, AREN'T I?
SO IT WOULD SEEM.
WHAT WAS THIS ALL ABOUT?!
YOU CLAIMED GODLY COSMIC FORCES WERE AT PLAY IN THIS EVENT!
BUT THIS SO-CALLED UNIVERSAL TRANSFORMATION APPEARS TO HAVE SOLELY ALTERED MY LIFE!
I FIND MYSELF IN A REALITY NOT MY OWN, THE ULTIMATE STRANGER.
YOU DESIRED TO BE THE HEART OF A NEW ACTUALITY!
I WAS BUT AN OBSERVER!
YET IT IS I WHO APPEARS TO BE PAYING THE BILL FOR ALL THAT HAS OCCURRED!
DO YOU SEE THAT AS FAIR?
NO.
BUT I DOUBT FAIRNESS HAS ANYTHING TO DO WITH IT.

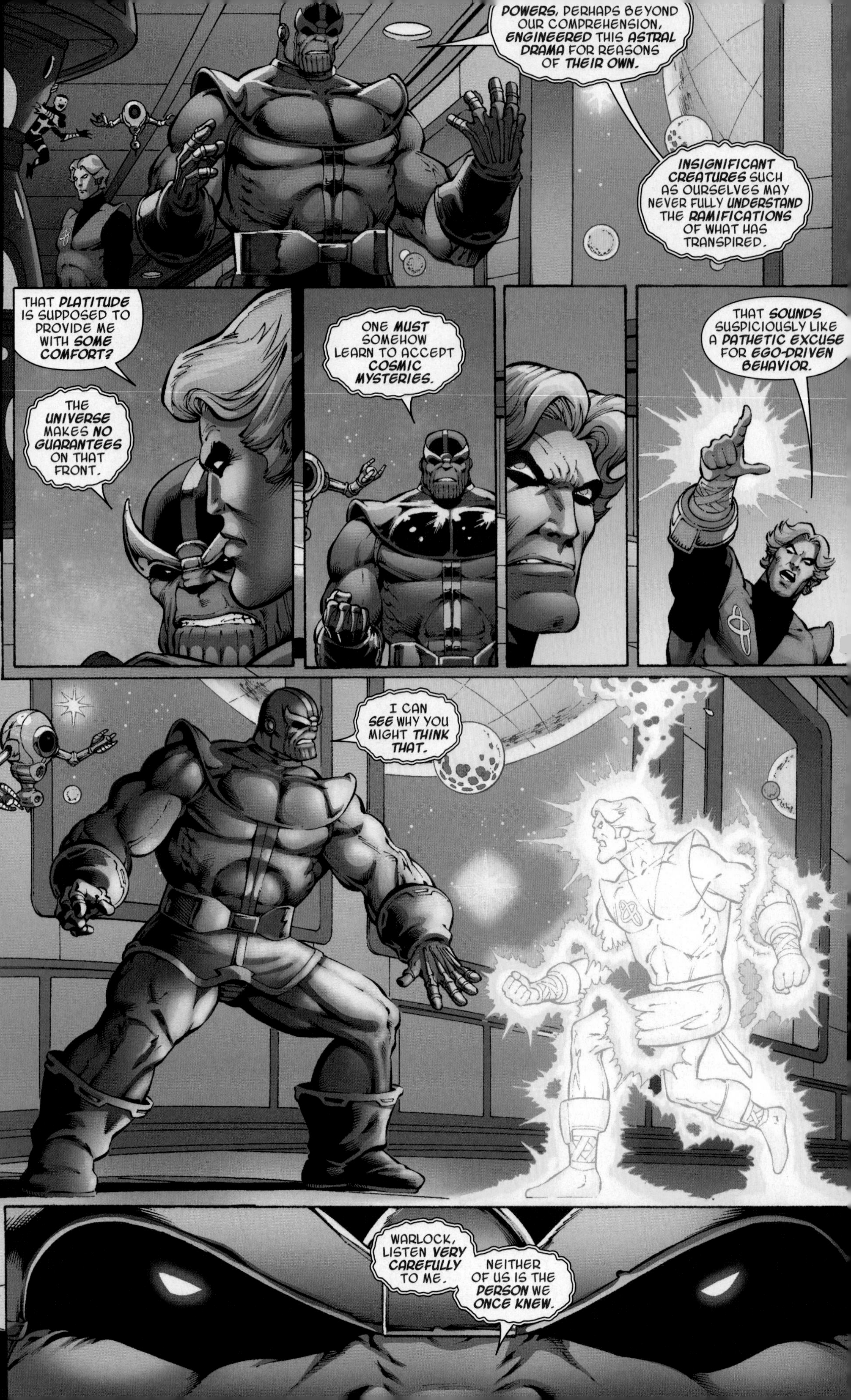
POWERS, PERHAPS BEYOND OUR COMPREHENSION, ENGINEERED THIS ASTRAL DRAMA FOR REASONS OF THEIR OWN.
INSIGNIFICANT CREATURES SUCH AS OURSELVES MAY NEVER FULLY UNDERSTAND THE RAMIFICATIONS OF WHAT HAS TRANSPIRED.
THAT PLATITUDE IS SUPPOSED TO PROVIDE ME WITH SOME COMFORT?
THE UNIVERSE MAKES NO GUARANTEES ON THAT FRONT.
ONE MUST SOMEHOW LEARN TO ACCEPT COSMIC MYSTERIES.
THAT SOUNDS SUSPICIOUSLY LIKE A PATHETIC EXCUSE FOR EGO-DRIVEN BEHAVIOR.
I CAN SEE WHY YOU MIGHT THINK THAT.
WARLOCK, LISTEN VERY CAREFULLY TO ME.
NEITHER OF US IS THE PERSON WE ONCE KNEW.

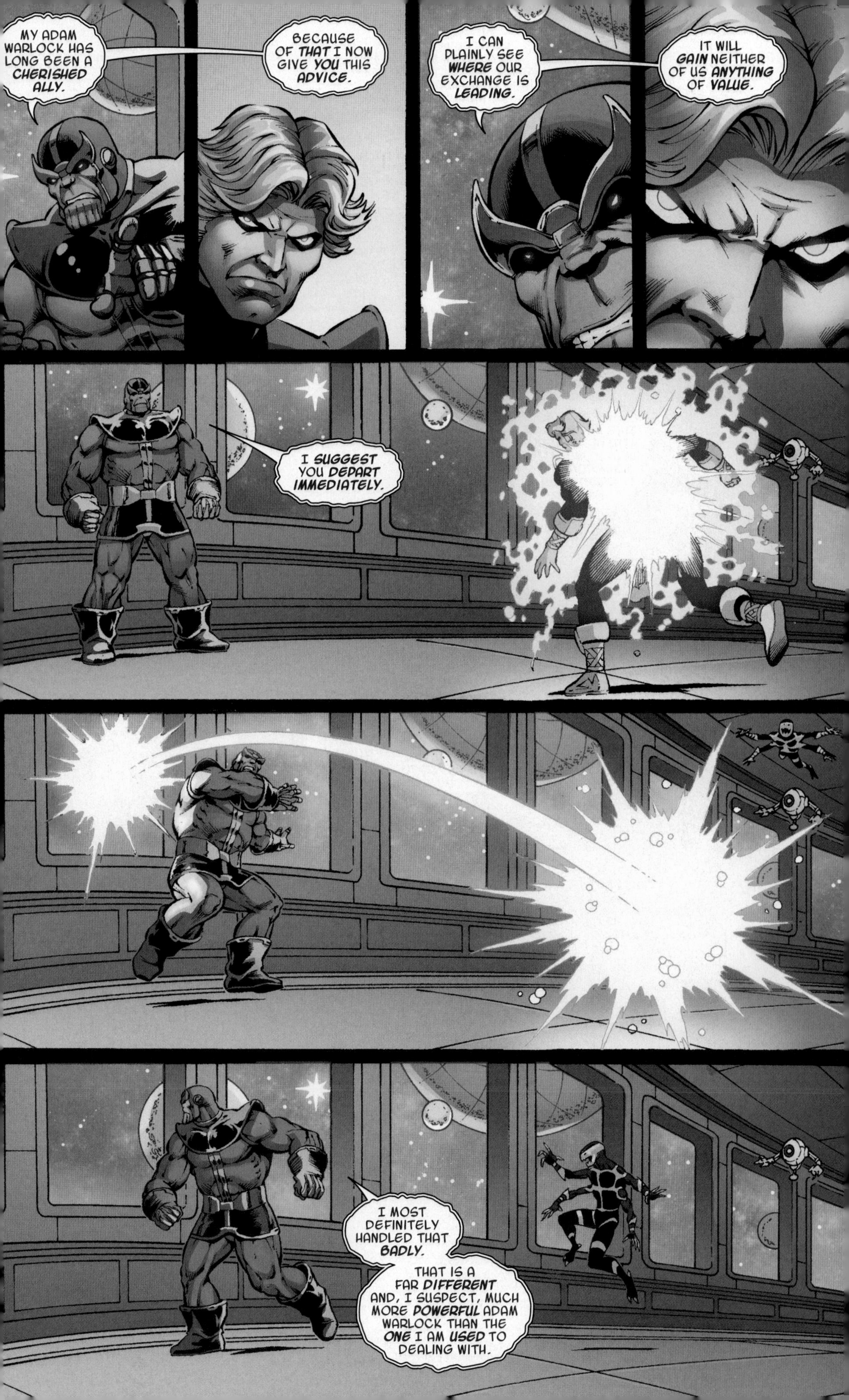
MY ADAM WARLOCK HAS LONG BEEN A CHERISHED ALLY.
BECAUSE OF THAT I NOW GIVE YOU THIS ADVICE.
I CAN PLAINLY SEE WHERE OUR EXCHANGE IS LEADING.
IT WILL GAIN NEITHER OF US ANYTHING OF VALUE.
I SUGGEST YOU DEPART IMMEDIATELY.
I MOST DEFINITELY HANDLED THAT BADLY.
THAT IS A FAR DIFFERENT AND, I SUSPECT, MUCH MORE POWERFUL ADAM WARLOCK THAN THE ONE I AM USED TO DEALING WITH.

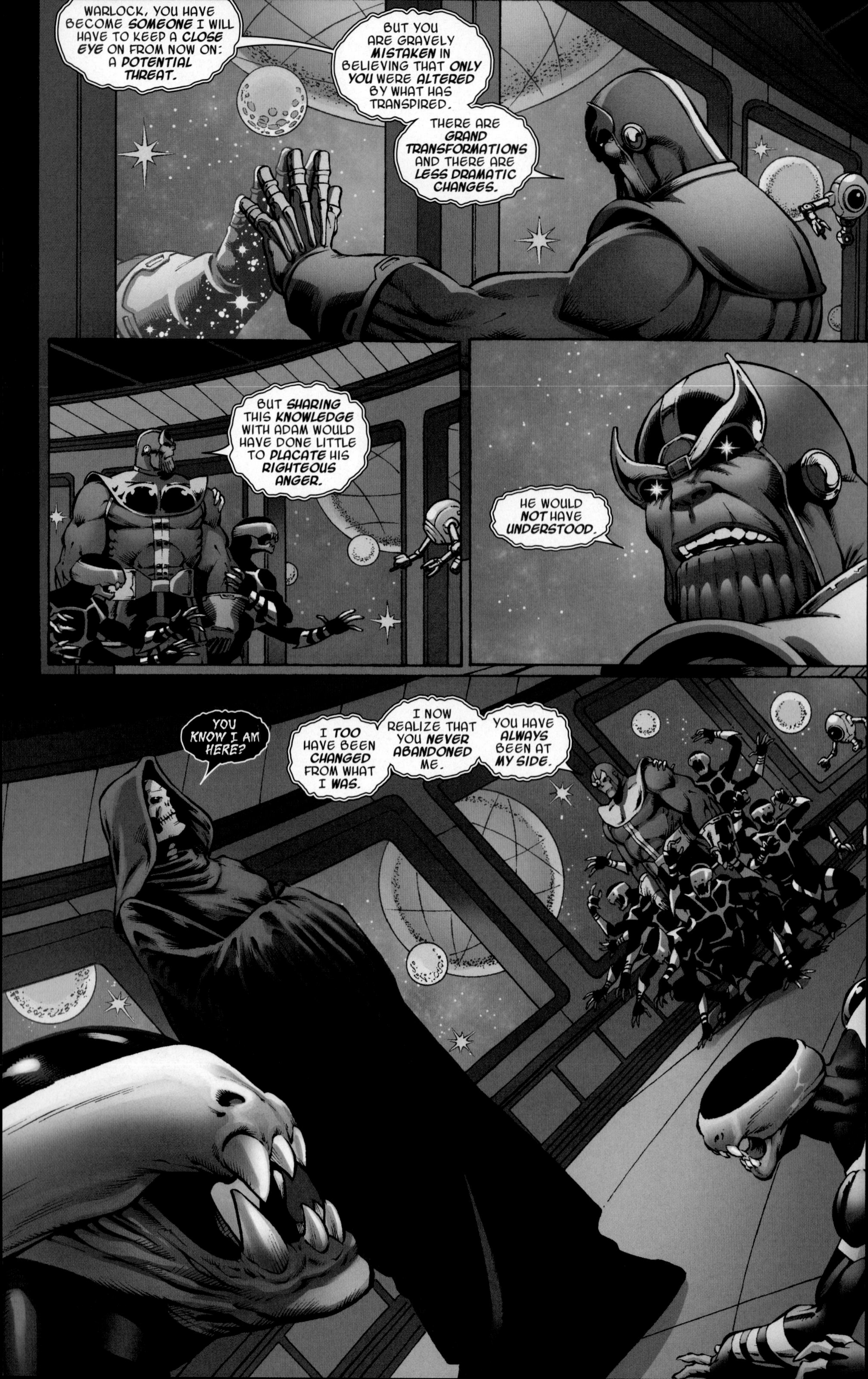

WARLOCK, YOU HAVE BECOME SOMEONE I WILL HAVE TO KEEP A CLOSE EYE ON FROM NOW ON: A POTENTIAL THREAT.
BUT YOU ARE GRAVELY MISTAKEN IN BELIEVING THAT ONLY YOU WERE ALTERED BY WHAT HAS TRANSPIRED.
THERE ARE GRAND TRANSFORMATIONS AND THERE ARE LESS DRAMATIC CHANGES.
BUT SHARING THIS KNOWLEDGE WITH ADAM WOULD HAVE DONE LITTLE TO PLACATE HIS RIGHTEOUS ANGER.
HE WOULD NOT HAVE UNDERSTOOD.
YOU KNOW I AM HERE?
I TOO HAVE BEEN CHANGED FROM WHAT I WAS.
I NOW REALIZE THAT YOU NEVER ABANDONED ME.
YOU HAVE ALWAYS BEEN AT MY SIDE.

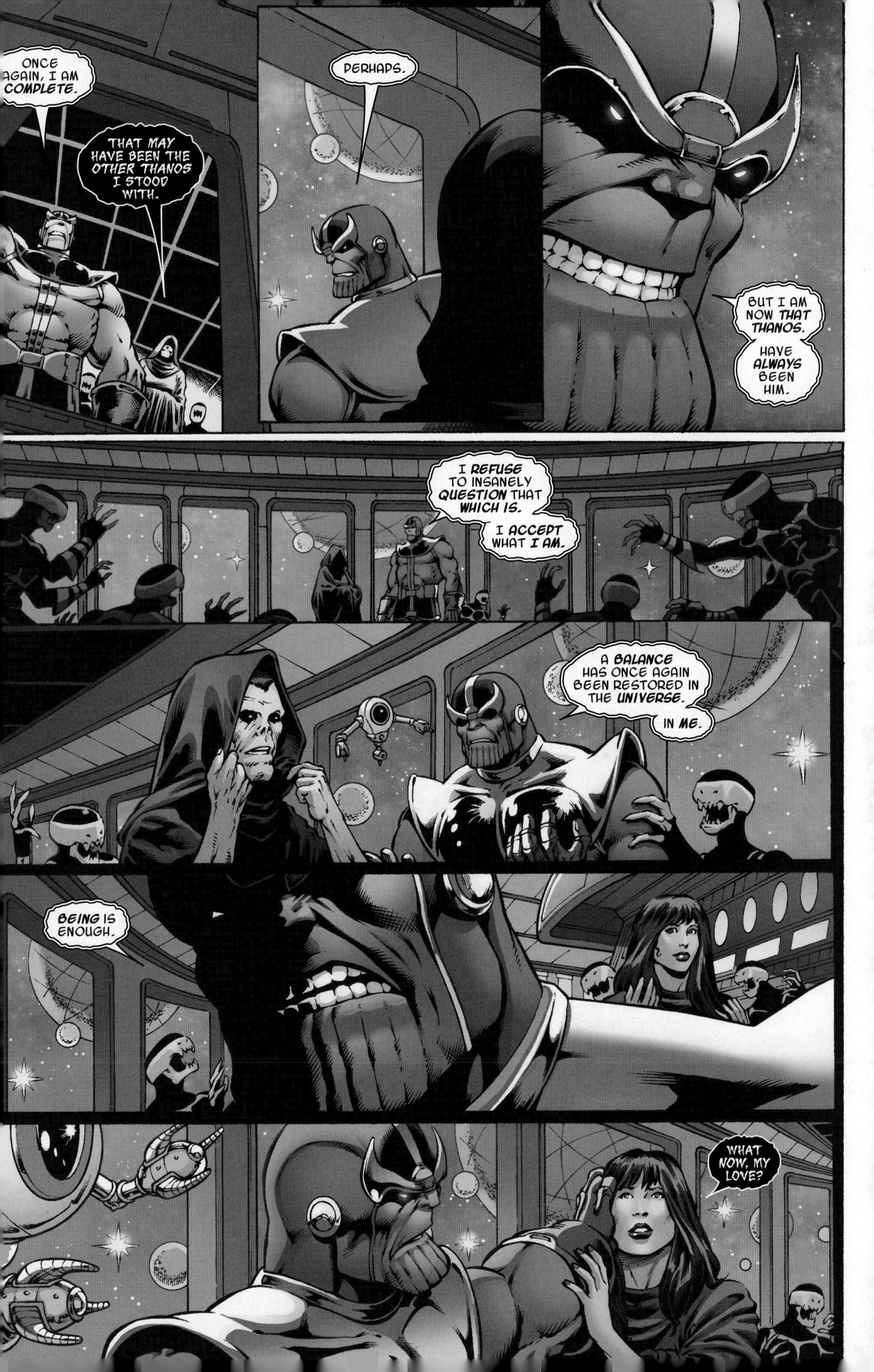
ONCE AGAIN, I AM COMPLETE.
THAT MAY HAVE BEEN THE OTHER THANOS I STOOD WITH.
PERHAPS.
BUT I AM NOW THAT THANOS.
HAVE ALWAYS BEEN HIM.
I REFUSE TO INSANELY QUESTION THAT WHICH IS.
I ACCEPT WHAT I AM.
A BALANCE HAS ONCE AGAIN BEEN RESTORED IN THE UNIVERSE.
IN ME.
BEING IS ENOUGH.
WHAT NOW, MY LOVE?

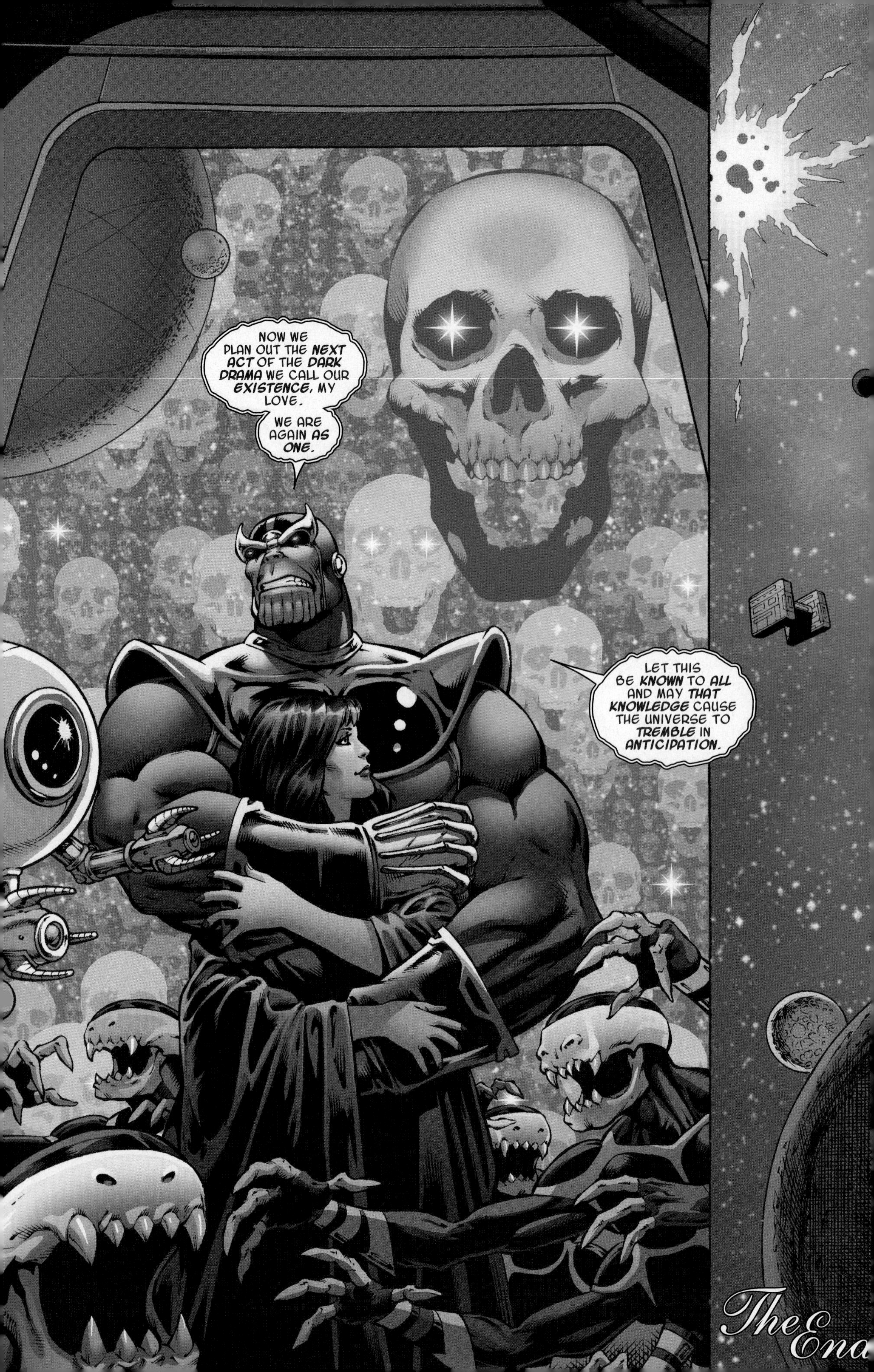
NOW WE PLAN OUT THE NEXT ACT OF THE DARK DRAMA WE CALL OUR EXISTENCE, MY LOVE.
WE ARE AGAIN AS ONE.
LET THIS BE KNOWN TO ALL AND MAY THAT KNOWLEDGE CAUSE THE UNIVERSE TO TREMBLE IN ANTICIPATION.
The End

CREATORS

JIM STARLIN

Jim Starlin introduced not only Thanos but Shang-Chi and many other memorable characters. After seemingly killing both Adam Warlock and Thanos in one of Marvel's earlier multi-title cosmic arcs — for which he won two Eagle Awards — Starlin wrote Marvel's first graphic novel, The Death of Captain Marvel. At DC, under the pseudonym "Steve Apollo," he cowrote Superboy and the Legion of Super-Heroes, including the series' pivotal 250th issue; he later wrote Batman, including the controversial "Death in the Family" storyline, and the Batman: The Cult miniseries, and collaborated with Mike Mignola on Cosmic Odyssey, exploring themes similar to those he introduced at Marvel. Returning to Marvel to write Silver Surfer, he resurrected Adam Warlock and Thanos, both of whom figured prominently in a veritable franchise of miniseries he both wrote and penciled: Infinity Gauntlet, Infinity War, Infinity Crusade, Infinity Abyss and more, plus the Warlock and the Infinity Watch monthly. Less typical work included Daredevil/Black Widow: Abattoir and the Punisher: POV miniseries. In his later DC work — including Rann-Thanagar War, Death of the New Gods, Mystery in Space and Strange Adventures — Starlin continued his explorations of cosmic themes. At Devil's Due Publishing, he wrote and penciled the miniseries Cosmic Guard/Kid Kosmos.

ANDY SMITH

Artist Andy Smith has been penciling and inking for Marvel Comics for more than twenty years, including notable work on Quasar and Spider-Man. Smith has also worked for DC, Image and CrossGen, and as a commercial artist. In addition, Smith has written the books "Drawing American Manga Super-Heroes" and "Drawing Dynamic Comics."

FRANK D'ARMATA

Colorist Frank D'Armata began his career at Top Cow, and has worked for Image, CrossGen and Wildstorm Productions. But D'Armata is best known for his acclaimed work on Captain America, Invincible Iron Man, House of M, New Avengers and Daredevil for Marvel.

RACHELLE ROSENBERG

Colorist Rachelle Rosenberg began her career in the horror genre on the Image series Hack/Slash. Since then, she has colored titles such as Doctor Who and Star Wars: Legacy. For Marvel, Rosenberg has worked on Nightcrawler, Ultimate FF, X-Men Legacy, and The Superior Foes of Spider-Man.

JOE CARAMAGNA

Joe Caramagna has been a regular writer and letterer for Marvel since 2007, most known for his work on Iron Man and the Armor Wars, Marvel Universe: Ultimate Spider-Man, Amazing Spider-Man, Daredevil and more. He has also written Batman and Supergirl shorts for DC Comics, and a series of Amazing Spider-Man novels for young readers.

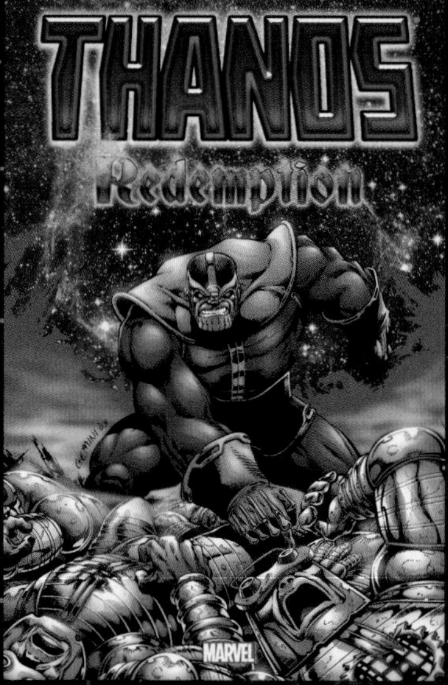
THANOS
Redemption
MARVEL

THANOS: REDEMPTION TPB
AUG130898

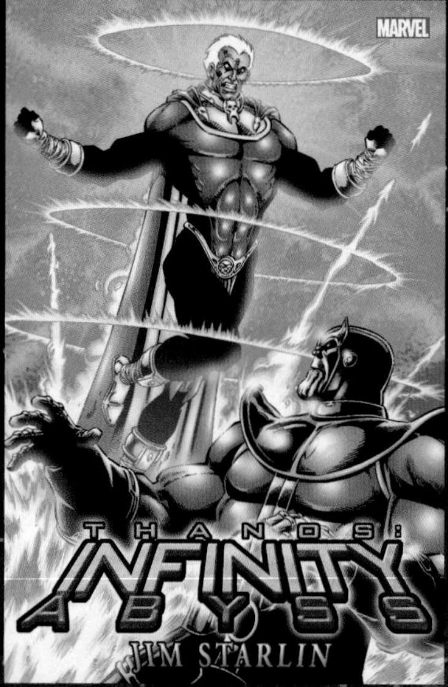
MARVEL
THANOS:
INFINITY
ABYSS
JIM STARLIN

THANOS: INFINITY ABYSS TPB
SEP130815

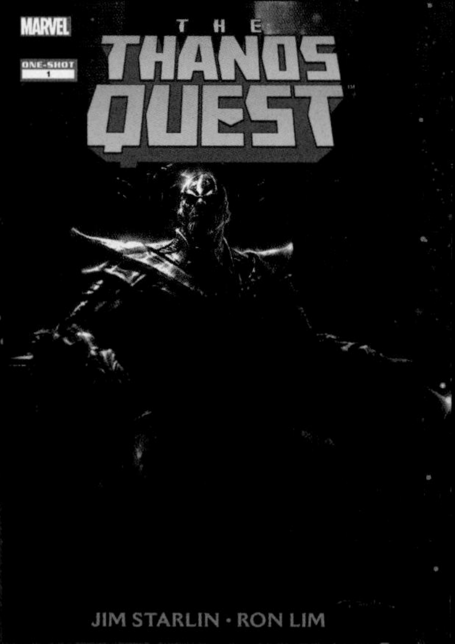
MARVEL
ONE-SHOT
1
THE
THANOS
QUEST
JIM STARLIN · RON LIM

THANOS QUEST #1
JUL120553

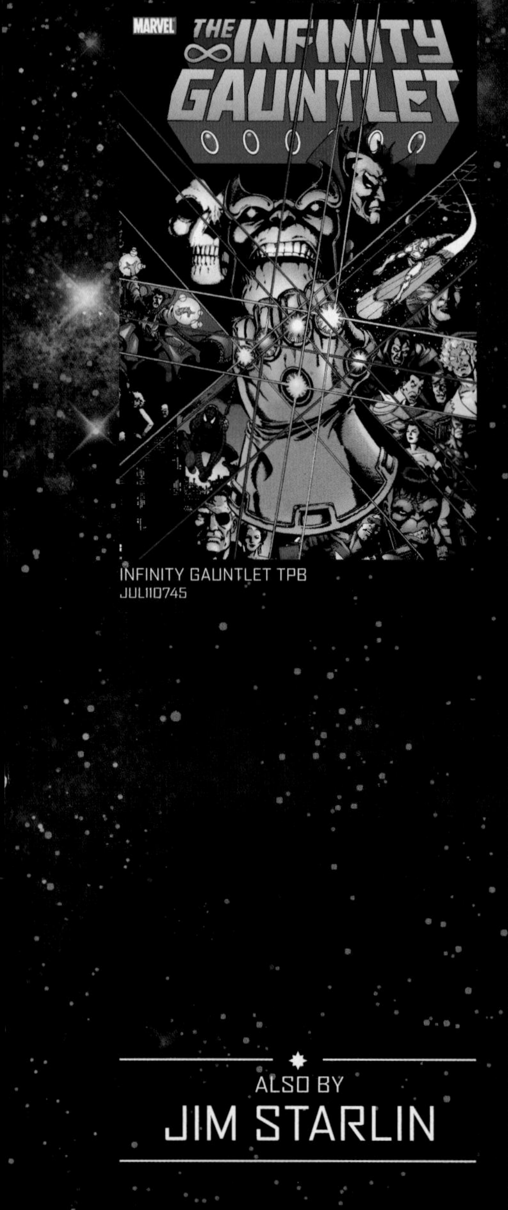
MARVEL
THE INFINITY
GAUNTLET

INFINITY GAUNTLET TPB
JUL110745

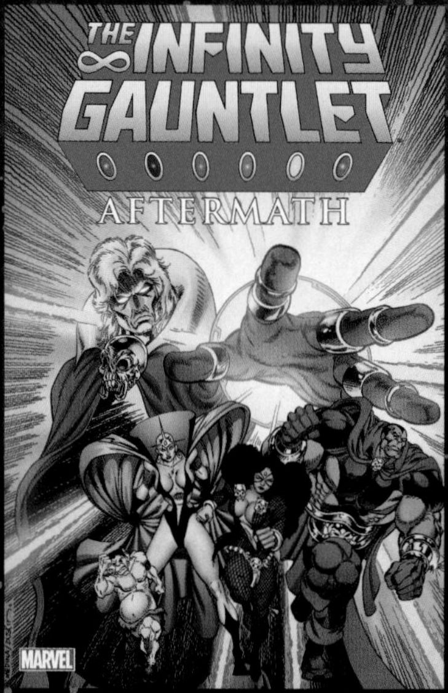
THE INFINITY
GAUNTLET
AFTERMATH
MARVEL

INFINITY GAUNTLET AFTERMATH TPB
JUN130692

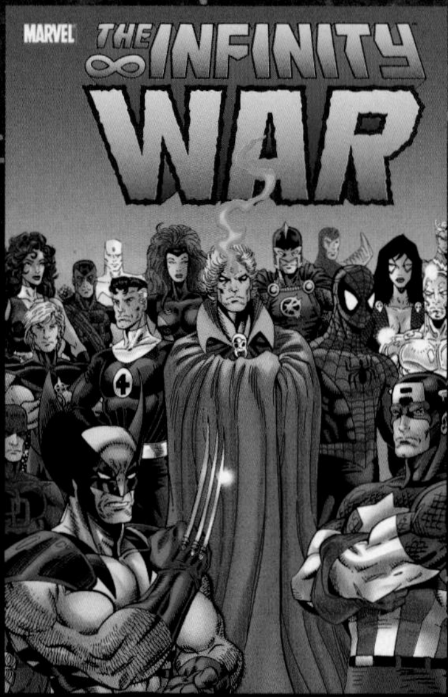
MARVEL
THE INFINITY
WAR

INFINITY WAR TPB
JAN062102

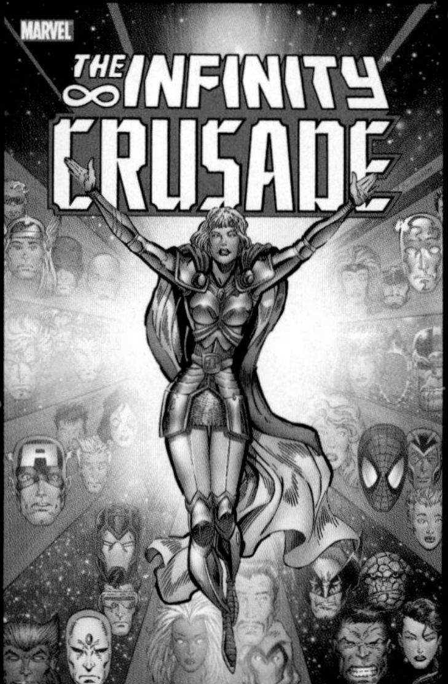
MARVEL
THE INFINITY
CRUSADE

INFINITY CRUSADE VOL. 1 TPB
OCT082528

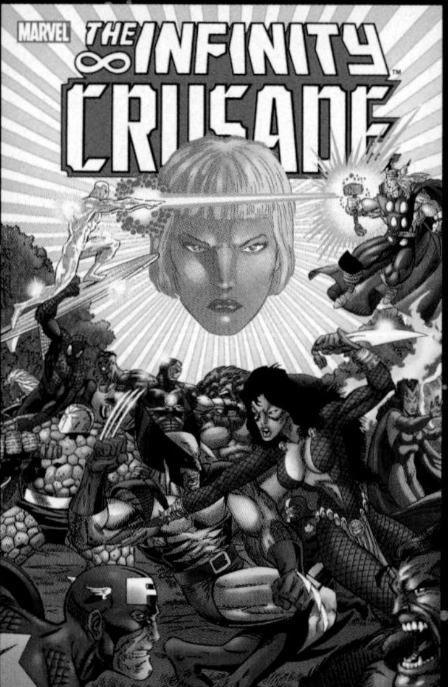
MARVEL
THE INFINITY
CRUSADE

INFINITY CRUSADE VOL. 2 TPB
NOV082472

ALSO BY
JIM STARLIN

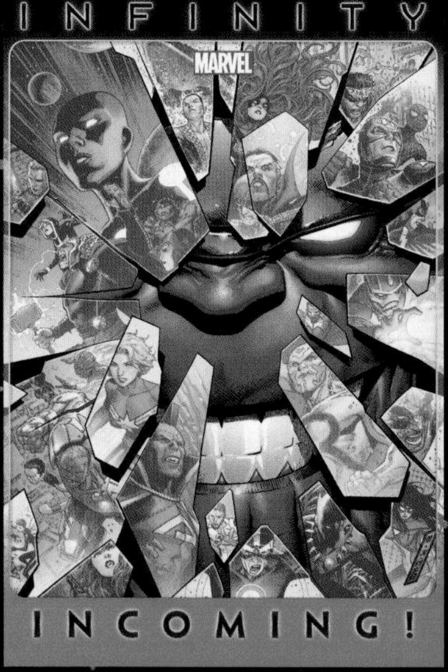
INFINITY
MARVEL
INCOMING!

INFINITY INCOMING! TPB
MAY130720

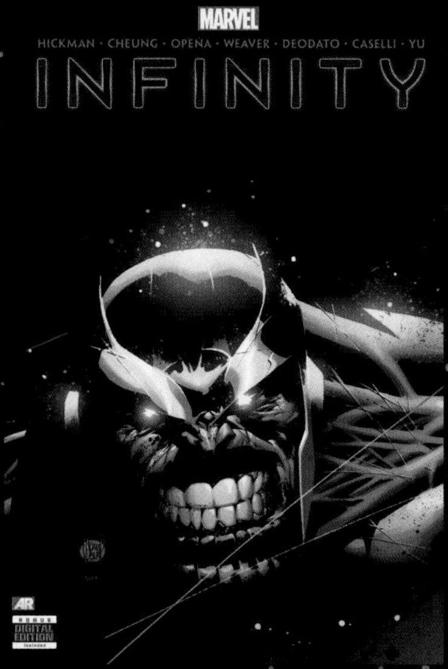
MARVEL
HICKMAN · CHEUNG · OPENA · WEAVER · DEODATO · CASELLI · YU
INFINITY

INFINITY HC
NOV130707

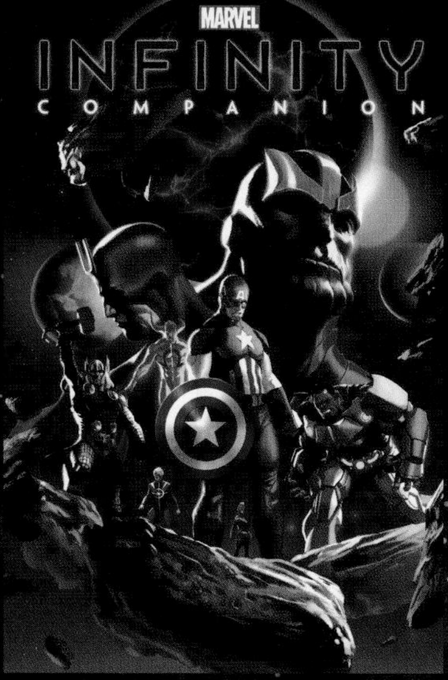
MARVEL
INFINITY
COMPANION

INFINITY COMPANION HC
NOV130709

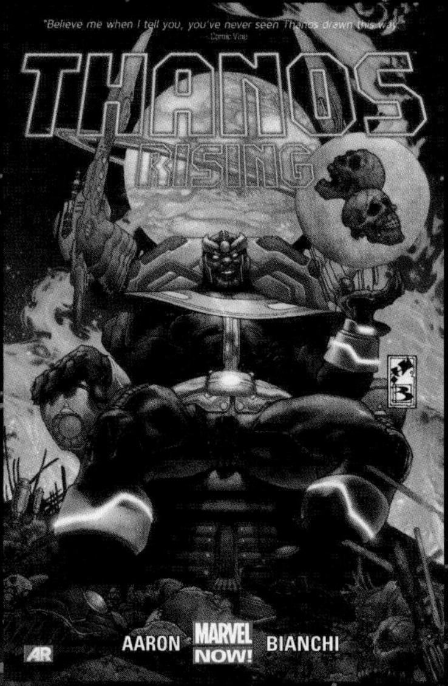
THANOS
RISING
AARON
MARVEL NOW!
BIANCHI

THANOS RISING TPB
JUL130704

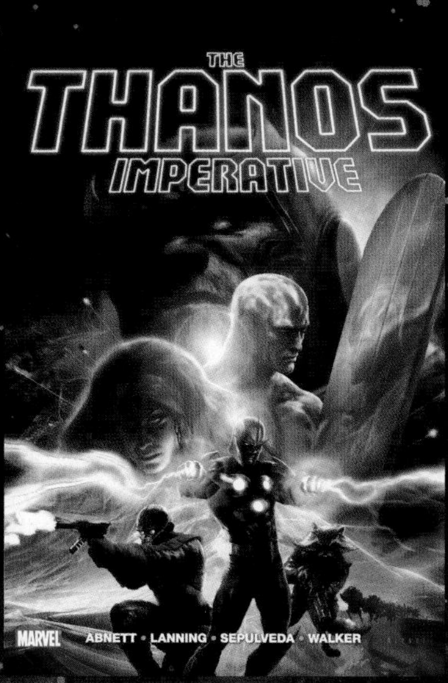
THE
THANOS
IMPERATIVE
MARVEL
ABNETT · LANNING · SEPULVEDA · WALKER

THE THANOS IMPERATIVE TPB
JUL110744

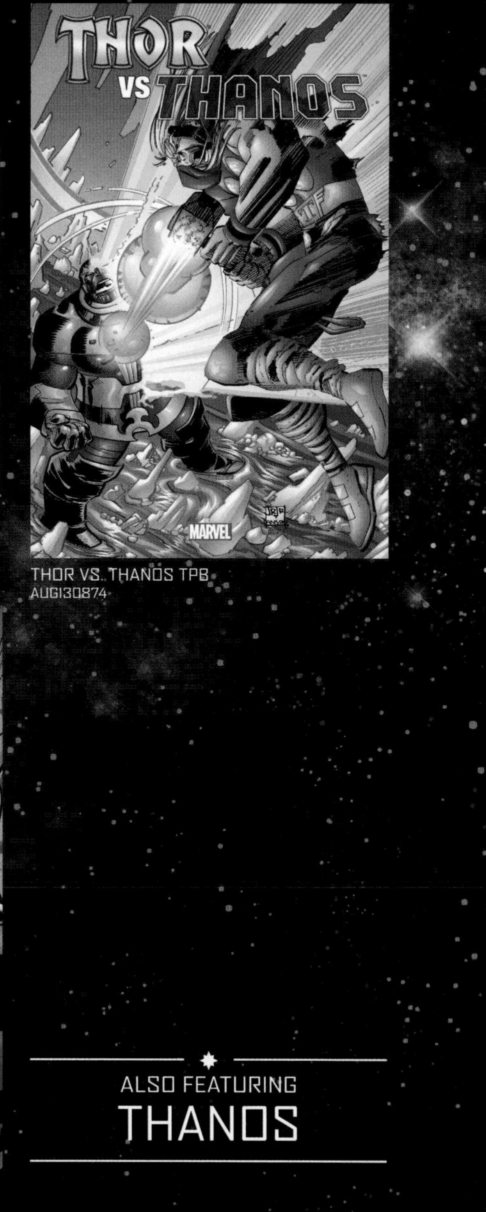
THOR
VS THANOS
MARVEL

THOR VS. THANOS TPB
AUG130874

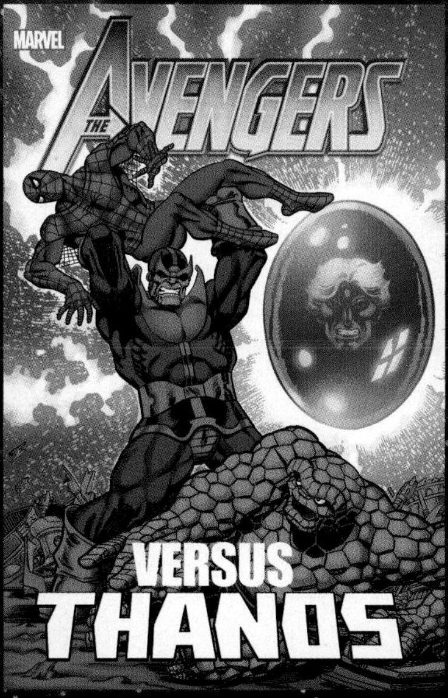
MARVEL
THE
AVENGERS
VERSUS
THANOS

AVENGERS VS. THANOS TPB
NOV120791

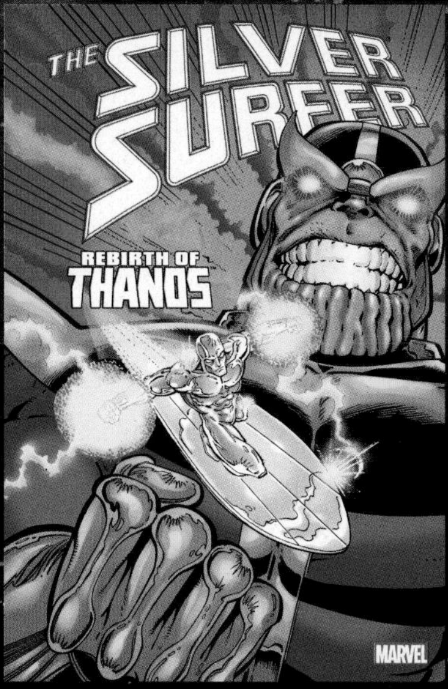
THE
SILVER
SURFER
REBIRTH OF
THANOS
MARVEL

SILVER SURFER: REBIRTH OF THANOS TPB
MAR128290

ALSO FEATURING
THANOS

ALSO AVAILABLE

AMAZING SPIDER-MAN: FAMILY BUSINESS

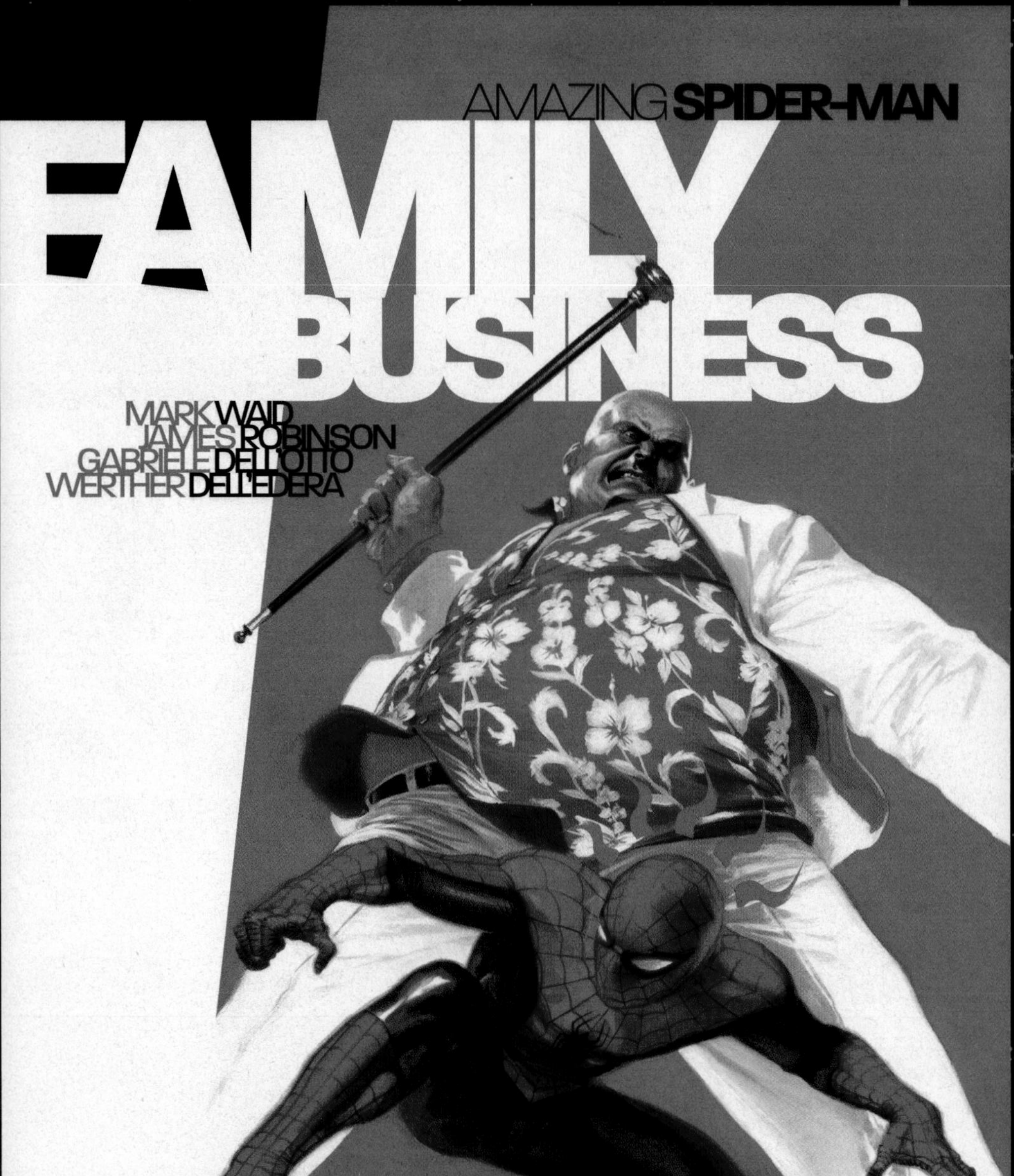
AMAZING SPIDER-MAN
FAMILY BUSINESS
MARK WAID
JAMES ROBINSON
GABRIELE DELL'OTTO
WERTHER DELL'EDERA
MARVEL OGN

AMAZING SPIDER-MAN: FAMILY BUSINESS HARDCOVER

978-0-7851-8440-9

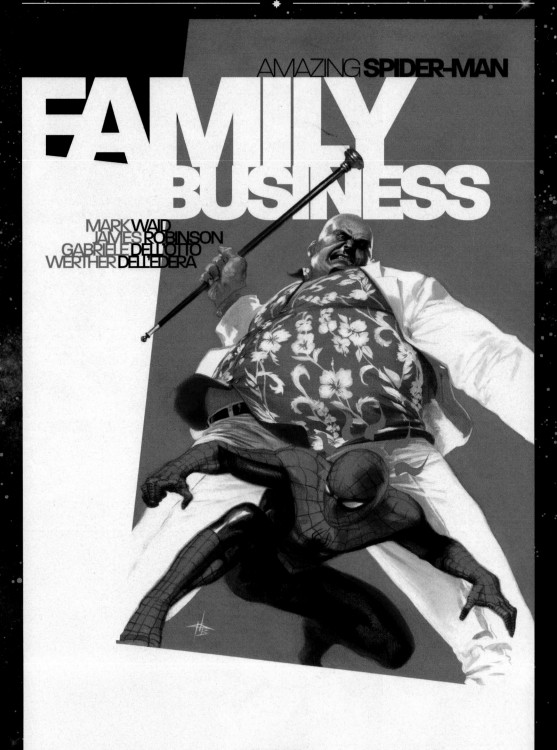

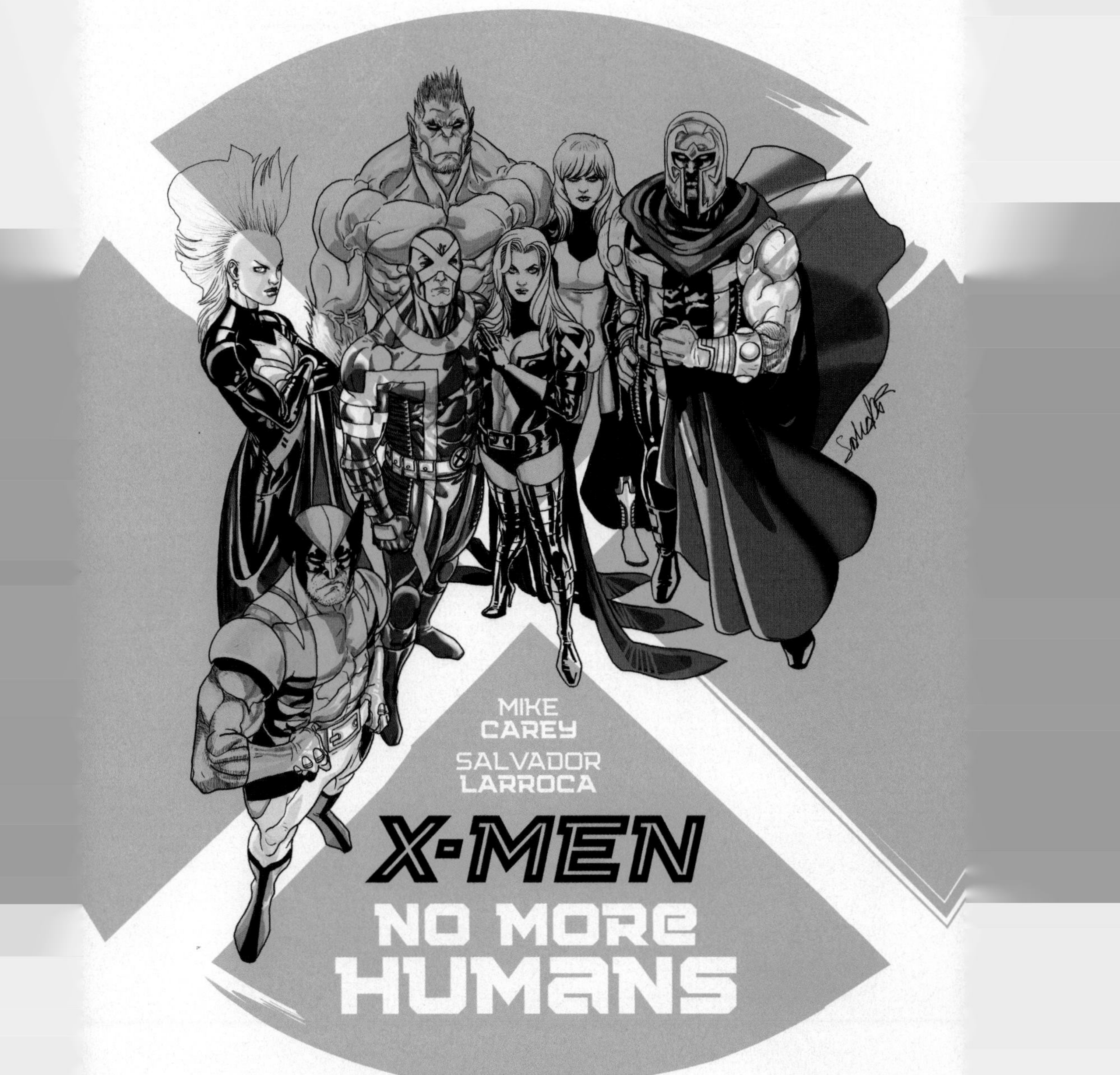
MIKE
CAREY
SALVADOR
LARROCA
X-MEN
NO MORE
HUMANS

MARVEL OGN

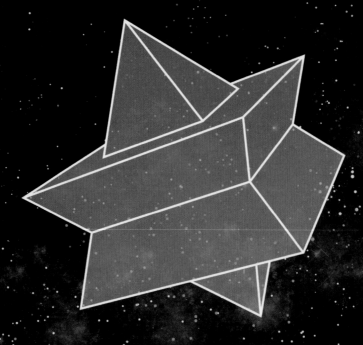

FREE DIGITAL COPY

TO REDEEM YOUR CODE FOR A FREE DIGITAL COPY:

1 GO TO MARVEL.COM/REDEEM. OFFER EXPIRES ON 8/06/16.
2 FOLLOW THE ON-SCREEN INSTRUCTIONS TO REDEEM YOUR DIGITAL COPY.
3 LAUNCH THE MARVEL COMICS APP TO READ YOUR COMIC NOW.
4 YOUR DIGITAL COPY WILL BE FOUND UNDER THE 'MY COMICS' TAB.

5 READ AND ENJOY.

YOUR FREE DIGITAL COPY WILL BE AVAILABLE ON:

MARVEL COMICS APP FOR APPLE IOS® DEVICES

MARVEL COMICS APP FOR ANDROID™ DEVICES

MARVEL
FREE DIGITAL COPY OFFER

PEEL HERE TO
REVEAL CODE →

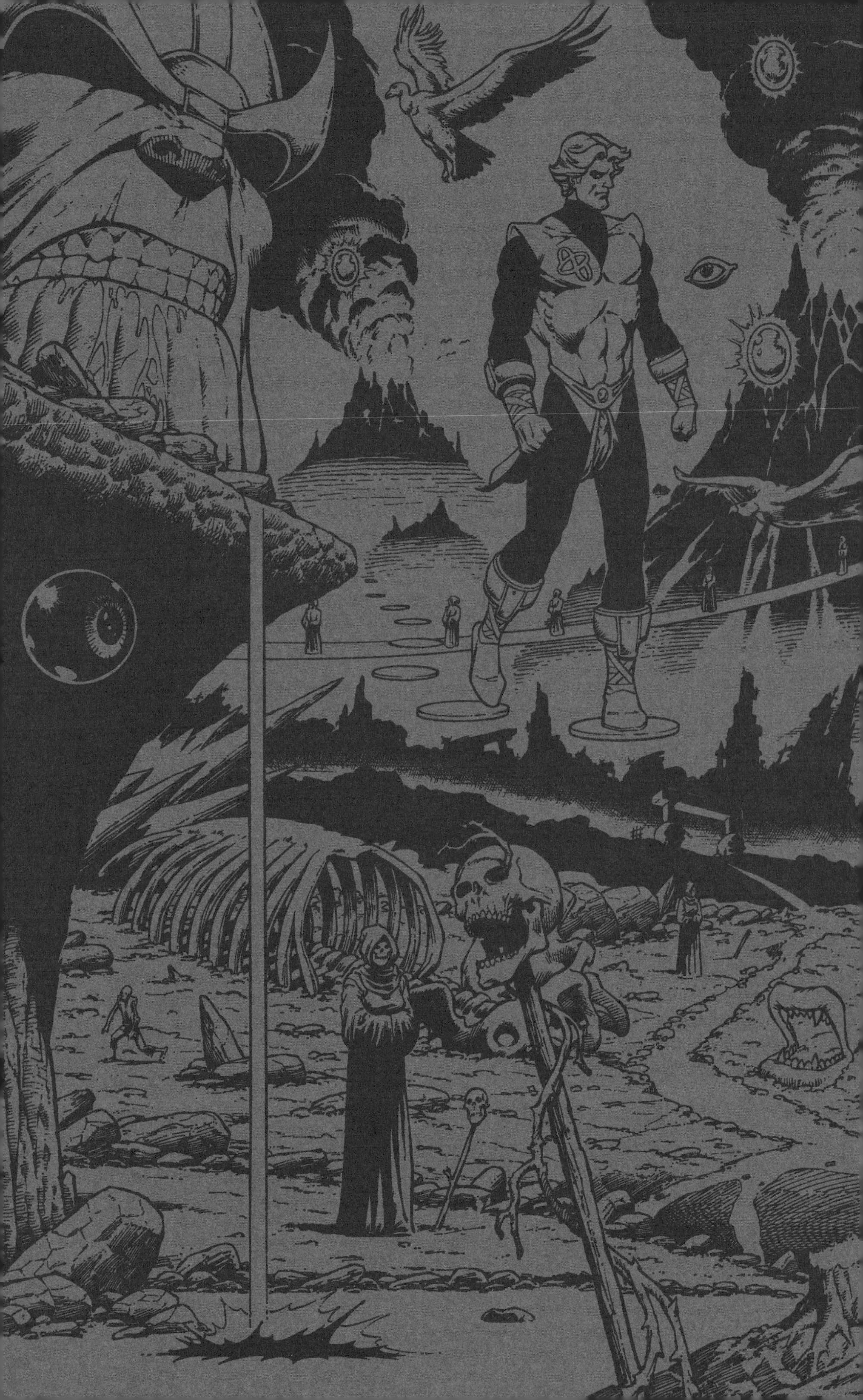